Release It!

Design and Deploy Production-Ready Software

Michael T. Nygard

The Pragmatic Bookshelf

Dallas, Texas • Raleigh, North Carolina

Many of the designations used by manufacturers and sellers to distinguish their products are claimed as trademarks. Where those designations appear in this book, and The Pragmatic Programmers, LLC was aware of a trademark claim, the designations have been printed in initial capital letters or in all capitals. The Pragmatic Starter Kit, The Pragmatic Programmer, Pragmatic Programming, Pragmatic Bookshelf, PragProg and the linking *g* device are trademarks of The Pragmatic Programmers, LLC.

Every precaution was taken in the preparation of this book. However, the publisher assumes no responsibility for errors or omissions, or for damages that may result from the use of information (including program listings) contained herein.

Our Pragmatic courses, workshops, and other products can help you and your team create better software and have more fun. For more information, as well as the latest Pragmatic titles, please visit us at *http://pragprog.com*.

Printed in the United States of America.
ISBN-13: 978-0-9787392-1-8
Printed on acid-free paper.
Book version: P5.1—August 2012

What readers are saying about
Release It!

Agile development emphasizes delivering production-ready code every iteration. This book finally lays out exactly what this really means for critical systems today. You have a winner here.

➤ **Tom Poppendieck**
Poppendieck.LLC

It's brilliant. Absolutely awesome. This book would've saved [Really Big Company] hundreds of thousands, if not millions, of dollars in a recent release.

➤ **Jared Richardson**
Agile Artisans, Inc.

Beware! This excellent package of experience, insights, and patterns has the potential to highlight all the mistakes you didn't know you have already made. Rejoice! Michael gives you recipes of how you redeem yourself right now. An invaluable addition to your Pragmatic bookshelf.

➤ **Arun Batchu**
Enterprise Architect, netrii LLC

Contents

Part III — General Design Issues

Part IV — Operations

Preface

You've worked hard on the project for more than a year. Finally, it looks like all the features are actually complete, and most even have unit tests. You can breathe a sigh of relief. You're done.

Or are you?

Does "feature complete" mean "production ready"? Is your system really ready to be deployed? Can it be run by operations staff and face the hordes of real-world users without you? Are you starting to get that sinking feeling that you'll be faced with late-night emergency phone calls or pager beeps? It turns out there's a lot more to development than just getting all the features in.

Too often, project teams aim to pass QA's tests, instead of aiming for life in Production (with a capital P). That is, the bulk of your work probably focuses on passing testing. But testing—even agile, pragmatic, automated testing— is not enough to prove that software is ready for the real world. The stresses and the strains of the real world, with crazy real users, globe-spanning traffic, and virus-writing mobs from countries you've never even heard of, go well beyond what we could ever hope to test for.

To make sure your software is ready for the harsh realities of the real world, you need to be prepared. I'm here to help show you where the problems lie and what you need to get around them. But before we begin, there are some popular misconceptions I'll discuss.

First, you need to accept that fact that despite your best laid plans, bad things will still happen. It's always good to prevent them when possible, of course. But it can be downright fatal to assume that you've predicted and eliminated all possible bad events. Instead, you want to take action and prevent the ones you can but make sure that your system as a whole can recover from whatever unanticipated, severe traumas might befall it.

Second, realize that "Release 1.0" is not the end of the development project but the beginning of the system's life on its own. The situation is somewhat like having a grown child leave its parents for the first time. You probably don't want your adult child to come and move back in with you, especially with their spouse, four kids, two dogs, and cockatiel.

Similarly, your design decisions made during development will greatly affect your quality of life after Release 1.0. If you fail to design your system for a production environment, your life after release will be filled with "excitement." And not the good kind of excitement. In this book, you'll take a look at the design trade-offs that matter and see how to make them intelligently.

And finally, despite our collective love of technology, nifty new techniques, and cool systems, in the end you have to face the fact that none of that really matters. In the world of business—which is the world that pays us—it all comes down to money. Systems cost money. To make up for that, they have to generate money, either in direct revenue or through cost savings. Extra work costs money, but then again, so does downtime. Inefficient code costs a *lot* of money, by driving up capital and operation costs. To understand a running system, you have to follow the money. And to stay in business, you need to make money—or at least not lose it.

It is my hope that this book can make a difference and can help you and your organization avoid the huge losses and overspending that typically characterize enterprise software.

Who Should Read This Book?

I've targeted this book at architects, designers, and developers of enterprise-class software systems—this includes websites, web services, and EAI projects, among others. To me, *enterprise-class* simply means that the software must be available, or the company loses money. These might be commerce systems that generate revenue directly through sales or perhaps critical internal systems that employees use to do their jobs. If anybody has to go home for the day because your software stops working, then this book is for you.

How the Book Is Organized

The book is divided into four parts, each introduced by a case study. Part 1 shows you how to keep your systems alive—maintaining system uptime. Distributed systems, despite promises of reliability through redundancy, exhibit availability more like "two eights" rather than the coveted "five nines."[1]

---

1. That is, 88% uptime instead of 99.999% uptime.

Stability is a necessary prerequisite to any other concerns. If your system falls over and dies every day, nobody is going to care about any aspects of the far future. Short-term fixes—and short-term thinking—will dominate in that environment. You'll have no viable future without stability, so you'll start by looking at ways to ensure you've got a stable base system from which to work.

Once you've achieved stability, your next concern is capacity. You'll look at that in Part 2, where you'll see how to measure the capacity of the system, learn just what *capacity* actually means, and learn how to optimize capacity over time. I'll show you a number of patterns and antipatterns to help illustrate good and bad designs and the dramatic effects they can have on your system's capacity (and hence, the number of late-night pager or cell calls you'll get).

In Part 3, you'll look at general design issues that architects should consider when creating software for the data center. Hardware and infrastructure design has changed significantly over the past ten years; for example, practices such as multihoming, which were once relatively rare, are now nearly universal. Networks have grown more complex—they're layered and intelligent. Storage area networking is commonplace. Software designs must account for and take advantage of these changes in order to run smoothly in the data center.

In Part 4, you'll examine the system's ongoing life as part of the overall information ecosystem. Too many production systems are like Schrodinger's cat—locked inside a box, with no way to observe its actual state. That doesn't make for a healthy ecosystem. Without information, it is impossible to make deliberate improvements.[2] Chapter 17, *Transparency*, on page 231 discusses the motives, technologies, and processes needed to learn from the system in production (which is the only place you *can* learn certain lessons). Once the health, performance, and characteristics of the system are revealed, you can act on that information. And in fact, that's not optional—you *must* take action in the light of new knowledge. Sometimes that's easier said than done, and in Chapter 18, *Adaptation*, on page 273 you'll look at the barriers to change and ways to reduce and overcome those barriers.

---

2. Random guesses might occasionally yield improvements but are more likely to add entropy than remove it.

About the Case Studies

I have included several extended case studies to illustrate the major themes of this book. These case studies are taken from real events and real system failures that I have personally observed. These failures were very costly—and embarrassing—for those involved. Therefore, I have obfuscated some information to protect the identities of the companies and people. I have also changed the names of the systems, classes, and methods. Only "nonessential" details have been changed, however. In each case, I have maintained the same industry, sequence of events, failure mode, error propagation, and outcome. The costs of these failures are not exaggerated. These are real companies, and this is real money. I have preserved those figures to underscore the seriousness of this material. Real money is on the line when systems fail.

Acknowledgments

This book grew out of a talk that I originally presented to the Object Technology User's Group.[3] Because of that, I owe thanks to Kyle Larson and Clyde Cutting, who volunteered me for the talk and accepted the talk, respectively. Tom and Mary Poppendieck, authors of two fantastic books on "lean software development"[4] have provided invaluable encouragement. They convinced me that I had a book waiting to get out. Special thanks also go to my good friend and colleague, Dion Stewart, who has consistently provided excellent feedback on drafts of this book.

Of course, I would be remiss if I didn't give my warmest thanks to my wife and daughters. My youngest girl has seen me working on this for half of her life. You have all been so patient with my weekends spent scribbling. Marie, Anne, Elizabeth, Laura, and Sarah, I thank you.

---

3. See http://www.otug.org.
4. See *Lean Software Development [PP03]* and *Implementing Lean Software Development [PP06]*.

CHAPTER 1

Introduction

Software design as taught today is terribly incomplete. It talks only about what systems *should* do. It doesn't address the converse—things systems should *not* do. They should not crash, hang, lose data, violate privacy, lose money, destroy your company, or kill your customers.

In this book, we will examine ways we can architect, design, and build software —particularly distributed systems—for the muck and tussle of the real world. We will prepare for the armies of illogical users who do crazy, unpredictable things. Our software will be under attack from the moment we release it. It needs to stand up to the typhoon winds of a flash mob, a Slashdotting, or a link on Fark or Digg. We'll take a hard look at software that failed the test and find ways to make sure your software survives contact with the real world.

Software design today resembles automobile design in the early 90s: disconnected from the real world. Cars designed solely in the cool comfort of the lab looked great in models and CAD systems. Perfectly curved cars gleamed in front of giant fans, purring in laminar flow. The designers inhabiting these serene spaces produced designs that were elegant, sophisticated, clever, fragile, unsatisfying, and ultimately short-lived. Most software architecture and design happens in equally clean, distant environs.

You want to own a car designed for the real world. You want a car designed by somebody who knows that oil changes are *always* 3,000 miles late; that the tires must work just as well on the last sixteenth of an inch of tread as on the first; and that you will certainly, at some point, stomp on the brakes while you're holding an Egg McMuffin in one hand and a cell phone in the other.

1.1　Aiming for the Right Target

Most software is designed for the development lab or the testers in the Quality Assurance (QA) department. It is designed and built to pass tests such as, "The customer's first and last names are required, but the middle initial is optional." It aims to survive the artificial realm of QA, not the real world of production.

When my system passes QA, can I say with confidence that it is ready for production? Simply passing QA tells me little about the system's suitability for the next three to ten years of life. It could be the Toyota Camry of software, racking up thousands of hours of continuous uptime. It could be the Chevy Vega (a car whose front end broke off on the company's own test track) or a Ford Pinto, prone to blowing up when hit in just the right way. It is impossible to tell from a few days or weeks of testing in QA what the next several years will bring.

Product designers in manufacturing have long pursued "design for manufacturability"—the engineering approach of designing products such that they can be manufactured at low cost and high quality. Prior to this era, product designers and fabricators lived in different worlds. Designs thrown over the wall to production included screws that could not be reached, parts that were easily confused, and custom parts where off-the-shelf components would serve. Inevitably, low quality and high manufacturing cost followed.

Does this sound familiar? We're in a similar state today. We end up falling behind on the new system because we're constantly taking support calls from the last half-baked project we shoved out the door. Our analog of "design for manufacturability" is "design for production." We don't hand designs to fabricators, but we do hand finished software to IT operations. We need to design individual software systems, and the whole ecosystem of interdependent systems, to produce low cost and high quality in operations.

1.2　Use the Force

Your early decisions make the biggest impact on the eventual shape of your system. The earliest decisions you make can be the hardest ones to reverse later. These early decisions about the system boundary and decomposition into subsystems get crystallized into the team structure, funding allocation, program management structure, and even time-sheet codes. Team assignments are the first draft of the architecture. (See *Conway's Law*, on page 124.) It's a terrible irony that these very early decisions are also the least informed. This is when your team is most ignorant of the eventual structure of the software in the beginning, yet that is when some of the most irrevocable decisions must be made.

Even on "agile" projects,[1] decisions are best made with foresight. It seems as if the designer must "use the force" to see the future in order to select the most robust design. Since different alternatives often have similar implementation costs but radically different lifecycle costs, it is important to consider the effects of each decision on availability, capacity, and flexibility. I'll show you the downstream effects of dozens of design alternatives, with concrete examples of beneficial and harmful approaches. These examples all come from real systems I've worked on. Most of them cost me sleep at one time or another.

1.3 Quality of Life

Release 1.0 is the beginning of your software's life, not the end of the project. Your quality of life after Release 1.0 depends on choices you make long before that vital milestone.

Whether you wear the support pager, sell your labor by the hour, or pay the invoices for the work, you need to know that you are dealing with a rugged, Baja-tested, indestructible vehicle that will carry your business forward, not a fragile shell of fiberglass that spends more time in the shop than on the road.

1.4 The Scope of the Challenge

The "software crisis" is now more than thirty years old. According to the *gold owners*, software still costs too much. (But, see *Why Does Software Cost So Much? [DeM95]* about that.) According to the *goal donors*, software still takes too long—even though schedules are measured in months rather than years. Apparently, the supposed productivity gains from the past thirty years have been illusory.

These terms come from the agile community. The gold owner is the one paying for the software. The goal donor is the one whose needs you are trying to fill. These are seldom the same person.

On the other hand, maybe some real productivity gains have gone into attacking larger problems, rather than producing the same software faster

---

1. I'll reveal myself here and now as a strong proponent of agile methods. Their emphasis on early delivery and incremental improvements means software gets into production quickly. Since production is the only place to learn how the software will respond to real-world stimuli, I advocate any approach that begins the learning process as soon as possible.

and cheaper. Over the past ten years, the scope of our systems expanded by orders of magnitude.

In the easy, laid-back days of client/server systems, a system's user base would be measured in the tens or hundreds, with few dozen concurrent users at most. Now, sponsors glibly toss numbers at us such as "25,000 concurrent users" and "4 million unique visitors a day."

Uptime demands have increased, too. Whereas the famous "five nines" (99.999%) uptime was once the province of the mainframe and its caretakers, even garden-variety commerce sites are now expected to be available 24 by 7 by 365.[2] Clearly, we've made tremendous strides even to consider the scale of software we build today, but with the increased reach and scale of our systems come new ways to break, more hostile environments, and less tolerance for defects.

The increasing scope of this challenge—to build software fast that's cheap to build, good for users, and cheap to operate—demands continually improving architecture and design techniques. Designs appropriate for small brochure-ware websites fail outrageously when applied to thousand-user, transactional, distributed systems, and we'll look at some of those outrageous failures.

1.5   A Million Dollars Here, a Million Dollars There

A lot is on the line here: your project's success, your stock options or profit sharing, your company's survival, and even your job. Systems built for QA often require so much ongoing expense, in the form of operations cost, downtime, and software maintenance, that they never reach profitability, let alone net positive cash for the business, which is reached only after the profits generated by the system pay back the costs incurred in building it. These systems exhibit low levels of availability, resulting in direct losses in missed revenue and sometimes even larger indirect losses through damage to the brand. For many of my clients, the direct cost of downtime exceeds $100,000 per hour.

In one year the difference between 98% uptime and 99.99% uptime adds up to more than $17 million.[3] Imagine adding $17 million to the bottom line just through better design!

---

2. That phrase has always bothered me. As an engineer, I expect it to either be "24 by 365" or be "24 by 7 by 52."

3. At an average $100,000 per hour, the cost of downtime for a tier-1 retailer.

During the hectic rush of the development project, you can easily make decisions that optimize development cost at the expense of operational cost. This makes sense only in the context of the project team being measured against a fixed budget and delivery date. In the context of the organization paying for the software, it's a bad choice. Systems spend much more of their life in operation than in development—at least, the ones that don't get canceled or scrapped do. Avoiding a one-time cost by incurring a recurring operational cost makes no sense. In fact, the opposite decision makes much more financial sense. If you can spend $5,000 on an automated build and release system that avoids downtime during releases, the company will avoid $200,000.[4] I think that most CFOs would not mind authorizing an expenditure that returns 4,000% ROI.

> **Don't avoid one-time development expenses at the cost of recurring operational expenses.**

Design and architecture decisions are also financial decisions. These choices must be made with an eye toward their implementation cost as well as their downstream costs. The fusion of technical and financial viewpoints is one of the most important recurring themes in this book.

1.6 Pragmatic Architecture

Two divergent sets of activities both fall under the term *architecture*. One type of architecture strives toward higher levels of abstraction that are more portable across platforms and less connected to the messy details of hardware, networks, electrons, and photons. The extreme form of this approach results in the "ivory tower"—a Kubrickesque clean room, inhabited by aloof gurus, decorated with boxes and arrows on every wall. Decrees emerge from the ivory tower and descend upon the toiling coders. "Use EJB container-managed persistence!" "All UIs shall be constructed with JSF!" "All that is, all that was, and all that shall ever be lives in Oracle!" If you've ever gritted your teeth while coding something according to the "company standards" that would be ten times easier with some other technology, then you've been the victim of an ivory-tower architect. I guarantee that an architect who doesn't bother to listen to the coders on the team doesn't bother listening to the users either. You've seen the result: users who cheer when the system crashes, because at least then they can stop using it for a while.

---

4. This assumes $10,000 per release (labor plus cost of planned downtime), four releases per year, and a five-year horizon. Most companies would like to do more than four releases per year, but I'm being conservative.

In contrast, another breed of architect rubs shoulders with the coders and might even be one. This kind of architect does not hesitate to peel back the lid on an abstraction or to jettison one if it does not fit. This pragmatic architect is more likely to discuss issues such as memory usage, CPU requirements, bandwidth needs, and the benefits and drawbacks of hyper-threading and CPU bonding.

The ivory-tower architect most enjoys an end-state vision of ringing crystal perfection, but the pragmatic architect constantly thinks about the dynamics of change. "How can we do a deployment without rebooting the world?" "What metrics do we need to collect, and how will we analyze them?" "What part of the system needs improvement the most?" When the ivory-tower architect is done, the system will not admit any improvements; each part will be perfectly adapted to its role. Contrast that to the pragmatic architect's creation, in which each component is good enough for the current stresses—and the architect knows which ones need to be replaced depending on how the stress factors change over time.

If you're already a pragmatic architect, then I've got chapters full of powerful ammunition for you. If you're an ivory-tower architect—and you haven't already stopped reading—then this book might entice you to descend through a few levels of abstraction to get back in touch with that vital intersection of software, hardware, and users: living in production. You, your users, and your company will be much happier when the time comes to finally release it!

Part I

Stability

CHAPTER 2

Case Study: The Exception That Grounded An Airline

Have you ever noticed that the incidents that blow up into the biggest issues start with something very small? A tiny programming error starts the snowball rolling downhill. As it gains momentum, the scale of the problem keeps getting bigger and bigger. A major airline experienced just such an incident. It eventually stranded thousands of passengers and cost the company hundreds of thousands of dollars. Here's how it happened.

It started with a planned failover on the database cluster that served the Core Facilities (CF).[1] The airline was moving toward a service-oriented architecture, with the usual goals of increasing reuse, decreasing development time, and decreasing operational costs. At this time, CF was in its first generation. The CF team planned a phased rollout, driven by features. It was a sound plan, and it probably sounds familiar—most large companies have some variation of this project underway now.

CF handled flight searches—a very common service for any airline application. Given a date, time, city, airport code, flight number, or any combination, CF could find and return a list of flight details. When this incident happened, the self-service check-in kiosks, IVR, and "channel partner" applications had been updated to use CF. Channel partner applications generate data feeds for big travel-booking sites. IVR and self-service check-in are both used to put passengers on airplanes—"butts in seats" in the vernacular. The development schedule had plans for new releases of the gate agents and call center

Interactive Voice Response: the dreaded telephone menu system

---

1. As always, all names, places, and dates are changed to protect the confidentiality of people and companies involved.

applications to transition to CF for flight lookup, but those had not been rolled out yet, which turned out to be a good thing, as you will soon see.

The architects of CF were well aware of how critical it would be. They built it for high availability. It ran on a cluster of J2EE application servers with a redundant Oracle 9i database. All the data was stored on a large external RAID array with off-site tape backups taken twice daily and on-disk replicas in a second chassis that were guaranteed to be at most five minutes old.

The Oracle database server would run on one node of the cluster at a time, with Veritas Cluster Server controlling the database server, assigning the virtual IP address, and mounting or unmounting filesystems from the RAID array. Up front, a pair of redundant hardware load balancers directed incoming traffic to one of the application servers. Calling applications like the self-service check-in kiosks and IVR system would connect to the front-end virtual IP address. So far, so good.

If you've done any website or web services work, Figure 1, *CF Deployment Architecture*, on page 11 probably looks familiar. It is a very common high-availability architecture, and it's a good one. CF did not suffer from any of the usual single-point-of-failure problems. Every piece of hardware was redundant: CPUs, fans, drives, network cards, power supplies, and network switches. The servers were even split into different racks in case a single rack got damaged or destroyed. In fact, a second location thirty miles away was ready to take over in the event of a fire, flood, bomb, or meteor strike.

2.1 The Outage

As was the case with most of my large clients, a local team of engineers dedicated to the account operated the airline's infrastructure. In fact, that team had been doing most of the work for more than three years when this happened. On the night this started, the local engineers had executed a manual database failover from CF database 1 to CF database 2. (See Figure 1, *CF Deployment Architecture*, on page 11.) They used Veritas to migrate the active database from one host to the other. This allowed them to do some routine maintenance to the first host. Totally routine. They had done this procedure dozens of times in the past.

Veritas Cluster Server orchestrates the failover. In the space of one minute, it can shut down the Oracle server on database 1, unmount the filesystems from the RAID array, remount them on database 2, start Oracle there, and reassign the virtual IP address to database 2. The application servers can't

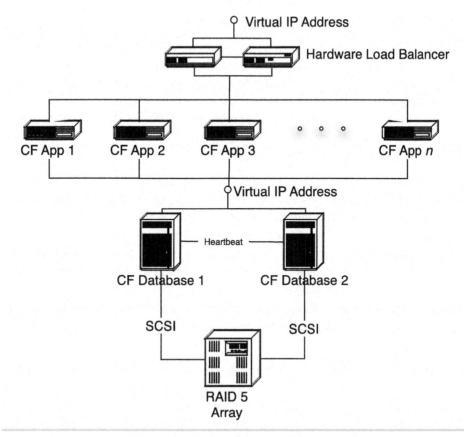

Figure 1—CF Deployment Architecture

even tell that anything has changed, because they are configured to connect to the virtual IP address only.

The client scheduled this particular change for a Thursday evening, at around 11 p.m., Pacific time. One of the engineers from the local team worked with the operations center to execute the change. All went exactly as planned. They migrated the active database from database 1 to database 2 and then updated database 1. After double-checking that database 1 was updated correctly, they migrated the database back to database 1 and applied the same change to database 2. The whole time, routine site monitoring showed that the applications were continuously available. No downtime was planned for this change, and none occurred. At about 12:30 a.m., the crew marked the change as "Completed, Success" and signed off. The local engineer headed for bed, after working a 22-hour shift. There's only so long you can run on double espressos, after all.

Nothing unusual occurred until two hours later.

At about 2:30 a.m., all the check-in kiosks went red on the monitoring console —every single one, everywhere in the country, stopped servicing requests at the same time. A few minutes later, the IVR servers went red too. Not exactly panic time, but pretty close, because 2:30 a.m. in Pacific time is 5:30 a.m. Eastern time, which is prime time for commuter flight check-in on the Eastern seaboard. The operations center immediately opened a Severity 1 case and got the local team on a conference call.

In any incident, my first priority is always to restore service. Restoring service takes precedence over investigation. If I can collect some data for post-mortem root cause analysis, that's great—unless it makes the outage longer. When the fur flies, improvisation is not your friend. Fortunately, the team had created scripts long ago to take thread dumps of all the Java applications and snapshots of the databases. This style of automated data collection is the perfect balance. It's not improvised, it does not prolong an outage, yet it aids post-mortem analysis. According to procedure, the operations center ran those scripts right away. They also tried restarting one of the kiosks' application servers.

The trick to restoring service is figuring out what to target. You can always "reboot the world" by restarting every single server, layer by layer. That's almost always effective, but it takes a *long* time. Most of the time, you can find one culprit that is really locking things up. In a way, it is like a doctor diagnosing a disease. You could treat a patient for every known disease, but that will be painful, expensive, and slow. Instead, you want to look at the symptoms the patient shows to figure out exactly which disease to treat. The trouble is that individual symptoms aren't specific enough. Sure, once in a while, some symptom points you directly at the fundamental problem, but not usually. Most of the time, you get symptoms—like a fever—that tell you nothing by themselves.

Hundreds of diseases can cause fevers. To distinguish between possible causes, you need more information from tests or observations.

In this case, the team was facing two separate sets of applications that were both completely hung. It happened at almost the same time, close enough that the difference could just be latency in the separate monitoring tools that the kiosks and IVR applications used. The most obvious hypothesis was that both sets of applications depended on some third entity that was in trouble. As you can see from Figure 2, *Common Dependencies*, on page 14, that was a big finger pointing at CF, the only common dependency shared by the kiosks and the IVR system. The fact that CF had a database failover three hours before this problem also made it highly suspect. Monitoring hadn't reported any trouble with CF, though. Log file scraping did not reveal any problems, and neither did URL probing. As it turns out, the monitoring application was only hitting a status page, so it did not really say much about the real health of the CF application servers. We made a note to fix that error through normal channels later.

Remember, restoring service was the first priority. This outage was approaching the one-hour SLA limit, so the team decided to restart each of the CF application servers. As soon as they restarted the first CF application server, the IVR systems began recovering. Once all CF servers were restarted, IVR was green, but the kiosks still showed red. On a hunch, the lead engineer decided to restart the kiosks' own application servers. That did the trick; the kiosks and IVR systems were all showing green on the board.

Service-level agreement: A contract between the service provide and the client, usually with substantial financial penalties for breaking the SLA

The total elapsed time for the incident was a little more than three hours.

2.2 Consequences

Three hours might not sound like much, especially when you compare that to some legendary outages. (EBay's 24-hour outage from 1999 comes to mind, for example.) The impact to the airline lasted a lot longer than just three hours, though. Airlines don't staff enough gate agents to check everyone in using the old systems. When the kiosks go down, the airline has to call in agents who are off-shift. Some of them are over their 40 hours for the week, incurring union-contract overtime (time and a half). Even the off-shift agents are only human, though. By the time the airline could get more staff on-site, they could deal only with the backlog. It took until nearly 3 p.m. to deal with the backlog.

It took so long to check in the early-morning flights that planes could not push back from their gates. They would have been half empty. Many travelers were late departing or arriving that day. Thursday happens to be the day that a lot of "nerd-birds" fly: commuter flights returning consultants to their home cities. Since the gates were still occupied, incoming flights had to be switched to other unoccupied gates. So, even travelers who were already checked in still got inconvenienced. They had to rush from their original gate to the reallocated gate.

The delays were shown on *Good Morning America* (complete with video of pathetically stranded single moms and their babies) and the Weather Channel's travel advisory.

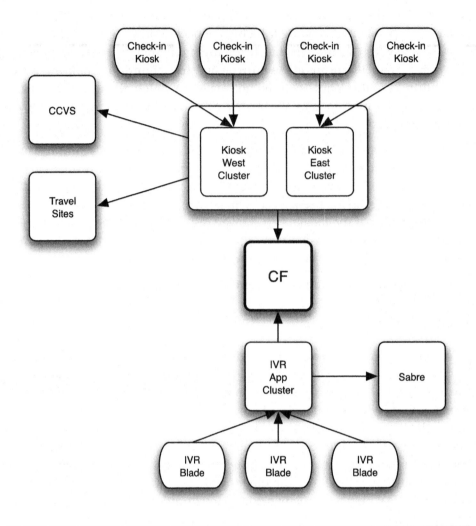

Figure 2—Common Dependencies

The FAA measures on-time arrivals and departures as part of the airline's annual report card. They also measure customer complaints sent to the FAA about an airline.

The CEO's compensation is partly based on the FAA's annual report card.

You know it's going to be a bad day when you see the CEO stalking around the operations center to find out who cost him his vacation home in St. Thomas.

2.3 Post-mortem

At 10:30 a.m. Pacific time, eight hours after the outage started, Tom,[2] our account representative, called me to come down for a post-mortem. Because the failure occurred so soon after the database failover and maintenance, suspicion naturally condensed around that action. In operations, "post hoc, ergo propter hoc"[3] turns out to be a good starting point most of the time. It's not always right, but it certainly provides a place to begin looking. In fact, when Tom called me, he asked me to fly there to find out why the database failover caused this outage.

Once I was airborne, I started reviewing the problem ticket and preliminary incident report on my laptop.

My agenda was simple: conduct a post-mortem investigation, and answer some questions:

- Did the database failover cause the outage? If not, what did?
- Was the cluster configured correctly?
- Did the operations team conduct the maintenance correctly?
- How could the failure have been detected before it became an outage?
- Most important, how do we make sure this never, ever happens again?

Of course, my presence there also served to demonstrate to the client that we were serious about responding to this outage. Not to mention, my investigation should also allay any fears about the local team whitewashing the incident. They wouldn't do such a thing, of course, but managing perception after a major incident can be as important as managing the incident itself.

> Manage perceptions after a major incident. It's as important as managing the incident itself.

A post-mortem is like a murder mystery. You have a set of clues. Some are reliable, such as server logs copied from the time of the outage. Some are unreliable, such as statements from people about what they saw. As with real witnesses, people will mix observations with speculation. They will present hypotheses as facts. The post-mortem can actually be harder to solve than a murder, because the body goes away. There is no corpse to autopsy, because the servers are back up and running. Whatever state they were in that caused the failure no longer exists. The failure might have left traces in the log files or monitoring data collected from that time, or it might not. The clues can be very hard to see.

---

2. Not his real name.
3. Literally "after this, therefore because of this." It refers to the common logical fallacy of attributing causation based on close timing. Also known as "you touched it last."

As I read the files, I made some notes about data to collect. From the application servers, I would need log files, thread dumps, and configuration files. From the database servers, I would need configuration files for the databases and the cluster server. I also made a note to compare the current configuration files to those from the nightly backup. The backup ran before the outage, so that would tell me whether any configurations were changed between the backup and my investigation. In other words, that would tell me whether someone was trying to cover up a mistake.

By the time I got to my hotel, my body said it was after midnight. All I wanted was a shower and a bed. What I got instead was a meeting with our account executive to brief me on developments while I was incommunicado in the air. My day finally ended around 1 a.m.

In the morning, fortified with quarts of coffee, I dug into the database cluster and RAID configurations. I was looking for common problems with clusters: not enough heartbeats, heartbeats going through switches that carry production traffic, servers set to use physical IP addresses instead of the virtual address, bad dependencies among managed packages, and so on. At that time, I didn't carry a checklist; these were just problems that I had seen more than once or heard about through the grapevine. I found nothing wrong. The engineering team had done a great job with the database cluster. Proven, textbook work. In fact, some of the scripts appeared to be taken directly from Veritas's own training materials.

Next, it was time to move on to the application servers' configuration. The local engineers had made copies of all the log files from the kiosk application servers during the outage. I was also able to get log files from the CF application servers. They still had log files from the time of the outage, since it was just the day before. Better still, there were thread dumps in both sets of log files. As a longtime Java programmer, I love Java thread dumps for debugging application hangs.

Armed with a thread dump, the application is an open book, if you know how to read it. You can deduce a great deal about applications for which you've never seen the source code. You can tell what third-party libraries an application uses, what kind of thread pools it has, how many threads are in each one, and what background processing the application uses. By looking at the classes and methods in each thread's stack trace, you can even tell what protocols the application uses.

It did not take long to decide that the problem had to be within CF. The thread dumps for the kiosks' application servers showed exactly what I would expect

Getting Thread Dumps

Any Java application will dump the state of every thread in the JVM when you send it a signal 3 (SIGQUIT) on UNIX systems or press Ctrl+Break on Windows systems.

To use this on Windows, you must be at the console, with a Command Prompt window running the Java application. Obviously, if you are logging in remotely, this pushes you toward VNC or Remote Desktop.

On UNIX, you can use kill to send the signal:

kill -3 18835

One catch about the thread dumps: they always come out on "standard out." Many canned start-up scripts do not capture standard out, or they send it to /dev/null. (For example, Gentoo Linux's JBoss package sets *JBOSS_CONSOLE* to /dev/null by default.) Log files produced with Log4J or java.util.logging cannot show thread dumps. You might have to experiment with your application server's start-up scripts to get thread dumps.

Here is a small portion of a thread dump:

```
"http-0.0.0.0-8080-Processor25" daemon prio=1 tid=0x08a593f0 \
  nid=0x57ac runnable [a88f1000..a88f1ccc]
    at java.net.PlainSocketImpl.socketAccept(Native Method)
    at java.net.PlainSocketImpl.accept(PlainSocketImpl.java:353)
    - locked <0xac5d3640> (a java.net.PlainSocketImpl)
    at java.net.ServerSocket.implAccept(ServerSocket.java:448)
    at java.net.ServerSocket.accept(ServerSocket.java:419)
    at org.apache.tomcat.util.net.DefaultServerSocketFactory.\
acceptSocket(DefaultServerSocketFactory.java:60)
    at org.apache.tomcat.util.net.PoolTcpEndpoint.\
acceptSocket(PoolTcpEndpoint.java:368)
    at org.apache.tomcat.util.net.TcpWorkerThread.\
runIt(PoolTcpEndpoint.java:549)
    at org.apache.tomcat.util.threads.ThreadPool$ControlRunnable.\
run(ThreadPool.java:683)
    at java.lang.Thread.run(Thread.java:534)

"http-0.0.0.0-8080-Processor24" daemon prio=1 tid=0x08a57c30 \
  nid=0x57ab in Object.wait() [a8972000..a8972ccc]
    at java.lang.Object.wait(Native Method)
    - waiting on <0xacede700> (a org.apache.tomcat.util.threads.\
ThreadPool$ControlRunnable)
    at java.lang.Object.wait(Object.java:429)
    at org.apache.tomcat.util.threads.ThreadPool$ControlRunnable.\
run(ThreadPool.java:655)
    - locked <0xacede700> (a org.apache.tomcat.util.threads.\
ThreadPool$ControlRunnable)
    at java.lang.Thread.run(Thread.java:534)
```

They do get verbose.

This fragment shows two threads, each named like http-0.0.0.0-8080-ProcessorN. Number 25 is in a runnable state, whereas thread 24 is blocked in Object.wait(). This trace clearly indicates that these are members of a thread pool. That some of the classes on the stacks are named ThreadPool$ControlRunnable() might also be a clue.

from the observed behavior during the incident. Out of the forty threads allocated for handling requests from the individual kiosks, all forty were blocked inside SocketInputStream.socketRead0(), a native method inside the internals of Java's socket library. They were trying vainly to read a response that would never come.

The kiosk application server's thread dump also gave me the precise name of the class and method that all forty threads had called: FlightSearch.lookupByCity(). I was surprised to see references to RMI and EJB methods a few frames higher in the stack. CF had always been described as a "web service." Admittedly, the definition of a web service was pretty loose at that time, but it still seems like a stretch to call a stateless session bean a "web service."

Remote Method Invocation (RMI) provides EJB with its remote procedure calls. EJB calls can ride over one of two transports: CORBA (dead as disco) or RMI. As much as I like RMI's programming model, it's really dangerous because calls cannot be made to time out. As a result, the caller is vulnerable to problems in the remote server.

2.4 The Smoking Gun

At this point, the post-mortem analysis agreed with the symptoms from the outage itself: CF appeared to have caused both IVR and kiosk check-in to hang. The biggest remaining question was still, "What happened to CF?"

The picture got clearer as I investigated the thread dumps from CF. CF's application server used separate pools of threads to handle EJB calls and HTTP requests. That's why CF was always able to respond to the monitoring application, even during the middle of the outage. The HTTP threads were almost entirely idle, which makes sense for an EJB server. The EJB threads, on the other hand, were all completely in use processing calls to Flight-Search.lookupByCity(). In fact, every single thread on every application server was blocked at exactly the same line of code: attempting to check out a database connection from a resource pool.

It was circumstantial evidence, not a smoking gun, but considering the database failover before the outage, it seemed that I was on the right track.

The next part would be dicey. I needed to look at that code, but the operations center had no access to the source control system. Only binaries were deployed to the production environment. That's usually a good security precaution, but it was a bit inconvenient at the moment. When I asked our account executive how we could get access to the source code, he was reluctant to take that step. Given the scale of the outage, you can imagine that there was plenty of blame floating in the air looking for someone to land on. Relations between the operations center and Development—never all that cozy—were more strained than usual. Everyone was on the defensive, wary of any attempt to point the finger of blame in their direction.

So, with no legitimate access to the source code, I did the only thing I could do. I took the binaries from production and decompiled them.[4] The minute I saw the code for the suspect EJB, I knew I had found the real smoking gun. This particular session bean turned out to be the only facility that CF implemented yet. Here is the actual code:

```java
package com.example.cf.flightsearch;
. . .
public class FlightSearch implements SessionBean {

  private MonitoredDataSource connectionPool;

  public List lookupByCity(. . .) throws SQLException, RemoteException {
    Connection conn = null;
    Statement stmt = null;

    try {
      conn = connectionPool.getConnection();
      stmt = conn.createStatement();

      // Do the lookup logic
      // return a list of results
    } finally {
      if (stmt != null) {
        stmt.close();
      }

      if (conn != null) {
        conn.close();
      }
    }
  }
}
```

Actually, at first glance, this method looks well constructed. Use of the try..finally block indicates the author's desire to clean up resources. In fact, this very cleanup block has appeared in some Java books on the market. Too bad it contains a fatal flaw.

---

4. My favorite tool for decompiling Java code is still JAD. It is fast and accurate, though it is beginning to creak and groan when used on Java 5 code.

It turns out that java.sql.Statement.close() can throw a SQLException. It almost never does. Oracle's driver does only when it encounters an IOException attempting to close the connection—following a database failover, for instance.

Suppose the JDBC connection was created before the failover. The IP address used to create the connection will have moved from one host to another, but the current state of TCP connections will not carry over to the second database host. Any socket writes will eventually throw an IOException (after the operating system and network driver finally decide that the TCP connection is dead). That means every JDBC connection in the resource pool is an accident waiting to happen.

Amazingly, the JDBC connection is still willing to create statements. To create a statement, the driver's connection object checks only its own internal status.[5] If the JDBC connection thinks it is still connected, then it will create the statement. Executing that statement will throw a SQLException when it does some network I/O. But, closing the statement will also throw a SQLException, because the driver attempts to tell the database server to release resources associated with that statement.

In short, the driver is willing to create a Statement Object that cannot be used. You might consider this a bug. Many of the developers at the airline certainly made that accusation. The key lesson to be drawn here, though, is that the JDBC specification allows java.sql.Statement.close() to throw SQLException, so your code has to handle it.

In the previous offending code, if closing the statement throws an exception, then the connection does not get closed, resulting in a resource leak. After forty of these calls, the resource pool is exhausted, and all future calls will block at connectionPool.getConnection(). That is exactly what I saw in the thread dumps from CF.

The entire globe-spanning, multibillion dollar airline with its hundreds of aircraft and tens of thousands of employees was grounded by one programmer's rookie error: a single uncaught SQLException.

2.5 An Ounce of Prevention?

When such staggering cost results from such a small error, the natural response is to say, "This must never happen again." But how can it be prevented? Would a code review have caught this bug? Only if one of the

---

5. This might be a quirk peculiar to Oracle's JDBC drivers. I've decompiled only Oracle's.

reviewers knew the internals of Oracle's JDBC driver or the review team spent hours on each method. Would more testing have prevented this bug? Perhaps. Once the problem was identified, the team performed a test in the stress test environment that did demonstrate the same error. The regular test profile didn't exercise this method enough to show the bug. In other words, once you know where to look, it's simple to make a test that finds it.

Ultimately, it is just fantasy to expect every single bug like this one to be driven out. Bugs will happen. They cannot be eliminated, so they must be survived instead.

The worst problem here is that the bug in one system could propagate to all the other affected systems. A better question to ask is, "How do we prevent bugs in one system from affecting everything else?" Inside every enterprise today is a mesh of interconnected, interdependent systems. They cannot—must not—allow bugs to cause a chain of failures. You're going to look at design patterns that can prevent this type of problem from spreading.

CHAPTER 3

Introducing Stability

New software emerges like a new college graduate, full of optimistic vigor, suddenly facing the harsh realities of the world outside the lab. Things happen in the real world that just do not happen in the lab, usually bad things. In the lab, all the tests are contrived by people who know what answer they expect to get. In the real world, the tests aren't designed to have answers. Sometimes they're just setting your software up to fail.

Enterprise software must be cynical. Cynical software expects bad things to happen and is never surprised when they do. Cynical software doesn't even trust itself, so it puts up internal barriers to protect itself from failures. It refuses to get too intimate with other systems, because it could get hurt.

The airline's Core Facilities project discussed in the previous chapter was not cynical enough. As so often happens, the team got caught up in the excitement of new technology and advanced architecture. It had lots of great things to say about leverage and synergy. Dazzled by the dollar signs, it didn't see the stop sign and took a turn for the worse.

Poor stability carries significant real costs. The obvious cost is lost revenue. The retailer I discussed in Chapter 1, *Introduction*, on page 1 loses $100,000 per hour of downtime, and that's during the off-season. Trading systems can lose that much in a single missed transaction!

A common rule of thumb says that it costs from $25 to $50 for an online retailer to acquire a customer. With 5,000 unique visitors per hour, assume 10 percent of those would-be visitors walk away for good. That means $12,500 to $25,000 in wasted customer acquisition costs.[1]

---

1. http://retailindustry.about.com/library/weekly/aa122599a.htm

Less tangible, but just as painful, is lost reputation. Tarnish to the brand might be less immediately obvious than lost customers, but try having your holiday-season operational problems reported in *BusinessWeek*. Millions of dollars in image advertising—touting online customer service—can be undone in a few hours by a batch of bad hard drives.

Good stability does not necessarily cost a lot. When building the architecture, design, and even low-level implementation of a system, there are many decision points that have high leverage over the system's ultimate stability. Confronted with these leverage points, two paths might both satisfy the functional requirements (aiming for QA). One will lead to hours of downtime every year while the other will not. The amazing thing is that the highly stable design usually costs the same to implement as the unstable one.

> A highly stable design usually costs the same to implement as an unstable one.

3.1 Defining Stability

To talk about stability, I need to define some terms. A *transaction* is an abstract unit of work processed by the system. This is not the same as a database transaction. A single unit of work might encompass many database transactions. In an ecommerce site, for example, one common type of transaction is "Customer Places Order." This transaction spans several pages, often including external integrations such as credit card verification. Transactions are the reason that the system exists. A single system can process just one type of transaction, making it a dedicated system. A *mixed workload* is a combination of different transaction types processed by a system.

When I use the word *system*, I mean the complete, interdependent set of hardware, applications, and services required to process transactions for users. A system might be as small as a single application, or it might be a sprawling, multitier network of applications and servers.

I use *system* when I mean a collection of hosts, applications, network segments, power supplies, and so on, that process transactions from end to end.

A resilient system keeps processing transactions, even when there are transient impulses, persistent stresses, or component failures disrupting normal processing. This is what most people mean when they just say *stability*. It's not just that your individual servers or applications stay up and running but rather that the user can still get work done.

The terms *impulse* and *stress* come from mechanical engineering. An impulse is a rapid shock to the system. An impulse to the system is when something whacks it with a hammer. In contrast, stress to the system is a force applied to the system over an extended period.

A flash mob pounding the Xbox 360 product detail page, thanks to a rumor about discounts, causes an impulse. Ten thousand new sessions, all arriving within one minute of each other, is very difficult to withstand. Getting Slashdotted is an impulse. Dumping twelve million messages into a queue at midnight on November 21st is an impulse. These are things that can fracture the system in the blink of an eye.

On the other hand, getting slow responses from your credit card processor, because it doesn't have enough capacity for all of its customers, is a stress on the system. In a mechanical system, a material changes shape when stress is applied. This change in shape is called the *strain*. Stress produces strain. The same thing happens with computer systems. The stress from the credit card processor will cause strain to propagate to other parts of the system, which can produce odd effects. It could manifest as higher RAM usage on the web servers or excess I/O rates on the database server or as some other far distant effect.

> Run longevity tests. It's the only way to catch longevity bugs.

A system with longevity keeps processing transactions for a long time. What is a long time? It depends. A useful working definition of *a long time* is the time between code deployments. If new code is deployed into production every week, then it doesn't matter if the system can run for two years without rebooting. On the other hand, a data collector in western Montana really shouldn't need to be rebooted by hand once a week. (Unless you want to live in western Montana, that is.)

3.2 Failure Modes

Sudden impulses and excessive strain both can trigger catastrophic failure. In either case, some component of the system will start to fail before everything else does. In *Inviting Disaster [Chi01]*, James R. Chiles refers to these as *cracks in the system*. He draws an analogy between a complex system on the verge of failure and a steel plate with a microscopic crack in the metal. Under stress, that crack can begin to propagate, faster and faster. Eventually, the crack will propagate faster than the speed of sound, and the metal breaks with an explosive sound. The original trigger and the way the crack spreads to the

Extending Your Life Span

The major dangers to your system's longevity are memory leaks and data growth. Both kinds of sludge will kill your system in production. Both are rarely caught during testing.

Testing makes problems visible so you can fix them (which is I why I always thank my testers when they find bugs). Following Murphy's law, whatever you do not test *against* will happen. Therefore, if you do not test for crashes right after midnight or out-of-memory errors in the application's forty-ninth hour of uptime, those crashes will happen. If you do not test for memory leaks that show up only after seven days, you will have memory leaks after seven days.

The trouble is that applications never run long enough in the development environment to reveal their longevity bugs. How long do you usually keep an application server running in your development environment? I'll bet the average life span is less than the length of a sitcom on TiVo.[a] In QA, it might run a little longer but is probably still getting recycled at least daily, if not more often. Even when it is up and running, it's not under continuous load. These environments are not conducive to long-running tests, such as leaving the server running for a month under daily traffic.

These sorts of bugs usually aren't caught by load testing either. A load test runs for a specified period of time and then quits. Load-testing vendors charge large dollars per hour, so nobody asks them to keep the load running for a week at a time. Your development team probably shares the corporate network, so you cannot disrupt such vital corporate activities as email and web browsing for days at a time.

So, how do you find these kinds of bugs? The only way you can catch them before they bite you in production is to run your own longevity tests. If you can, set aside a developer machine. Have it run JMeter, Marathon, or some other load-testing tool. Don't hit the system hard; just keep driving requests all the time. (Also, be sure to have the scripts slack for a few hours a day to simulate the slow period during the middle of the night. That will catch connection pool and firewall timeouts.)

Sometimes the economics don't justify setting up a complete environment. If not, at least try to test important parts while stubbing out the rest. It's still better than nothing.

If all else fails, production becomes your longevity testing environment by default. You'll definitely find the bugs there, but it's not a recipe for a happy lifestyle.

---

a. Once you skip commercials and the opening and closing credits: about 21 minutes.

rest of the system, together with the result of the damage, are collectively called a *failure mode*.

No matter what, your system will have a variety of failure modes. Denying the inevitability of failures robs you of your power to control and contain them. Once you accept that failures will happen, you have the ability to design your system's reaction to specific failures. Just as auto engineers create *crumple zones*—areas designed to protect passengers by failing first—you can create safe failure modes that contain the damage and protect the rest of the system. This sort of self-protection determines the whole system's resilience.

Chiles calls these protections *crackstoppers*. Like building crumple zones into cars to absorb impacts and keep passengers safe, you can decide what features of the system are indispensable and build in failure modes that keep cracks away from those features. If you do not design your failure modes, then you will get whatever unpredictable—and usually dangerous—ones happen to emerge.

3.3 Cracks Propagate

Let's see how this applies to the grounded airline I investigated before. The airline's Core Facilities project had not designed its failure modes. The crack started at the improper handling of the SQLException, but it could have been stopped at many other points. Let's look at some examples, from low-level detail to high-level architecture.

Because the pool was configured to block requesting threads when no resources were available, it eventually tied up all request-handling threads. (This happened independently in each application server instance.) The pool could have been configured to create more connections if it was exhausted. It could also have been configured to block callers for a limited time, instead of blocking forever when all connections were checked out. Either of these would have stopped the crack from propagating.

At the next level up, a problem with one call in CF caused the calling applications on other hosts to fail. Because CF exposed its services as Enterprise JavaBeans (EJBs), it used RMI. By default, RMI calls will never time out. In other words, the callers blocked waiting to read their responses from CF's EJBs. The first twenty callers to each instance received exceptions: a SQLException wrapped in an InvocationTargetException wrapped in a RemoteException, to be precise. After that, the calls started blocking.

The client could have been written to set a timeout on the RMI sockets.[2] At a certain point in time, CF could also have decided to build an HTTP-based web service instead of EJBs. Then, the client could set a timeout on its HTTP

---

2. For example, by installing a socket factory that calls Socket.setSoTimeout() on all new sockets it creates.

requests.[3] The clients might also have written their calls so the blocked threads could be jettisoned, instead of having the request-handling thread make the external integration call. None of these were done, so the crack propagated from CF to all systems that used CF.

At a still larger scale, the CF servers themselves could have been partitioned into more than one service group. That would keep a problem within one of the service groups from taking down all users of CF. (In this case, all service groups would have cracked in the same way, but that would not always be the case.) This is another way of stopping cracks from propagating into the rest of the enterprise.

Looking at even larger architecture issues, CF could have been built using request/reply message queues. In that case, the caller would know that a reply might never arrive. It would have to deal with that case, as part of handling the protocol itself. Even more radically, the callers could be searching for flights by looking for entries in a tuplespace that matched the search criteria. CF would keep the tuplespace populated with flight records. The more tightly coupled the architecture, the greater the chance this coding error can propagate. Conversely, the less coupled architectures act as shock absorbers, diminishing the effects of this error instead of amplifying them.

Any of these approaches could have stopped the SQLException problem from spreading to the rest of the airline. Sadly, the designers had not considered the possibility of "cracks" when they created the shared services.

3.4   Chain of Failure

Underneath every system outage, there is a chain of events like this. One small thing leads to another, which leads to another. Looking at the entire chain of failure after the fact, the failure seems inevitable. If you tried to estimate the probability of that exact chain of events occurring, it would look incredibly improbable. But, it looks improbable only if you consider the probability of each event independently. A coin has no memory; each toss has the same probability, independent of previous tosses. The combination of events causing the failure is not independent. A failure in one point or layer actually increases the probability of other failures. If the database gets slow, then the application servers are *more* likely to run out of memory. Because the layers are coupled, the events are not independent.

---

3.   Unless it used java.net.URL and java.net.URLConnection, though. Until Java 5, it was impossible to set a timeout on HTTP calls made through the standard Java library.

At each step in the chain of failure, the crack can be accelerated, slowed, or stopped. High levels of complexity provide more directions for the cracks to propagate in.

Tight coupling accelerates cracks. For instance, the tight coupling of EJB calls allowed a resource exhaustion problem in CF to create larger problems in its callers. Coupling the request-handling threads to the external integration calls in those systems caused a remote problem to turn into downtime.

One way to prepare for every possible failure is to look at every external call, every I/O, every use of resources, and every expected outcome and ask, "What are all the ways this can go wrong?" Think about the different types of impulse and stress that can be applied:

- What if I can't make the initial connection?
- What if it takes ten minutes to make the connection?
- What if I can make the connection and then it gets disconnected?
- What if I can make the connection and I just can't get any response from the other end?
- What if it takes two minutes to respond to my query?
- What if 10,000 requests come in at the same time?
- What if my disk is full when I try to log the error message about the SQLException that happened because the network was bogged down with a worm?

I'm getting tired already, and that's just the beginning of everything that can go wrong. So, the exhaustive brute-force approach is impractical for anything but life-critical systems or Mars rovers. What if you actually have to deliver in this decade? You need to look at some patterns that let you create shock absorbers to relieve those stresses.

3.5 Patterns and Antipatterns

I've dealt with hundreds of production failures. Each one was unique. (They were mostly unique, anyway, since I try not to have the same failure happen twice!) I can't think of two incidents where the precise chain of failure happened the same way: same triggers, same fracture, same propagation. Over time, however, patterns of failure do emerge. A certain brittleness along an axis, a tendency for *this* problem to amplify *that* way. These are the stability antipatterns. Chapter 4, *Stability Antipatterns*, on page 31 deals with these patterns of failure.

If there are systematic patterns of failure, you might imagine that some common solutions would apply. You would be correct. Chapter 5, *Stability Patterns*, on page 89 deals with design and architecture patterns to defeat the antipatterns. These patterns cannot prevent cracks in the system. Nothing can. There will always be some set of conditions that can trigger a crack. These patterns stop cracks from propagating. They help contain damage and preserve partial functionality instead of allowing total crashes.

It should come as no surprise that these patterns and antipatterns interact with each other. The antipatterns have a tendency to reinforce each other. Like matching garlic, silver, and fire to their respective movie monsters,[4] each of the patterns alleviates specific problems.

The following figure maps the most important of these interactions. You'll start now by looking at the common sources of failure: the antipatterns.

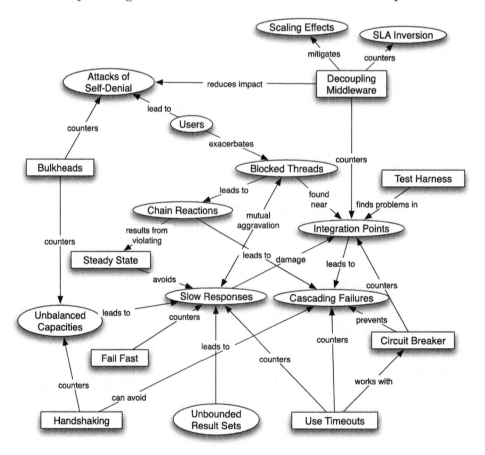

---

4.   That would be vampires, werewolves, and Frankenstein's monster.

CHAPTER 4

Stability Antipatterns

Once upon a time, application crashes were just about the most common type of bug, with operating system crashes a near second. I could make snide remarks about how little has changed, but that would be dishonest. Applications rarely crash these days, thanks in large part to the wide adoption of Java, PHP, Ruby, and other interpreted languages. Operating systems have generally gotten more stable and reliable due to the hard work of many thousands of programmers. We used to think of a hundred concurrent users as representing a large system; now we think in the tens of thousands. Instead of application uptime in the hours, we now look for months of continuous uptime. The breadth of our applications' reach has exploded, first as we integrate systems within the enterprise and then again as we integrate across enterprises.

Of course, this also means bigger challenges. As we integrate the world, tightly coupled systems are the rule rather than the exception. Big systems serve more users by commanding more resources; but, in many failure modes, big systems fail faster than small systems. The size and the complexity of these systems push us to what *Inviting Disaster [Chi01]* calls the *technology frontier*, where the twin specters of highly interactive complexity and tight coupling conspire to turn rapidly moving cracks into full-blown failures.

Highly interactive complexity arises when systems have enough moving parts and hidden, internal dependencies that most operators' mental models are either incomplete or just plain wrong. In *The Design of Everyday Things [Nor88]*, Don Norman describes the disconnect between the users' mental model and the implementation model that can occur when the implementation is invisible and the surface appearance is not obvious. He describes his experience with the two dials in his refrigerator that appear to directly control the temperature in the refrigeration section and the freezer section. Adjusting the dials under that mental model resulted in frozen milk and thawed meat, because the actual mechanism was controlling the proportion of chilled air sent to each section. In a system exhibiting highly interactive complexity, the operator's instinctive actions will have results ranging from ineffective to actively harmful. With the best of intentions, the operator can take an action, based on his own mental model of how the system functions, that triggers a completely unexpected linkage. Such linkages contribute to *problem inflation*, turning a minor issue into a major incident. Hidden linkages in cooling monitoring and control systems are partly to blame for the Three Mile Island reactor incident.[1] These hidden linkages often appear obvious during the post-mortem analysis but are in fact devilishly difficult to anticipate.

Tight coupling allows cracks in one part of the system to propagate themselves —or multiply themselves—across layer or system boundaries. In the physical world, you can think of a catwalk held up by four bolts threaded through a metal plate. The catwalk, the nuts and bolts, the plate, and the ceiling are obviously tightly coupled. (In fact, that's sort of the point of the bolts!) The failure of a single bolt will radically increase the stress on the other bolts, the ceiling, and the catwalk. This increased stress makes it extremely likely that another component in the system will fail—probably the catwalk itself. In your systems, tight coupling can appear within application code, in calls between systems, or anyplace a resource has multiple consumers.

In this chapter, we'll look at eleven stability antipatterns I've observed. These are common forces that I've seen at the root cause of more than one system failure. Some of these are like the guy who goes into the doctor and says, "Doc, whenever I do this, it hurts," and hits himself in the head with a hammer. Quoth the doctor, "Don't do that!" Each of the antipatterns will create, accelerate, or multiply cracks in the system. These bad behaviors are to be avoided.

In all cases, however, the main point to remember is that things will break. Don't pretend you can eliminate every possible source of failure, because either nature or nurture will create bigger failures to wreck your systems. Assume the worst, because cracks happen.

> Antipatterns create, accelerate, or multiply cracks in the system.

---

1. *Inviting Disaster [Chi01]*, pages 37–63.

4.1   Integration Points

 I haven't seen a "pure-website" project since about 1996. If your projects are like mine, they have probably been enterprise integration projects that happen to have an HTML-based front end. Indeed, despite lip service, companies didn't really get off the starting line for enterprise integration until they needed to create dynamic websites. Those projects were the impetus that finally forced many companies to integrate systems that have never played well together. Look at the system context diagram from any of these projects, and you'll see the site squatting in the center of the diagram with lines stretching in every direction. Feeds come in from inventory, pricing, content management, CRM, ERP, MRP, SAP, WAP, BAP, BPO, R2D2, and C3P0. Data extracts fly off toward CRM, fulfillment, booking, authorization, fraud checking, address normalization, scheduling, shipping, and so on. Reports are generated (one hopes) showing business statistics to business people, technical statistics to technical people, and management statistics to management.

Integration points are the number-one killer of systems. Every single one of those feeds presents a stability risk. Every socket, process, pipe, or remote procedure call can and will hang. Even database calls can hang, in ways obvious and subtle. Every feed into the system can hang it, crash it, or generate other impulses at the worst possible time. You'll look at some of the specific ways these integration points can go bad and what you can do about them.

Socket-Based Protocols

Many higher-level integration protocols run over sockets. In fact, pretty much everything except named pipes and shared-memory IPC is socket based. The higher protocols introduce their own failure modes, but they are all susceptible to failures at the socket layer.

The simplest failure mode occurs when the remote system refuses connections. The calling system must deal with connection failures. Usually, this is not much of a problem, since everything from C to Java to Ruby has clear ways to indicate a connection failure—either a -1 return value in C or an exception in Java, C#, and Ruby. Because the API makes it clear that connections don't always work, programmers deal with that case.

One wrinkle to watch out for, though, is that it can take a *long* time to discover that you can't connect. Hang on for a quick dip into the details of TCP/IP networking.

How Many Feeds?

I was helping launch a replatform/rearchitecture project for a huge retailer. It came time to identify all the production firewall rules so we could open holes in the firewall to allow authorized connections to the production system. We had already gone through the usual suspects: the web servers' connections to the application server, the application server to the database server, the cluster manager to the cluster nodes, and so on.

When it came time to add rules for the feeds in and out of the production environment, we were pointed at the project manager for enterprise integration. That's right, the site rebuild project had its own project manager dedicated to integration. That was our second clue that this was not going to be a simple task. (The first clue was that nobody else could tell us what all the feeds were.) The PM understood exactly what we needed. He pulled up his database of integrations and ran a custom report to give us the connection specifics.

On one hand, I was impressed that he had a fully populated database to keep track of the various feeds (synchronous/asynchronous, batch or trickle feed, source system, frequency, volume, cross-reference numbers, business stakeholder, and so on). On the other hand, I was dismayed that he *needed* a database to keep track of it!

It probably comes as no surprise, then, that the site was plagued with stability problems when it launched. It was like having a newborn baby in the house; I was awakened up every night at 3 a.m. for the latest crash or crisis. We kept documenting the spots where the app crashed and feeding them back to the maintenance team for correction. I never kept a tally, but I'm sure that every single synchronous integration point caused at least one outage.

Every architecture diagram ever drawn has boxes and arrows, like the ones in Figure 3, *Simplest Topology: Direct Connection*, on page 35. Like a lot of other things we work with, this arrow is an abstraction for a network connection. Really, though, that means it's an abstraction for an abstraction. A network "connection" is a logical construct—an abstraction—in its own right. All you will ever see on the network itself are packets.[2] This is the Internet Protocol (IP) part of TCP/IP. Transmission Control Protocol (TCP) is an agreement about how to make something that looks like a continuous connection out of discrete packets. Figure 4, *Three-Way Handshake*, on page 35 shows the "three-way handshake" that TCP defines to open a connection.

The connection starts when the caller (the client in this scenario, even though it is itself a server for other applications) sends a SYN packet to a port on the

---

2. Of course, a "packet" is an abstraction, too. On the wire, it's just electrons. Between electrons and a TCP connection, there are many layers of abstraction. Fortunately, we get to choose whichever level of abstraction is useful at any given point in time.

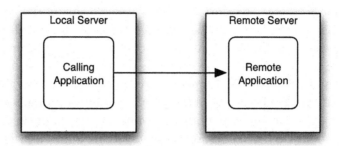

Figure 3—Simplest Topology: Direct Connection

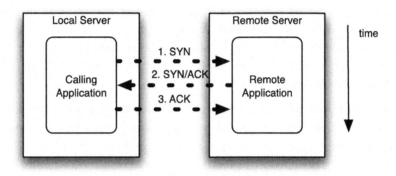

Figure 4—Three-Way Handshake

remote server. If nobody is listening to that port, the remote server immediately sends back a TCP "reset" packet to indicate that nobody's home. The calling application then gets an exception or a bad return value. All this happens very quickly, in less than ten milliseconds if both machines are plugged into the same switch.

If there is an application listening to the destination port, then the remote server sends back a SYN/ACK packet, indicating its willingness to accept the connection. The caller gets the SYN/ACK and sends back its own ACK. These three packets have now established the "connection," and the applications can send data back and forth.[3]

Suppose, though, that the remote application is listening to the port but is absolutely hammered with connection requests, until it cannot service the

---

3. TCP also defines the "simultaneous open" handshake, in which both machines send SYN packets to each other before a SYN/ACK. This is relatively rare in systems that are based on client/server interactions.

incoming connections. The port itself has a *listen queue* that defines how many pending connections (SYN sent, but no SYN/ACK replied) are allowed by the network stack. Once that listen queue is full, further connection attempts are refused quickly. The listen queue is the worst place to be. While the socket is in that partially formed state, whichever thread called open() is blocked inside the OS kernel until the remote application finally gets around to accepting the connection or until the connection attempt times out. Connection timeouts vary from one operating system to another, but they are usually measured in *minutes*! The calling application's thread could be blocked waiting for the remote server to respond for ten minutes!

Nearly the same thing happens when the caller can connect and send its request but the server takes a long time to read the request and send a response. The read() call will just block until the server gets around to responding. In Java, the default is to block forever. You have to call Socket.set-SoTimeout() if you want to break out of the blocking call. In that case, be prepared for an IOException.

Networks failures can hit you in two ways: fast or slow. Fast network failures cause immediate exceptions in the calling code. "Connection refused" is a very fast failure; it takes a few milliseconds to come back to the caller. Slow failures, such as a dropped ACK, let threads block for minutes before throwing exceptions. The blocked thread can't process other transactions, so overall capacity is reduced. If all threads end up getting blocked, then for all practical purposes, the server is down. Clearly, a slow response is a lot worse than no response.

The 5 a.m. Problem

One of the sites I launched developed this very nasty pattern of hanging completely at almost exactly 5 a.m. every day. This was running on around thirty different instances, so something was happening to make all thirty different application server instances hang within a five-minute window (the resolution of our URL pinger). Restarting the application servers always cleared it up, so there was some transient effect that tipped the site over at that time. Unfortunately, that was just when traffic started to ramp up for the day. From midnight to 5 a.m., there were only about 100 transactions per hour of interest, but the numbers ramped up quickly once the East Coast started to come online (one hour ahead of us Central Time folks). Restarting all the application servers just as people started to hit the site in earnest was what you'd call a suboptimal approach.

On the third day this occurred, I took thread dumps from one of the afflicted application servers. The instance was up and running, but all request-handling threads were blocked inside the Oracle JDBC library, specifically inside of OCI calls. (We were using the thick-client driver for its superior failover features.) In fact, once I eliminated the threads that were just blocked trying to enter a synchronized method, it looked as if the active threads were all in low-level socket read or write calls.

The next step was tcpdump and ethereal.[4] The odd thing was how little that showed. A handful of packets were being sent from the application servers to the database servers, but with no replies. Also nothing was coming from the database to the application servers. Yet, monitoring showed that the database was alive and healthy. There were no blocking locks, the run queue was at zero, and the I/O rates were trivial.

By this time, we had to restart the application servers. Our first priority is restoring service. We do data collection when we can, but not at the risk of breaking an SLA. Any deeper investigation would have to wait until it happened again. None of us doubted that it would happen again.

Service-level agreement: a contractual obligation to provide a service to a measurable, quantitative level. Financial penalties accompany the violation of an SLA.

Sure enough, the pattern repeated itself the next morning. Application servers locked up tight as a drum, with the threads inside the JDBC driver. This time, I was able to look at traffic on the databases' network. Zilch. Nothing at all. The utter absence of traffic on that side of the firewall was like Sherlock Holmes' dog that *didn't* bark in the night—the absence of activity was the biggest clue. I had a hypothesis. Quick decompilation of the application server's resource pool class confirmed that my hypothesis was plausible.

I said before that socket connections are an abstraction. They exist only as objects in the memory of the computers at the endpoints. Once established, a TCP connection can exist for days *without a single packet* being sent by either side.[5] As long as both computers have that socket state in memory, the "connection" is still valid. Routes can change, and physical links can be severed and reconnected. It doesn't matter; the "connection" persists as long as the two computers at the endpoints think it does.

There was a time when that all worked beautifully well. These days, a bunch of paranoid little bastions have broken the philosophy and implementation of the whole Net. I'm talking about firewalls, of course.

---

4. Ethereal has since been renamed Wireshark.
5. Assuming you set suitably perverse timeouts in the kernel.

Packet Capture

Abstractions provide great conciseness of expression. We can go much faster when we talk about fetching a document from a URL than if we have to discuss the tedious details of connection setup, packet framing, acknowledgments, receive windows, and so on. With every abstraction, however, there comes a time when you must peel the onion, shed some tears, and see what's really going on—usually when something is going wrong. Whether for problem diagnosis or performance tuning, packet capture tools are the only way to understand what is really happening on the network.

tcpdump is a common UNIX tool for capturing packets from a network interface. Running it in "promiscuous" mode instructs the network interface card (NIC) to receive all packets that cross its wire—even those addressed to other computers. (In a data center, the NIC is almost certainly connected to a switch port that is assigned to a virtual LAN [VLAN]. In that case, the switch guarantees that the NIC receives packets bound for addresses only in that VLAN. This is an important security measure, because it prevents bad guys from doing exactly what we're doing: sniffing the wire to look for "interesting" bits of information.) Wireshark[a] is a combination sniffer and protocol analyzer. It can sniff packets on the wire, as tcpdump does. Wireshark goes farther, though, by unpacking the packets for us. Through its history, Wireshark has experienced numerous security flaws—some trivial, some serious. At one point, a specially crafted packet sent across the wire (by a piece of malware on a compromised desktop machine, for example) could trigger a buffer overflow and execute arbitrary code of the attacker's choice. Since Wireshark must run as root to put the NIC into promiscuous mode—as any packet capture utility must—that exploit allowed the attacker to gain root access on a network administrator's machine.

Beyond the security issues, Wireshark is a big, heavy GUI program. On UNIX, it requires a bunch of X libraries (which might not even be installed on a headless system). On any host, it takes up a lot of RAM and CPU cycles to parse and display the packets. That is a burden that should not be on the production servers. For these reasons, it is best to capture packets noninteractively using tcpdump and then move the capture file to a nonproduction environment for analysis.

The screenshot below shows Ethereal analyzing a capture from my home network. The first packet shows an address routing protocol (ARP) request. This happens to be a question from my wireless bridge to my cable modem. The next packet was a surprise: an HTTP query to Google, asking for a URL called /safebrowsing/lookup with some query parameters. The next two packets show a DNS query and response, for the "michaelnygard.dyndns.org" hostname. Packets five, six, and seven are the three-phase handshake for a TCP connection setup. We can trace the entire conversation between my web browser and server. Note that the pane below the packet trace shows the layers of encapsulation that the TCP/IP stack created around the HTTP request in the second packet. The outermost frame is an Ethernet packet. The Ethernet packet contains an IP packet, which in turn contains a TCP packet. Finally, the payload of the TCP packet is an HTTP request. The exact bytes of the entire packet appear in the third pane.

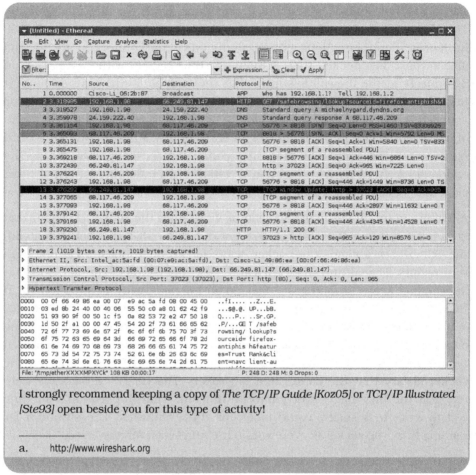

I strongly recommend keeping a copy of *The TCP/IP Guide [Koz05]* or *TCP/IP Illustrated [Ste93]* open beside you for this type of activity!

---

a. http://www.wireshark.org

A firewall is nothing but a specialized router. It routes packets from one set of physical ports to another. Inside each firewall, a set of access control lists define the rules about which connections it will allow. The rules say such things as "connections originating from 192.0.2.0/24 to 192.168.1.199 port 80 are allowed." When the firewall sees an incoming SYN packet, it checks it against its rule base. The packet might be allowed (routed to the destination network), rejected (TCP reset packet sent back to origin), or ignored (dropped on the floor with no response at all). If the connection is allowed, then the firewall makes an entry in its own internal table that says something like "192.0.2.98:32770 is connected to 192.168.1.199:80." Then all future packets, in either direction, that match the endpoints of the connection are routed between the firewall's networks.

So far, so good. How is this related to my 5 a.m. wake-up calls?

The key is that table of established connections inside the firewall. It's finite. Therefore, it does not allow infinite duration connections, even though TCP itself does allow them. Along with the endpoints of the connection, the firewall also keeps a "last packet" time. If too much time elapses without a packet on a connection, the firewall assumes that the endpoints are dead or gone. It just drops the connection from its table, as shown in Figure 5, *Idle Connection Dropped by Firewall*, on page 41. But, TCP was never designed for that kind of intelligent device in the middle of a connection. There's no way for a third party to tell the endpoints that their connection is being torn down. The endpoints assume their connection is valid for an indefinite length of time, even if no packets are crossing the wire.

After that point, any attempt to read or write from the socket on either end does *not* result in a TCP reset or an error due to a half-open socket. Instead, the TCP/IP stack sends the packet, waits for an ACK, doesn't get one, and retransmits. The faithful stack tries and tries to reestablish contact, and that firewall just keeps dropping the packets on the floor, without so much as an "ICMP destination unreachable" message. (That could let bad guys probe for active connections by spoofing source addresses.) My Linux system, running on a 2.6 series kernel, has its tcp_retries2 set to the default value of 15, which results in a *twenty-minute* timeout before the TCP/IP stack informs the socket library that the connection is broken. The HP-UX servers we were using at the time had a thirty-minute timeout. That application's one-line call to write to a socket could block for thirty minutes! The situation for reading from the socket is even worse. It could block forever.

When I decompiled the resource pool class, I saw that it used a last-in, first-out strategy. During the slow overnight times, traffic volume was light enough that one single database connection would get checked out of the pool, used, and checked back in. Then the next request would get the same connection, leaving the thirty-nine others to sit idle until traffic started to ramp up. They were idle well over the one-hour idle connection timeout configured into the firewall.

Once traffic started to ramp up, those thirty-nine connections per application server would get locked up immediately. Even if the one connection was still being used to serve pages, sooner or later it would be checked out by a thread that ended up blocked on a connection from one of the other pools. Then the one good connection would be held by a blocked thread. Total site hang.

Once we understood all the links in that chain of failure, we had to find a solution. The resource pool has the ability to test JDBC connections for validity before checking them out. It checked validity by executing a SQL

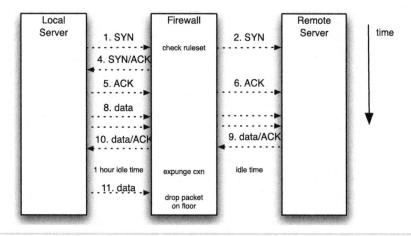

Figure 5—Idle Connection Dropped by Firewall

query like SELECT SYSDATE FROM DUAL. Well, that would just make the request-handling thread hang anyway. We could also have the pool keep track of the idle time of the JDBC connection and discard any that were older than one hour. Unfortunately, that involves sending a packet to the database server to tell it that the session is being torn down. Hang.

We were starting to look at some really hairy complexities, such as creating a "reaper" thread to find connections that were *close* to getting too old and tearing them down before they timed out. Fortunately, a sharp DBA recalled just the thing. Oracle has a feature called *dead connection detection* that you can enable to discover when clients have crashed. When enabled, the database server sends a ping packet to the client at some periodic interval. If the client responds, then the database knows it is still alive. If the client fails to respond after a few retries, the database server assumes the client has crashed and frees up all the resources held by that connection.

We weren't that worried about the client crashing, but the ping packet itself would be enough to reset the firewall's "last packet" time for the connection, keeping the connection alive. Dead connection detection kept the connection alive, which let me sleep through the night.

Next, we'll look at problems with HTTP-based protocols, including web services.

HTTP Protocols

Service-oriented architectures are a hot topic these days, certainly if you listen to application server vendors. One reason to pursue SOA is the renewed hope of getting the reusability that RPC, OOP, CORBA, and EJB have not delivered on. Another commonly cited reason is more efficient use of data center resources by providing shared hardware for commonly used services. Other organizations desire the flexibility and nimbleness that SOA promises.

Whether based on the WS-I family of protocols, SOAP, XML-RPC, or REST, the common feature of service-oriented architecture is HTTP.[6] All of these ultimately involve shipping some chunk of XML as an HTTP request and waiting for an HTTP response.

Of course, all HTTP-based protocols use sockets so are vulnerable to all of the problems described previously. HTTP adds its own flavor of issue, mainly centered around the client library. Any Java developer has a built-in HTTP client available through the java.net.URL and java.net.URLConnection classes.

```
Line 1  URL url = new URL("http://www.google.com/search?q=foo");
     2  URLConnection conn = url.openConnection();
     3  HttpURLConnection httpConnection = (HttpURLConnection)conn;
     4  httpConnection.setRequestProperty("User-Agent",
     5  "Mozilla/5.0 (Macintosh; U; PPC Mac OS X Mach-O; en-US; rv:1.8.0.1) " +
     6  "Gecko/20060111 Firefox/1.5.0.1");
     7  InputStream response = httpConnection.getInputStream();
```

Java's highly generic URL class tries to hide the differences between HTTP, HTTPS, FTP, and other protocols. In line 1 we construct a query URL to hit Google. Opening the connection on line 2 doesn't actually send the request; it just acts as a factory method to create the concrete subclass of URLConnection that does the real work. We have to downcast the returned URLConnection to that specific class to call the setRequestProperty() on line 4.[7] Finally, in line 7, the HttpURLConnection actually opens a socket to the remote host, sends the HTTP request, waits for and parses the HTTP response, and returns an Input-Stream on the bytes of the response body.

There's a lot going on in line 7. This is where the HttpURLConnection actually connects to the remote server. Everything before this was just setup in local memory. Prior to Java 1.5, there was no chance to set any parameters, so we had to resort to tricks like installing a custom SocketImplFactory. Fortunately, the JDK now lets us control the connection timeout, but there is still no read timeout. The remote system could dribble back one byte per second for the next ten years, and your thread would still be stuck on that one call.

---

6. Technically, SOAP and the WS-I protocols allow for other message transports, but, in practice, only TIBCO and IBM MQ devotees are using them. More people should be using asynchronous message transport.

7. We have to lie about our user agent, or else Google will return a 403 "Forbidden" response!

A cynical system would never put up with such an unprotected call. Fortunately, other available HTTP clients allow much more control. For example, the Apache Jakarta Common's HttpClient package offers granular control over both the connection and read timeouts, not to mention request headers, response headers, and cookie policies.

Vendor API Libraries

It would be nice to think that enterprise software vendors *must* have hardened their software against bugs, just because they've sold it and deployed it for lots of clients. That might be true of the server software they sell, but it's rarely true for their client libraries. Usually, software vendors provide client API libraries that have a lot of problems and often have hidden stability risks. These libraries are just code, coming from regular developers. They have all the variability in quality, style, and safety that you see from any other random sampling of code.

The worst part about these libraries is that you have so little control over them. About the best thing you can do is decompile the code, find issues, and report them as bugs. If you have enough clout to apply pressure to the vendor, then you might be able to get a bug fix to their client library, assuming, of course, that you are on the latest version of their software. In the past, I have been known to fix their bugs and recompile my own version for temporary use while waiting for the patched version from the vendor.

The prime stability killer with vendor API libraries is all about blocking. Whether it's an internal resource pool, socket read calls, HTTP connections, or just plain old Java serialization, vendor API libraries are peppered with unsafe coding practices.

Here's a classic example. Whenever you have threads that need to synchronize on multiple resources, you have the potential for deadlock. Thread 1 holds lock A and needs lock B, while thread 2 has lock B and needs lock A. The classic recipe for avoiding this deadlock is to make sure you always acquire the locks in the same order and release them in the reverse order. Of course, this helps only if you *know* that the thread will be acquiring both locks and you can control the order in which they are acquired. Let's take an example in Java. This illustration could be from some kind of message-oriented middleware library:

```
stability_anti_patterns/UserCallback.java
public interface UserCallback {
  public void messageReceived(Message msg);
}
```

```
stability_anti_patterns/Connection.java
public interface Connection {
    public void registerCallback(UserCallback callback);

    public void send(Message msg);
}
```

I'm sure this looks quite familiar. Is it safe? No idea. Without knowing what thread messageReceived() gets called on, you cannot be sure what monitors the thread will be holding. It could have a dozen synchronized methods on the stack already. Deadlock minefield.

In fact, even though the UserCallback interface does not declare messageReceived() as synchronized (you can't declare an interface method as synchronized), the implementation might make it synchronized. Depending on the threading model inside the client library and how long your callback method takes, synchronizing the callback method could block threads inside the client library. Like a plugged drain, those blocked threads can cause threads calling send() to block. Odds are that means request-handling threads will be tied up. As always, once all the request-handling threads are blocked, your application might as well be down.

Countering Integration Point Problems

A stand-alone system that doesn't integrate with anything is rare, not to mention almost useless. What can you do to make integration points safer? The most effective patterns to combat integration point failures are Circuit Breaker and Decoupling Middleware.

Testing helps, too. Cynical software should handle violations of form and function, such as badly formed headers or abruptly closed connections. To make sure your software is cynical enough, you should make a *test harness*—a simulator that provides controllable behavior—for each integration test. Setting the test harness to spit back canned responses facilitates functional testing. It also provides isolation from the target system when you are testing. Finally, each such test harness should also allow you to simulate various kinds of system and network failure.

> Combat integration point failures with the Circuit Breaker and Decoupling Middleware patterns.

This test harness will immediately help with functional testing. To test for stability, you also need to flip all the switches on the harness while the system is under considerable load. This load can come from a bunch of workstations running JMeter or Marathon, but it definitely requires much more than a handful of testers clicking around on their desktops.

Remember This

Beware this necessary evil

Every integration point will eventually fail in some way, and you need to be prepared for that failure.

Prepare for the many forms of failure

Integration point failures take several forms, ranging from various network errors to semantic errors. You will not get nice error responses delivered through the defined protocol; instead, you'll see some kind of protocol violation, slow response, or outright hang.

Know when to open up abstractions

Debugging integration point failures usually requires peeling back a layer of abstraction. Failures are often difficult to debug at the application layer, because most of them violate the high-level protocols. Packet sniffers and other network diagnostics can help.

Failures propagate quickly

Failure in a remote system quickly becomes your problem, usually as a cascading failure when your code isn't defensive enough.

Apply patterns to avert Integration Points problems

Defensive programming via Circuit Breaker, Timeouts, Decoupling Middleware, and Handshaking will all help you avoid the dangers of Integration Points.

4.2 Chain Reactions

 In Section 8.1, *Defining Capacity*, on page 135, I'll talk a lot about the two main flavors of scalability: horizontal and vertical scaling. *Horizontal scaling* refers to adding capacity by adding servers. This is the Google and Amazon approach. A web farm is an example of horizontal scaling—each server adds nearly the same amount of capacity as the previous server. The alternative, *vertical scaling*, means building bigger and bigger servers: replacing x86 pizza boxes with four-way, eight-way, and then thirty-two-way servers. This is the approach Oracle would love to see you use. Each type of scaling works best under different circumstances.

If your system scales horizontally, then you will have load-balanced farms or clusters where each server runs the same applications. The multiplicity of machines provides you with fault tolerance through redundancy. A single

Searching...

I was dealing with a retailer's primary online brand. It has a huge catalog—half a million SKUs in 100 different categories. For its site, search isn't just useful; it's necessary. To handle all the customers during the holidays, the retailer was running a dozen search engines sitting behind a hardware load balancer. The application servers were configured to connect to a virtual IP address[a] instead of specific search engines. The load balancer then distributed the application servers' queries out to the search engines. It also performed health checks to discover which servers were alive and responsive so it could make sure to send queries only to search engines that were alive.

Those health checks turned out to be useful. The search engine had some bug that caused a memory leak. Under regular traffic (not a holiday season), the search engines would start to go dark right around noon. Because each engine had been taking the same proportion of load throughout the morning, they would all crash at about the same time. As each search engine went dark, the load balancer would send their share of the queries to the remaining servers, causing them to run out of memory even faster. When I looked at a chart of their "last response" time stamps, I could see an accelerating pattern of crashes very clearly. The gap between the first crash and the second would be five or six minutes. Between the second and third would be just three or four minutes. The last two would go down within seconds of each other.

This particular system also suffered from cascading failures and blocked threads. Losing the last search server caused the entire front end to lock up completely.

Until we got an effective patch from the vendor (which took months), we had to follow a daily regime of restarts that bracketed the peak hours: 11 a.m., 4 p.m., and 9 p.m.

---

a.   See Section 11.3, *Virtual IP Addresses*, on page 190 for more about load balancing and virtual IP addresses.

machine or process can completely bonk while the remainder continues serving transactions.

Single point of failure (SPOF): Any device, node, or cable that, when removed, results in the complete failure of a larger system. For example, a server with only one power supply and a network switch with no redundancy are both SPOFs.

Still, even though horizontal clusters are not susceptible to single points of failure (except in the case of attacks of self-denial, see *Attacks of Self-Denial*, on page 69), they can exhibit a load-related failure mode. When one node in a load-balanced group fails, the other nodes must pick up the slack. For example, in the eight-server farm shown in Figure 6, *Eight-Way Horizontal Farm*, on page 47, each node handles 12.5% of the total load.

After one server pops off, you have the distribution shown in Figure 7, *Formerly an eight-way cluster*, on page 47. Each of the remaining seven servers must handle about 14.3% of the total load. Even though each server has to take only 1.8% more of the total workload, that server's load increases by about

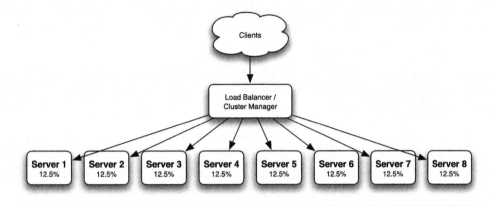

Figure 6—Eight-Way Horizontal Farm

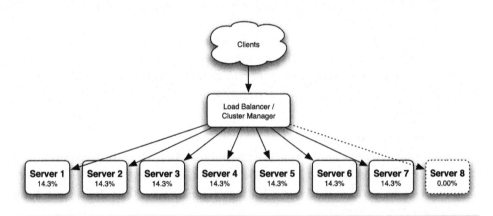

Figure 7—Formerly an eight-way cluster

15%. In the degenerate case of a failure in a two-node cluster, the survivor's workload doubles. It has its original load (50% of the total) plus the dead node's load (50% of the total).

If the first server failed because of some load-related condition, such as a memory leak or intermittent race condition, the surviving nodes become more likely to fail. With each additional server that goes dark, the remaining stalwarts get more and more burdened and therefore are more and more likely to also go dark.

A chain reaction occurs when there is some defect in an application—usually a resource leak or a load-related crash. We're already talking about a homogeneous layer, so that defect is going to be in each of the servers. That means the only way you can eliminate the chain reaction is to fix the underlying defect. Splitting a layer into multiple pools—as in the Bulkhead pattern—can sometimes help by splitting a single chain reaction into two separate chain reactions that occur at different rates.

What effect could a chain reaction have on the rest of the system? Well, for one thing, a chain reaction failure in one layer can easily lead to a cascading failure in a calling layer.

Chain reactions are sometimes caused by blocked threads. This happens when all the request-handling threads in an application get blocked and that application stops responding. Incoming requests will then get distributed out to the applications on other servers in the same layer, increasing their chance of failure.

 Remember This

One server down jeopardizes the rest

A chain reaction happens because the death of one server makes the others pick up the slack. The increased load makes them more likely to fail. A chain reaction will quickly bring an entire layer down. Other layers that depend on it must protect themselves, or they will go down in a cascading failure.

Hunt for resource leaks

Most of the time, a chain reaction happens when your application has a memory leak. As one server runs out of memory and goes down, the other servers pick up the dead one's burden. The increased traffic means they leak memory faster.

Hunt for obscure timing bugs

Obscure race conditions can also be triggered by traffic. Again, if one server goes down to a deadlock, the increased load on the others makes them more likely to hit the deadlock too.

Defend with Bulkheads

Partitioning servers, with Bulkheads, can prevent Chain Reactions from taking out the entire service—though they won't help the callers of whichever partition does go down. Use Circuit Breaker on the calling side for that.

4.3   Cascading Failures

 The standard system architecture for enterprise systems, including websites and web services, comprises a collection of functionally distinct farms or clusters that are interconnected through some form of load balancing. We usually refer to the individual farms as *layers*—for example, as in Figure 8, *Layers Often Found in Commerce Systems*, on page 50—even though they might not really be a single stack.

In a service-oriented architecture, these look even less like traditional layers and more like a directed, acyclic graph.

System failures start with a crack. That crack comes from some fundamental problem. Various mechanisms can retard or stop the crack, which are the topics of the next chapter. Absent those mechanisms, the crack can progress and even be amplified by some structural problems. A cascading failure occurs when a crack in one layer triggers a crack in a calling layer.

A cascading failure occurs when problems in one layer cause problems in callers.

An obvious example is a database failure. If an entire database cluster goes dark, then any application that calls the database is going to experience problems of some kind. If it handles the problems badly, then the application layer will start to fail. One system I saw would tear down any JDBC connection that ever threw a SQLException. Each page request would attempt to create a new connection, get a SQLException, try to tear down the connection, get another SQLException, and then vomit a stack trace all over the user.

Cascading failures require some mechanism to transmit the failure from one layer to another. The failure "jumps the gap" when bad behavior in the calling layer gets triggered by the failure condition in the called layer.

Cascading failures often result from resource pools that get drained because of a failure in a lower layer. Integration Points without Timeouts is a surefire way to create Cascading Failures.

Just as integration points are the number-one source of cracks, cascading failures are the number-one crack accelerator. Preventing cascading failures is the very key to resilience. The most effective patterns to combat cascading failures are Circuit Breaker and Timeouts.

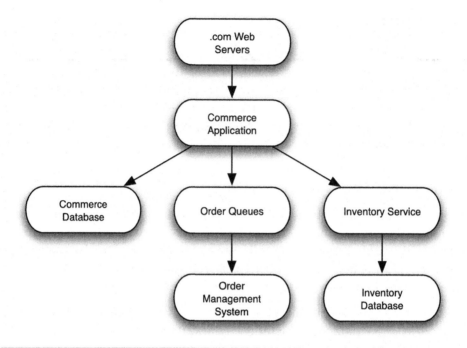

Figure 8—Layers Often Found in Commerce Systems

 Remember This

Stop cracks from jumping the gap

A cascading failure occurs when cracks jump from one system or layer to another, usually because of insufficiently paranoid integration points. A cascading failure can also happen after a chain reaction in a lower layer. Your system surely calls out to other enterprise systems; make sure you can stay up when they go down.

Scrutinize resource pools

A cascading failure often results from a resource pool, such as a connection pool, that gets exhausted when none of its calls return. The threads that get the connections block forever; all other threads get blocked waiting for connections. Safe resource pools always limit the time a thread can wait to check out a resource.

Defend with Timeouts and Circuit Breaker

A cascading failure happens *after* something else has already gone wrong. Circuit Breaker protects your system by avoiding calls out to the troubled integration point. Using Timeouts ensures that you can come back from a call out to the troubled one.

> ## Hammer Time
>
> The layer-jumping mechanism often takes the form of blocked threads, but I've also seen the reverse—an overly aggressive thread. In one case, the calling layer would get a quick error, but, because of a historical precedent, it would assume that the error was just an irreproducible, transient error in the lower layer. At some point, the lower layer was suffering from a race condition that would make it kick out an error once in a while for no good reason. The upstream developer decided to retry the call when that happened. Unfortunately, the lower layer didn't provide enough detail to distinguish between the transient error and a more serious one. As a result, once the lower layer started to have some real problems (losing packets from the database because of a failed switch), the caller started to pound it more and more. The more the lower layer whined and cried, the more the upper layer yelled, "I'll give you something to cry about!" and hammered it even harder. Ultimately, the calling layer was using 100% of its CPU making calls to the lower layer and logging failures in calls to the lower layer. A circuit breaker would really have helped here.

4.4 Users

Users are a terrible thing.[8] Systems would be infinitely more stable without them. The human users of a system have this knack for creative destruction. When your system is teetering on the brink of disaster like a car on a cliff in a movie, some user will be the seagull landing on the hood. Down she goes! Human users have a gift for doing exactly the worst possible thing at the worst possible time.

> Users are a terrible thing.

Worse yet, other systems that call ours march remorselessly forward like an army of Terminators, utterly unsympathetic about how close we are to crashing.

Traffic

Every user consumes some system resources. Unless you are building a peer-to-peer system such as BitTorrent, your system's capacity is limited. It scales with the amount of hardware and bandwidth you've bought, not the number of users you've attracted.

As traffic grows, it will eventually surpass your capacity.[9] Then comes the biggest question: How does your system react to excessive demand?

---

8. Obviously, I'm being somewhat tongue-in-cheek. Although users do present numerous risks to stability, they are also the reason our systems exist.
9. If traffic isn't growing, then you have other problems to worry about!

In Section 8.1, *Defining Capacity*, on page 135, we will see the definition of capacity: when transactions take too long to execute, it means that the demand on your system has exceeded its capacity. Internally to your system, however, there are some harder limits. Passing those limits makes cracks in the system, and cracks always propagate faster under stress.

One such hard limit is memory available, particularly in Java or J2EE systems. Excess traffic can stress the memory system in several ways. First and foremost, in web systems, every user has a session. The session stays resident in memory for a certain length of time after the last request from that user. Every additional user means more memory.

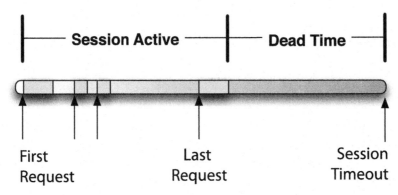

During that dead time, the session still occupies valuable memory. A session is not a magic "Bag of Holding."[10] Every object you put into the session sits there in memory, tying up precious bytes that could be serving some other user.

When memory gets short, a large number of very surprising things can happen. Probably the least offensive is throwing an OutOfMemoryError exception at the user. If things are really bad, the logging system might not even be able to log the error. For example, Log4j and java.util.logging both create objects to represent a log event. If no memory is available to create the log event, then nothing gets logged. (This, by the way, is a great argument for external monitoring in addition to log file scraping.) A supposedly recoverable low-memory situation will rapidly turn into a serious stability problem. In fact, if you are making

> Every user consumes more memory.

---

10. In case you didn't play Dungeons & Dragons, a Bag of Holding was much bigger on the inside than on the outside. Things you put into it were available but weighed almost nothing. It was a convenient explanation for characters that could keep two broadswords, a mace, full-plate armor, and half a million gold pieces with them all the time.

any native calls, then a low-memory condition will cause "malloc" to fail in the native code, for example, inside a Type 2 JDBC driver. It seems that few programmers of native code do good error checking, because I've seen JVM crashes result from native calls during a memory crisis.

Your best bet is to keep as little in the session as possible. For example, it's a bad idea to keep an entire set of search results in the session for pagination. It's better if you requery the search engine for each new page of results. For every object you put in the session, consider that it might never be used again. It could spend the next thirty minutes uselessly taking up memory and putting your system at risk.

It would be wonderful if there was a way to keep things in the session (therefore in memory) when memory is plentiful but automatically be more frugal when memory is tight. Good news! There is a way to do exactly that. java.lang.ref.SoftReference objects hold a reference to some other payload object.

You construct a SoftReference with the large or expensive object as an argument. The SoftReference object actually is a Bag of Holding. It keeps the payload for later use.

```
MagicBean hugeExpensiveResult = ...; SoftReference ref = new
SoftReference(hugeExpensiveResult);

session.setAttribute(EXPENSIVE_BEAN_HOLDER, ref);
```

This is not a transparent change. Any JSPs or servlets that access this object will know that they are going through a layer of indirection. If memory gets low, the garbage collector is allowed to reclaim the payload of a SoftReference, so long as there is no hard reference to that payload.

```
Reference reference = (Reference)session.getAttribute(EXPENSIVE_BEAN_HOLDER);
MagicBean bean = (MagicBean) reference.get();
```

What is the point of adding this level of indirection? When memory gets low, the garbage collector is allowed to reclaim any "softly reachable" objects. An object is softly reachable if the only references to it are held by SoftReference objects. The expensive object in Figure 9, *SoftReference and Its Payload*, on page 54 is softly reachable. The expensive object in Figure 10, *Strongly Reachable Payload Object*, on page 54, on the other hand, *not* softly reachable. It is strongly reachable because of the hard reference from the servlet.

The actual decision about when to reclaim softly reachable objects, how many of them to reclaim, and how many to spare is totally up to the garbage collector. The only guarantee is this: all softly reachable objects will be reclaimed before an OutOfMemoryError is thrown.

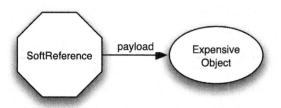

Figure 9—SoftReference and Its Payload

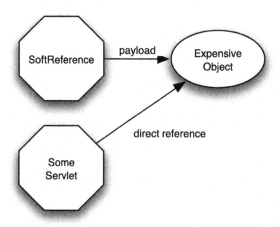

Figure 10—Strongly Reachable Payload Object

In other words, the garbage collector will take advantage of all the help you give it before it gives up. Be careful to note that it is the payload object that gets garbage collected, not the SoftReference itself. After the payload gets garbage collected, any calls to SoftReference.get() will return null. Any code that uses the payload object must be prepared to deal with a null payload, as shown in Figure 11, *SoftReference After Payload Is Garbage Collected*, on page 55. It can choose to recompute the expensive result, redirect the user to some other activity, or take any other protective action.

SoftReference is a useful way to respond to changing memory conditions, but it does add complexity. Generally, it's best to just keep things out of the session. Use the SoftReference approach when you cannot keep large or expensive objects out of the session. SoftReferences let you serve more users with the same amount of memory.

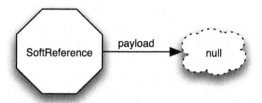

Figure 11—SoftReference After Payload Is Garbage Collected

Expensive to Serve

Some users are way more demanding than others. Ironically, these are usually the ones you want more of. For example, in a retail system, users who browse a couple of pages, maybe do a search, and then go away are both the bulk of users and the easiest to serve. Their content can usually be cached (however, see *Use Caching Carefully*, on page 176 for important cautions about caching). Serving their pages usually does not involve external integration points. You will likely do some personalization, maybe some clickstream tracking, and that's about it.

But then there's that user who actually wants to buy something. Unless you've licensed the one-click checkout patent, checkout probably takes four or five pages. That's already as many pages as a typical user's entire session. On top of that, checking out can involve several of those troublesome integration points: credit card authorization, sales tax calculation, address standardization, inventory lookups, and shipping. In fact, more buyers don't just increase the stability risk for the front-end system, they can place back-end or downstream systems at risk too. (See *Unbalanced Capacities*, on page 75.) Increasing the conversion rate might be good for the profit-and-loss statement, but it is definitely hard on the systems.

There is no effective defense against expensive users. They are not a direct stability risk, but the increased stress they produce increases the likelihood of triggering cracks elsewhere in the system. Still, I don't recommend measures to keep them off the system, since they are usually the ones who generate revenue. So, what should you do?

The best thing you can do about expensive users is test aggressively. Identify whatever your most expensive transactions are, and double or triple the proportion of those transactions. If your retail system expects a 2% conversion rate (which is about standard for retailers), then your load tests should test for a 4%, 6%, or 10% conversion rate.

Conversion rate: the percentage of site visitors who actually buy something.

> ## Total Conversion
>
> If a little is good, then a lot must be better, right? In other words, why not test for a 100% conversion rate? As a stability test, that's not a bad idea. I wouldn't use the results to plan capacity for regular production traffic, though. By definition, these are the most expensive transactions. Therefore, the average stress on the system is guaranteed to be less than what this test produces. Build the system to handle nothing but the most expensive transactions, and you will spend ten times too much on hardware.

Unwanted Users

We would all sleep easier if the only users to worry about were the ones handing us their credit card numbers. In keeping with the general theme of "weird, bad things happen in the real world," there are definitely weird, bad users out there.

Some of them don't mean to be bad. For example, I've seen badly configured proxy servers start re-requesting a user's last URL over and over again. I was able to identify the user's session by its cookie and then trace the session back to the registered customer. Logs showed that the user was legitimate. For some reason, fifteen minutes after the user's last request, the request started reappearing in the logs. At first, these requests were coming in every thirty seconds. They kept accelerating, though. Ten minutes later, we were getting four or five requests *every second*. These requests had the user's identifying cookie but not his session cookie. So, each request was creating a new session. It strongly resembled a DDoS attack except that it came from one particular proxy server on one Navy base.

DDoS: distributed denial-of-service attack. Many computers ganging up on a site with the purpose of saturating the bandwidth, CPU, or memory of the site's servers. Think Gulliver and the Lilliputians.

Once again, we see that sessions are the Achilles heel of web applications. Want to bring down nearly any dynamic web application? Pick a deep link from the site, and start requesting it, without sending cookies. Don't even wait for the response; just drop the socket connection as soon as you've sent the request. Web servers never tell the application servers that the end user stopped listening for an answer. The application server just keeps on processing the request. It sends the response back to the web server, which funnels it into the bit bucket. In the meantime, the 100 bytes of the HTTP request causes the application server to create a session (which may consume several kilobytes of memory in the application server). Even a desktop machine on a broadband connection can generate hundreds of thousands of sessions on the application servers.

In extreme cases, such as the flood of sessions originating from the Navy base, you can run into problems worse than just heavy memory consumption. In our case, the business users wanted to know how often their most loyal customers came back. The developers wrote a little interceptor that would update the "last login" time whenever a user's profile got loaded into memory from the database. During these session floods, though, the request presented a user ID cookie but no session cookie. That meant each request was treated like a new login, loading the profile from the database and attempting to update the "last login" time.

Imagine 100,000 transactions all trying to update the same row of the same table in the same database. Somebody is bound to get deadlocked. Once a single transaction with a lock on the user's profile got hung (because of the need for a connection from a different resource pool), all the other database transactions on that row got blocked. Pretty soon, every single request-handling thread got used up with these bogus logins. As soon as that happens, the site is down.

So, one kind of bad user just blunders around leaving disaster in his wake. There are more crafty sorts, however, who deliberately do abnormal things that just happen to have undesirable effects. The first group isn't deliberately malicious; they just do damage inadvertently. This next group belongs in its own category.

There is an entire parasitic industry that exists by consuming resources from other companies' websites. Collectively known as *competitive intelligence* companies, these outfits leech data out of your system one web page at a time.

These companies will argue that their service is no different from a grocery store sending someone into a competing store with a list and a clipboard. There is a big difference, though. Given the rate that they can request pages, it's more like sending a battalion of people into the store with clipboards. They would crowd out the aisles so legitimate shoppers could not get in.

Worse yet, these rapid-fire screen scrapers do not honor session cookies, so if you are not using URL rewriting to track sessions, each new page request will create a new session. Like a flash mob, pretty soon the capacity problem will turn into a stability problem. The battalion of price checkers could actually knock down the store.

Session Tracking

HTTP is a singularly unlikely protocol. If you were tasked with creating a protocol to facilitate arts, sciences, commerce, free speech, words, pictures, sound, and video, one that could weave the vastness of human knowledge and creativity into a single web, it is unlikely that you would arrive at HTTP. HTTP is stateless, for one thing. To the server, each new requester emerges from the swirling fog and makes some demand like "GET /site/index.jsp." Once answered, they disappear back into the fog without so much as a "thank you." Should one of these rude, demanding clients reappear, the server, in perfectly egalitarian ignorance, does not recognize it has seen them before.

Some clever folks at Netscape found a way to graft an extra bit of data into the protocol. Netscape originally conceived this data, called *cookies* (for no compelling reason), as a way to pass state back and forth from client to server, and vice versa. Cookies are a clever hack. They allowed all kinds of new applications, such as personalized portals (a big deal back then) and shopping sites. Security-minded application developers quickly realized, however, that unencrypted cookie data was open to manipulation by hostile clients. After all, just because some browser sends a User-Agent string that says "Mozilla," that doesn't mean it actually *is* Mozilla. (As of version 7 beta 1, Internet Explorer *still* claims to be Mozilla and probably always will. Its User-Agent string is "Mozilla/4.0 [compatible; MSIE 7.0b; Windows NT 6.0].") So, security dictates that the cookie either cannot contain actual data or must be encrypted. At the same time, high-volume sites found that passing real state in cookies uses up lots of expensive bandwidth and CPU time. Encrypting the cookies was right out.

So, cookies started being used for smaller pieces of data, just enough to tag a user with a persistent cookie or a temporary cookie to identify a session.

A *session* is an abstraction that makes building applications easier. All the user really sends are a series of HTTP requests. The web server receives these and, through a series of machinations, returns an HTTP response. There is no "begin a session" request by which the web browser can indicate it is about to start sending requests, and there is no "session finished" request. (The web server could not trust that such an indicator would be sent anyway.)

Sessions are all about caching data in memory. Early CGI applications had no need for a session, since they would fire up a new process (usually a Perl script) for each new request. That worked fine. There's nothing quite as safe as the "fork, run, and die" model. To reach higher volumes, however, developers and vendors turned to long-running application servers, such as Java application servers and long-running Perl processes via mod_perl. Instead of waiting for a process fork on each request, the server is always running, waiting for requests. With the long-running server, you can cache state from one request to another, reducing the number of hits to the database. Then, you need some way to identify a request as part of a session. Cookies work well for this.

Application servers handle all the cookie machinery for you, presenting a nice programmatic interface with some resemblance to a Map or Dictionary. As usual, though, the trouble with invisible machinery is that it can go horribly wrong when misused.

> When that invisible machinery involves layers of kludges meant to make HTTP look like a real application protocol, it can really tip over badly. For example, home-brew shopping bots do not handle session cookies properly. Each request creates a new session, consuming memory for no good reason. If the web server is configured to ask the application server for every URL, not just ones within a mapped context, then sessions can get created by requests for nonexistent pages. As you will see in *Capacity Killers*, keeping a tight reign on your sessions is vital to scalability.

Keeping out legitimate robots is fairly easy through the use of the robots.txt file.[11] Keep in mind, though, that robots.txt is nothing but a request from your site to the incoming robot. The robot has to ask for the file and choose to respect your wishes. It's a social convention—not even a standard—and definitely not enforceable. Some sites also choose to redirect robots and spiders, based on the User-Agent header. In the best cases, these agents get redirected to a static copy of the product catalog, or the site generates pages without prices. (The idea is to be searchable by the big search engines but not reveal pricing. That way, you can personalize the prices, run trial offers, partition the country or the audience to conduct market tests, and so on.) In the worst case, the site just sends the agent into a dead end.

The Spider Trap

Around 1998, when AltaVista was the big thing, I saw a site get brought down by a developer's bad case of "clever." He built what he called a *spider trap*. It was a page with some randomly generated links. The link text was some plausible-sounding phrase from a Markov chain-based generator. The URL had a big random hash in it, but effectively, it led back to the same page. So, the indexer kept seeing pages with differing content leading to new links. He thought that by tying up the spider in this spider trap, he would keep it off of the rest of his site, thereby keeping his content from being deep-linked from search engines. Just to be sure the spider would stay trapped, he put five of these random links on each page.

The trap worked like a charm. Once AltaVista hit the site, the spider kept requesting page after page of random links. In fact, they appeared to run multiple threads, because we'd see the number of requests increase geometrically. And there was the problem. Just accept this fact as an absolute law of the Net. Search engines always have more bandwidth than you. The indexer used up *all* of the company's bandwidth. It blew right through the committed rate, used up the allowed burst rate, and pegged against the bandwidth cap. By the time we discovered why our users were complaining about the site being slow, the spider trap had cost us more than $10,000 in bandwidth charges. The spider trap is like a Rube Goldberg machine set up to pull the trigger on a shotgun. It is really nothing more than an elaborate way to DDoS yourself. (See *Attacks of Self-Denial*, on page 69.)

I think he ended up selling the Markov chain text generator as a business plan writer.

---

11. See http://www.w3.org/TR/html4/appendix/notes.html#h-B.4.1.1.

So, the robots most likely to respect robots.txt are the ones that might actually generate traffic (and revenue) for you, while the leeches ignore it completely.

I've seen only two approaches work.

The first is technical. Once you identify a screen scraper, block it from your network. If you're using a content distribution network such as Akamai, this is a service it can provide for you. Otherwise, you can do it at the outer firewalls. Some of the leeches are honest. Their requests come from legitimate IP addresses with real reverse DNS entries. ARIN (http://www.arin.net) is your friend here. Blocking the honest ones is easy. Others stealthily mask their source addresses or make requests from dozens of different addresses. Some of these even go so far as to change their User-Agent strings around from one request to the next. (When a single IP address claims to be running Internet Explorer on Windows, Opera on Mac, and Firefox on Linux in the same five-minute window, something is up. Sure, it could be an ISP-level supersquid or somebody running a whole bunch of virtual emulators. When these requests are sequentially spidering an entire product category, it's more likely to be a screen scraper.) You may end up blocking quite a few subnets, so it's good idea to periodically expire old blocks to keep your firewalls performing well. This is a form of Circuit Breaker.

The second approach is legal. Write some "terms of use" for your site that say users can view content only for personal or noncommercial purposes. Then, when the screen scrapers start hitting your site, sic the lawyers on them. (Obviously, this requires enough legal firepower to threaten them effectively.) Neither of these is a permanent solutions. Consider it pest control—once you stop, the infestation will resume.

Malicious Users

The final group of undesirable users are the truly malicious. These bottom-feeding mouth breathers just *live* to kill your baby. Nothing excites them more than destroying the very thing you've put blood, sweat, and tears into building. Personally, I think they were the kids who always got their sand castles kicked over when they were little. That deep-seated bitterness compels them to do the same thing to others that was done to them.

Truly talented crackers who can analyze your defenses, develop a customized attack, and infiltrate your systems without being spotted are blessedly rare. You may be targeted by such a cracker for a variety of reasons, but the odds are against it. You usually have to incur their wrath for some reason or another. The overwhelming majority of malicious users are *script kiddies*.

Don't let the diminutive name fool you. Script kiddies are dangerous because of their sheer numbers. Although the odds are low that you will be targeted by a true cracker, your systems are probably being probed by script kiddies right now.

Script kiddie: An attacker who does not create his or her own attacks but downloads and employs tools created by "real" crackers.

This book is not about information security or online warfare. A robust approach to defense and deterrence is beyond the scope of this book. I will restrict my discussion to the intersection of security and stability as it pertains to system and software architecture. The primary risk to stability is the now-classic distributed denial-of-service (DDoS) attack. The attacker causes many computers, widely distributed across the Net, to start generating load on your site.[12] Sometimes this load takes the form of raw TCP connections, with no application-level protocol involved. Other attacks attempt to cripple your network devices by breaking the TCP/IP protocol in devious ways. Well-configured, modern network gear can guard against these attacks.

Newer attacks vector in against the applications rather than the network gear. These force you to saturate your own outbound bandwidth, denying service to legitimate users, and racking up huge bandwidth charges.

As you have seen before, session management is the most vulnerable point of a J2EE- or Rails-based web application. Application servers are particularly fragile when hit with a DDoS, so saturating the bandwidth might not even be the worst issue you have to deal with. A specialized Circuit Breaker can help to limit the damage done by any particular host. This also helps protect you from the accidental traffic floods too.

Cisco, Juniper, CheckPoint, and other network vendors all have products that detect and mitigate DDoS attacks. Configuring and monitoring of these products properly is essential. For instance, many administrators set a limit of fifteen connections per minute from a single source IP address (based on an example used in Cisco's documentation). By that definition, every AJAX application is a denial-of-service attack. (Given some of the abusive applications I've seen slap-happy AJAX developers create, that may not be far from the truth.)

---

12. The load typically comes from a *botnet,* or network of compromised computers. A daemon on the compromised computer subscribes to an IRC channel, through which the botnet master issues commands. Some script kiddies have been found to control botnets with tens of thousands of nodes, and there are rumors of nets with a million compromised nodes. Most of these are personal Windows machines running outdated operating systems.

Remember This

Users consume memory

Each user's session requires some memory. Minimize that memory to improve your capacity. Use a session only for caching so you can purge the session's contents if memory gets tight.

Users do weird, random things

Users in the real world do things that you won't predict (or sometimes understand). If there's a weak spot in your application, they'll find it through sheer numbers. Test scripts are useful for functional testing but too predictable for stability testing. Hire a bunch of chimpanzees to hammer on keyboards for more realistic testing.

Malicious users are out there

Become intimate with your network design; it should help avert attacks. Make sure your systems are easy to patch—you'll be doing a lot of it. Keep your frameworks up-to-date, and keep yourself educated. There's no excuse for a successful SQL injection attack in 2007.

Users will gang up on you

Sometimes they come in really, really big mobs. Picture the Slashdot editors giggling as they point toward your site, saying, "Release the legions!" Large mobs can trigger hangs, deadlocks, and obscure race conditions. Run special stress tests to hammer deep links or hot URLs.

4.5 Blocked Threads

Interpreted languages such as Java and Ruby almost never really crash. Sure, they get application errors, but it's relatively rare to see the interpreter or virtual machine crash. I still remember when a rogue pointer in C could reduce the whole machine to a navel-gazing heap. (Anyone else remember Amiga's "Guru Meditation" errors?) Here's the catch about interpreted languages, though. The interpreter can be running, and the application can still be totally deadlocked, doing nothing useful.

As often happens, adding complexity to solve one problem creates the risk of entirely new failure modes. Multithreading makes application servers scalable enough to handle the web's largest sites, but it also introduces the possibility of concurrency errors. The most common failure mode for applications built in these languages is *navel-gazing*—a happily running interpreter with every single thread sitting around waiting for Godot. Multithreading is complex enough that entire books are written about it.[13] Moving away from the "fork, run, and die" execution model brings you vastly higher capacity but only by introducing a new risk to stability.

The majority of system failures I've dealt with do not involve outright crashes. The process runs and runs but does nothing because every thread available for processing transactions is blocked waiting on some impossible outcome.

Blocked threads can happen anytime you check resources out of a connection pool, deal with caches or object registries, or make calls to external systems. If the code is structured properly, a thread will occasionally block whenever two (or more) threads try to access the same critical section at the same time. This is normal. Assuming that the code was written by someone sufficiently skilled in multithreaded programming, then you can always guarantee that the threads will eventually unblock and continue. If this describes you, then you are in a highly skilled minority.

The problem has four parts:

- Error conditions and exceptions create too many permutations to test exhaustively.

- Unexpected interactions can introduce problems in previously safe code.

- Timing is crucial. The probability that the app will hang goes up with the number of concurrent requests.

- Developers never hit their application with 10,000 concurrent requests.

Taken together, these conditions mean that it is very, very hard to find hangs during development. You cannot rely on "testing them out of the system." The best way to improve your chances is to carefully craft your code. Use a small set of primitives in known patterns. It's best if you download a well-crafted, proven library.[14]

Incidentally, this is another reason why I oppose anyone rolling their own connection pool class. It is always more difficult than you think to make a reliable, safe, high-performance connection pool. If you've ever tried writing unit tests to prove safe concurrency, you know how hard it is to achieve

---

13. The only book Java programmers actually need, however, is the excellent *Concurrent Programming in Java [Lea00]*, by Doug Lea.

14. If you are using Java 5 and you are not using the primitives in java.util.concurrent, then shame on you. If you are not using Java 5, then download the util.concurrent library from http://gee.cs.oswego.edu/dl/classes/EDU/oswego/cs/dl/util/concurrent/intro.html. It's the same library before adoption into the JCP.

The System Isn't Down! It's Just in a Funk!

I've probably tried 100 times to explain the distinction between saying "The system crashed" and "The system is hung." I finally gave up when I realized that it's a distinction only an engineer bothers with. It's like a physicist trying to explain where the photon goes in the two-slit experiment from quantum mechanics. Only one observable variable really matters—whether the system is able to process transactions or not. The business sponsor would frame this question, "Is it generating revenue?"

From the user's perspective, a system they can't use might as well be a smoking crater in the earth. The simple fact that the server process is running doesn't help the user get work done, books bought, flights found, and so on.

That is why I advocate supplementing internal monitors (such as log file scraping, process monitoring, and port monitoring) with external monitoring. A mock client somewhere (not in the same data center) can run synthetic transactions on a regular basis. That client experiences the same view of the system that real users experience. When that client cannot process the synthetic transactions, then there is a problem, whether or not the server process is running.

confidence in the pool. Once you start trying to expose metrics, as I discuss in Section 17.2, *Designing for Transparency*, on page 240, rolling your own connection pool goes from a fun Computer Science 101 exercise to a tedious grind.

If you find yourself synchronizing methods on your domain objects, you should probably rethink the design. Find a way that each thread can get its own copy of the object in question. This is important for two reasons. First, if you are synchronizing the methods to ensure data integrity, then your application will break when it runs on more than one server. In-memory coherence doesn't matter if there's another server out there changing the data. Second, your application will scale better if request-handling threads never block each other.

> Distrust synchronized methods on domain objects.

Spot the Blocking

Can you find the blocking call in the following code?

```
String key = (String)request.getParameter(PARAM_ITEM_SKU);
Availability avl = globalObjectCache.get(key);
```

You might suspect that globalObjectCache is a likely place to find some synchronization. You would be correct, but the point is that nothing in the calling code tells you that one of these calls is blocking and the other is not. In fact, the interface that globalObjectCache implemented didn't say anything about synchronization either.

In Java, it is possible for a subclass to declare a method synchronized that is unsynchronized in its superclass or interface definition. Object-oriented purists will tell you that this violates the Liskov Substitution principle. They are correct.

You cannot transparently replace an instance of the superclass with the synchronized subclass. This might seem like nit-picking, but it can be vitally important.

The basic implementation of the GlobalObjectCache interface is a relatively straightforward object registry:

```
public synchronized Object get(String id) {
  Object obj = items.get(id);
  if(obj == null) {
    obj = create(id);
    items.put(id, obj);
  }

  return obj;
}
```

You should hear mental alarm bells when you see the "synchronized" keyword on a method. While one thread is executing this method, any other callers of the method will be blocked. In this case, synchronizing the method is the right thing to do.[15] It executes quickly, and even if there is some contention between threads trying to get into this method, they should all be served fairly quickly.

(A word of caution, however. GlobalObjectCache could easily become a capacity constraint if every transaction uses it heavily. See *Resource Pool Contention*, on page 149 for an example of the effect that blocked requests have on throughput.)

Part of the system needed to check the in-store availability of items by making expensive inventory availability queries to a remote system. These external calls took a few seconds to execute. The results were known to be valid for at least fifteen minutes because of the way the inventory system worked.

---

15. Some of you Java programmers might have seen an idiom called the *double-checked lock* that is meant to avoid synchronizing the whole method. Unfortunately, it just doesn't work. See http://www.cs.umd.edu/~pugh/java/memoryModel/DoubleCheckedLocking.html for a complete rundown of why it doesn't work and why all the attempts to fix the pattern also don't work.

Synchronization and the Liskov Substitution Principle

In object theory, the Liskov Substitution principle (see *Family Values: A Behavioral Notion of Subtyping [LW93]*) states that any property that is true about objects of a type T should also be true for objects of any subtype of T. In other words, a method without side effects in a base class should also be free of side effects in derived classes. A method that throws the exception E in base classes should throw only exceptions of type E (or subtypes of E) in derived classes.

Java does not allow other declared violations of the substitution principle. It is not clear whether the ability to add synchronization in a subclass was a deliberate weakening of Liskov or whether it was just an oversight.

Since nearly 25% of the inventory lookups were on the week's "hot items" and there could be as many as 4,000 (worst case) concurrent requests against the undersized, overworking inventory system, the developer decided to cache the resulting Availability object.

The developer decided that the right metaphor was a read-through cache. On a hit, it would return the cached object. On a miss, it would do the query, cache the result, and then return it. Following good object orientation principles, the developer decided to create an extension of GlobalObjectCache, overriding the get() method to make the remote call. It was a textbook design. The new RemoteAvailabilityCache was a cache proxy, as described in *Pattern Languages of Program Design 2 [VCK96]*, pages 111–112. It even had a time stamp on the cached entries so they could be expired when the data became too stale. This was an elegant design, but it wasn't enough.

The problem with this design had nothing to do with the functional behavior. Functionally, RemoteAvailabilityCache was a nice piece of work. In times of stress, however, it had a nasty failure mode. The inventory system was undersized (see *Unbalanced Capacities*, on page 75), so when the front end got busy, the back end would be flooded with requests. Eventually, it crashed. At that point, any thread calling RemoteAvailabilityCache.get() would block, because one single thread was inside the create() call, waiting for a response that would never come. There they sit, Estragon and Vladimir, waiting endlessly for Godot.

This example shows how these antipatterns interact perniciously to accelerate the growth of cracks. The conditions for failure were created by the blocking threads and unbalanced capacities. The lack of timeouts in the integration points caused the failure in one layer to become a cascading failure. Ultimately, this combination of forces brought down the entire site.

> No one designed this failure mode in, but no one designed it *out* either.

Obviously, the business sponsors would laugh if you asked them, "Should the site crash if it can't check availability for in-store pickup?" If you asked the architects or developers, "Will the site crash if it can't check availability?" they would assert that it would not. Even the developer of RemoteAvailabilityCache would not expect the site to hang if the inventory system stopped responding. No one designed this failure mode into the combined system, but no one designed it *out* either.

Third-Party Libraries

Third-party libraries are notorious sources of blocking threads. Ironically, client libraries for enterprise-class software often do their own resource pooling inside the library. These often make request threads block forever when there is a problem. Of course, these never allow you to configure their failure modes, like what to do when all connections are tied up waiting for replies that will never come.

Your first problem with these libraries is determining exactly how they behave. I recommend writing some small test cases that deliberately try to break the library. Have the test case connect to a really devious test harness (see *Test Harness*, on page 110) that ties up all connections, and then see what the vendor's library does with calls from more and more threads. Try issuing the same query or call twenty times in parallel, and see what happens. If the vendor library is doing its own connection pooling, then you will see a drop in throughput once the number of requests exceeds the size of the connection pool. (Take a look at *Resource Pool Contention*, on page 149 to see what that looks like.) You will probably be able to provoke a deadlock inside the vendor library. It is a sad fact of the universe, however, that you cannot prove a negative. Even if you can't force a deadlock in the library during testing, it might still be vulnerable.

If the library breaks easily, you need to protect your request-handling threads. If the library allows you to set timeouts, use them. If not, you might have to resort to some complex structure such as a pool of worker threads external to the vendor library that the request-handling thread can ask to execute the dangerous operation. If the call makes it through the library in time, then the worker thread and the original request handling-thread rendezvous on a result object. If the call does not complete in time, the request-handling thread abandons the call, even though the worker thread might eventually complete. Once you're in this territory, beware. Here there be dragons. You'll need a good command of concurrent programming, thread pooling, and your language's specific threading model to pull this off, and it will still be a kludge.

Before you go down this path, spend some time beating up your vendor for a better client library.

A blocked thread is often found near an integration point. They can quickly lead to chain reactions. Blocked threads and slow responses can create a positive feedback loop, amplifying a minor problem into a total failure.

 ## Remember This

The Blocked Threads antipattern is the proximate cause of most failures

Application failures nearly always relate to Blocked Threads in one way or another, including the ever-popular "gradual slowdown" and "hung server." The Blocked Threads antipattern leads to Chain Reactions and Cascading Failures.

Scrutinize resource pools

Like Cascading Failures, the Blocked Threads antipattern usually happens around resource pools, particularly database connection pools. A deadlock in the database can cause connections to be lost forever, and so can incorrect exception handling.

Use proven primitives

Learn and apply safe primitives. It might seem easy to roll your own producer/consumer queue; it isn't. Any library of concurrency utilities has more testing than your newborn queue.

Defend with Timeouts

You cannot prove that your code has no deadlocks in it, but you can make sure that no deadlock lasts forever. Avoid Java's infinite wait() method; use the version that takes a timeout parameter. Always use Timeouts, even if it means you have to catch InterruptedException.

Beware the code you cannot see

All manner of problems can lurk in the shadows of third-party code. Be very wary. Test it yourself. Whenever possible, acquire and investigate the code for surprises and failure modes.[16]

---

16. You might also prefer open source libraries to closed source for this very reason. I do.

4.6   Attacks of Self-Denial

Self-denial is only occasionally a virtue in people and never in systems. A *self-denial attack* describes any situation in which the system—or the extended system that includes humans—conspires against itself.

The classic example of a self-denial attack is the email from marketing to a "select group of users" that contains some privileged information or offer. These things replicate faster than the Anna Kournikova Trojan (or the Morris worm if you're really old-school). Any special offer meant for a group of 10,000 users is guaranteed to attract millions. The community of networked bargain hunters can detect and share a reusable coupon code in milliseconds.

One great instance of self-denial occurred when the Xbox 360 was just becoming available for preorder. It was clear that demand would far outstrip supply in the United States, so when a major electronics retailer sent out an email promoting preorders, it helpfully included the exact date and time that the preorder would open. This email hit FatWallet, TechBargains, and probably other big deal-hunter sites the same day. It also thoughtfully included a deep link that accidentally bypassed Akamai, guaranteeing that every image, JavaScript file, and style sheet would be pulled directly from the origin servers.

One minute before the appointed time, the entire site lit up like Chernobyl chocolate milk, and then it went dark. It was gone in sixty seconds.

Amazon ran into trouble with the Xbox 360, too. In November 2006, Amazon decided to offer 1,000 units for just $100. News of the offer spread far and wide. Not surprisingly, the 1,000 units sold within five minutes. Unfortunately, nothing else sold during that time, because millions of visitors hammered on their Reload buttons, trying to load the special offer page and score a huge discount on the hot console.

Apparently, Amazon had not created a dedicated cluster of servers to handle the special offer (see *Bulkheads*, on page 96). The special offer, probably intended as a loss leader or traffic generator, generated more bad publicity than it did revenue. I can only hope Amazon got some good information about weak spots in its architecture—though finding out about them the day before Black Friday hardly seems worth it.

Everyone who has ever worked a retail site has a story like this. Sometimes it's the coupon code that gets reused a thousand times or the pricing error that makes one SKU get ordered as many times as all other products combined. As Paul Lord says, "Good marketing can kill you at any time."

Not every self-inflicted wound can be blamed on the marketing department (although we sure can try). In a horizontal layer that has some shared resources, it is possible for a single rogue server to damage all the others. For example, in an ATG-based[17] infrastructure, there is always one lock manager that handles distributed lock management to ensure cache coherency. (Any server that wants to update a RepositoryItem with distributed caching enabled must acquire the lock, update the item, release the lock, and then broadcast a cache invalidation for the item.) This lock manager is a singular resource. As the site scales horizontally, the lock manager becomes a bottleneck and then finally a risk. If a popular item is inadvertently modified (because of a programming error, for example), then you can end up with thousands of request-handling threads on hundreds of servers all serialized waiting for a write lock on one item.

> Good marketing can kill you at any time.

You can avoid machine-induced self-denial by building a "shared-nothing" architecture. (See ``Shared Nothing'', on page 75.) Where that is impractical, apply decoupling middleware to reduce the impact of excessive demand, or make the shared resource itself horizontally scalable through redundancy and a backside synchronization protocol. You can also design a fallback mode for the system to use when the shared resource is not available or responding. For example, if a lock manager that provides pessimistic locking is not available, the application can fall back to using *optimistic locking.*

> Optimistic locking: Modify objects freely, and detect collisions when saving them. Pessimistic locking: Require positive locks on objects before modifying them. Pessimistic' is safer, but it's slower and requires more coordination.

If you have plenty of time to prepare and are using hardware load balancing for traffic management, you can set aside a portion of your infrastructure to handle the promotion or traffic surge. Of course, this works only if the extraordinary traffic is directed at a portion of the system. (Think promotional pricing or lingerie fashion show.) In this case, even if the dedicated portion melts down, at least the rest of the system's regular behavior is available.

In this case, when dedicated servers go dark, be sure to apply Fail Fast. That way, other front-end resources, such as web server and load balancer connections, are not tied up waiting for a useless or nonexistent response.

As for the human-facilitated attacks, training, education, and communication are the keys. At the very least, if you keep the lines of communication open, you might have a chance to protect the systems from the coming surge. You might even be able to help them achieve their goals without jeopardizing the system.

---

17. ATG Commerce Suite, a competing J2EE application server and commerce framework. See http://www.atg.com.

Remember This

Keep the lines of communication open

Attacks of Self-Denial originate inside your own organization, when clever marketers cause self-inflicted wounds by creating their own flash mobs and traffic spikes. You can aid and abet these marketing efforts and protect your system at the same time, but only if you know what's coming. Make sure nobody sends mass emails with deep links. Create static "landing zone" pages for the first click from these offers. Watch out for embedded session IDs in URLs.

Protect shared resources

Programming errors, unexpected scaling effects, and shared resources all create risks when traffic surges. Watch out for *Fight Club* bugs, where increased front-end load causes exponentially increasing back-end processing.

Expect rapid redistribution of any cool or valuable offer

Anybody who thinks they'll release a special deal for limited distribution is asking for trouble. There's no such thing as limited distribution. Even if you limit the number of times a fantastic deal can be redeemed, you'll still get crushed with people hoping beyond hope that they, too, can get an Xbox 360 for $99.[18]

4.7 Scaling Effects

In biology, the square-cube law explains why we'll never see elephant-sized spiders. The bug's weight scales with volume, so it goes as $O(n^3)$. The strength of the leg scales with the area of the cross section, so it goes as $O(n^2)$.

If you make the critter ten times as large, that makes the strength-to-weight ratio one-tenth of the small version, and the legs just won't hold it up.

We run into scaling effects all the time. Anytime you have a "many-to-one" or "many-to-few" relationship, you can be hit by scaling effects when one side increases. For instance, a database server that holds up just fine when two application servers call it might crash miserably when you add the next eight application servers.

---

18. If you're reading this after the Xbox 360 gets down to $99 dollars, then substitute the next "next-gen" game console.

In the development environment, every application looks like one server. In QA, pretty much every system looks like one or two servers. When you get to production, though, some applications are really, really small, and some are medium, large, or humongous. Because the development and test environments rarely replicate production sizing, it can be hard to see where scaling effects will bite you.

Point-to-Point Communications

One of the worst places that scaling effects will bite you is with point-to-point communication. Point-to-point communication between application servers probably works just fine when there are only one or two instances communicating, as in the image below.

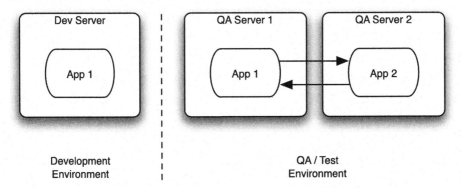

With point-to-point connections, each instance has to talk directly to every other instance, as in the image below.

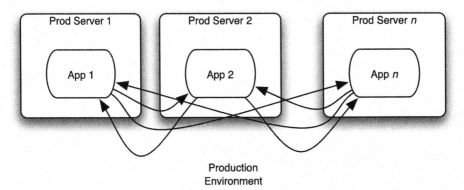

The total number of connections goes up as the square of the number of instances. Scale that up to a hundred instances, and the $O(n^2)$ scaling becomes quite painful. This is a multiplier effect driven by the number of application instances. Depending on the eventual size of your system, $O(n^2)$

scaling might be fine. Either way, you should know about this effect before your system hits production.

Unfortunately, unless you are Microsoft or Google, it is unlikely that you can build a test farm the same size as your production environment. This type of defect cannot be tested out; it must be designed out.

This is one of those times where there is no "best" choice, just a good choice for a particular set of circumstances. If the application will only ever have two servers, then point-to-point communication is perfectly fine.[19] As the number of servers grows, then a different communication strategy is needed. Depending on your infrastructure, you can replace point-to-point communication with the following:

- UDP broadcasts
- TCP or UDP multicast
- Publish/subscribe messaging
- Message queues

Broadcasts do the job but are not bandwidth efficient. They also cause some additional load on servers that are not interested in the messages, since the servers' NIC gets the broadcast and must notify the TCP/IP stack. Multicasts are more efficient, since they permit only the interested servers to receive the message. Publish/subscribe messaging is better still, since a server can pick up a message even if it wasn't listening at the precise moment the message was sent. Of course, publish/subscribe messaging often brings in some serious infrastructure cost. This is a great time to apply the XP principle that says, "Do the simplest thing that will work."

Shared Resources

Another scaling effect that can jeopardize stability is the "shared resource" effect. Commonly seen in the guise of a service-oriented architecture or "common services" project, the shared resource is some facility that all members of a horizontally scalable layer need to use. With some application servers, the shared resource will be a cluster manager or lock manager. When the shared resource gets overloaded, it will become a bottleneck limiting capacity (see Section 8.1, *Defining Capacity*, on page 135). Figure 12, *Many-to-One Dependencies*, on page 74 should give you an idea of how the callers can put a hurting on the shared resource.

---

19. As long as the communication is written so it won't block when the other server dies! (See *Blocked Threads*, on page 62.)

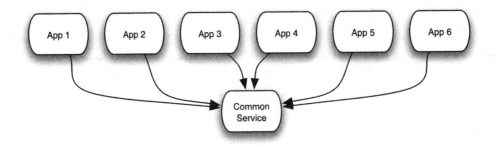

Figure 12—Many-to-One Dependencies

When the shared resource is redundant and nonexclusive—meaning it can service several of its consumers at once—then there is no problem. If it saturates, you can add more, thus scaling the bottleneck.

Too often, though, the shared resource will be allocated for exclusive use while a client is processing some unit of work. In these cases, the probability of contention scales with the number of transactions processed by the layer and the number of clients in that layer. (See *Resource Pool Contention*, on page 149 for an illustration of the effect that contention has on throughput.) When the shared resource saturates, you get a connection backlog. When the backlog exceeds the listen queue, you get failed transactions. At that point, nearly anything can happen. It depends on what function the caller needs the shared resource to provide. Particularly in the case of cache managers (providing coherency for distributed caches), failed transactions lead to stale data or, worse, loss of data integrity.

 ## Remember This

Examine production versus QA environments to spot Scaling Effects

You get bitten by Scaling Effects when you move from small one-to-one development and test environments to full-sized production environments. Patterns that work fine in small environments or one-to-one environments might slow down or fail completely when you move to production sizes.

Watch out for point-to-point communication

Point-to-point communication scales badly, since the number of connections increases as the square of the number of participants. Consider how large your system can grow while still using point-to-point connections —it might be sufficient. Once you're dealing with tens of servers, you will probably need to replace it with some kind of one-to-many communication.

"Shared Nothing"

The most scalable architecture is the *shared-nothing* architecture. Each server operates independently, without need for coordination or calls to any centralized services. In a shared nothing architecture, capacity scales more or less linearly with the number of servers.

The trouble with a shared nothing architecture is that it might scale better at the cost of failover. For example, consider session failover. A user's session resides in memory on an application server. When that server goes down, the next request from the user will be directed to another server. Obviously, we would like that transition to be invisible to the user, so the user's session should be loaded into the new application server. That requires some kind of coordination between the original application server and *some* other device. Perhaps the application server sends the user's session to a session backup server after each page request. Maybe it serializes the session into a database table or shares its sessions with another designated application server. There are numerous strategies for session failover, but they all involve getting the user's session off the original server. Most of the time, that implies some level of shared resources.

You can approximate a shared-nothing architecture by reducing the fan in of shared resources, that is, cutting down the number of servers calling on the shared resource. In the example of session failover, you could do this by designating pairs of application servers that each act as the failover server for the other.

Watch out for shared resources

Shared resources can be a bottleneck, a capacity constraint, and a threat to stability. If your system must use some sort of shared resource, stress test it heavily. Also, be sure its clients will keep working if the shared resource gets slow or locks up.

4.8 Unbalanced Capacities

The trade press is bursting with stories about utility computing. The concept is fabulous: as demand on your application changes, it automatically gets more CPU, memory, and I/O resources assigned to it. Who does the assigning? Some entity in the infrastructure monitors your application's performance and adds resources whenever it sees that performance doesn't meet the required service levels. This "master control program" lurks in the background, measuring your system's performance and dynamically reallocating resources. It is supposed to guarantee that you will never have a resource crunch again. Of course, it also bills you according to your usage—the same way you pay for water, sewer, and electrical utilities. It sounds fantastic, as in "it's a fantasy." The trade magazines are in cahoots with the vendors, who sense that they can sell a whole lot of products to make all this happen. True utility computing centers are on the horizon, but right now, the only real ones are a pale approximation of this vision.

In the world that the other 99.9% of us inhabit, production systems are deployed to some relatively fixed set of resources. Applications run on operating systems, which run on hardware.[20] The hardware contains network interfaces, which have cables plugged into them. The other end of the cable plugs into a switch. In a traditional data center, adding capacity to a production system requires weeks. (Validate the hardware request; check port availability, cooling capacity, power capacity, and rack space; procure the hardware; file change tickets; rack, stack, and cable the device; install the operating system; update the asset management database; allocate LUNs on the SAN; configure filesystems; deploy applications; and add applications to the cluster.) In a crisis, it can be done in days, particularly if you can rob someone else's servers for a while, thereby skipping the whole procurement and installation phase. Three years ago, I saw six extra servers get recabled, reinstalled, and reconfigured with new applications, all in a single heroic 36-hour marathon by one rock-star engineer. Todd, my hat is off to you. Those six extra servers rescued the launch and turned it from an unmitigated disaster to simply a mitigated disaster.

All of which is to say that—barring crises of the most extreme sort—you are more or less stuck with the amount of resources you have. It is infeasible to add resources for demand spikes of short duration (that is, a few hours or days). Although the system's capacity can change over time because of code releases, tuning, optimization, network reconfiguration, or architecture changes, at any particular point in time, it is essentially static.

This produces the potential for a failure mode in multitiered systems or systems that rely on other applications in the enterprise.

> Over short periods of time, your hardware capacity is fixed.

In Figure 13, *Unbalanced Capacities*, on page 77, the front-end website has 3,000 request-handling threads available. During peak usage,

---

20. Increasingly, the "hardware" may be a virtual machine. Nevertheless, in practice, adding, removing, or migrating virtual machines in response to changes in demand happens much slower than you might think. The most aggressive operations team I know of rebalances virtual machines only daily—and they expect that to slow down because virtual machine migration is being brought under a more rigorous change control process.

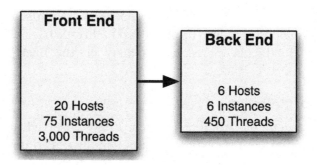

Figure 13—Unbalanced Capacities

the majority of these will be serving product catalog pages or search results. Some smaller number will be in various corporate "telling" pages. A few will be involved in a checkout process. Of the threads serving a checkout-related page, a tiny fraction will be querying the scheduling system to see whether the item can be installed in the customer's home by a local service team. You can do some math and science to predict how many threads could be making simultaneous calls to the scheduling system. The math is not hard, though it does rely on statistics and numerous assumptions, which is a notoriously easy-to-manipulate combination. But, as long as the scheduling system can service enough simultaneous requests to meet that demand prediction, then you'd think it should be sufficient.

Not necessarily.

Suppose marketing executes an attack of self-denial by offering the free installation of any big-ticket appliance for one day only. Suddenly, instead of a tiny fraction of a fraction of front-end threads involving scheduling queries, you could see two times, four times, or ten times as many. The fact is that the front end always has the ability to overwhelm the back end, because their capacities are not balanced.

It might be impractical to evenly match capacity in each system for a lot of reasons. In this example, it would be a gross misuse of capital to build up the scheduling system to the same size as the website, just on the off chance that it will someday need it. The infrastructure would be 99% idle except for one day out of five years!

So if you can't build the scheduling system large enough to meet the potentially overwhelming demand from the front end, then you must build both the front and back ends to be resilient in the face of a tsunami of requests. For the front end, Circuit Breaker will help by relieving the pressure on the back end when responses get slow or connections get refused. For the back end, use Handshaking to inform the front end to throttle back on the requests. Also consider Bulkheads to reserve capacity on the back end for other transaction types.

Drive Out Through Testing

Unbalanced capacities is another problem rarely observed during QA. The main reason is that QA for every system is usually scaled down to just two servers. So during integration testing, there are two servers representing the front-end system and two servers representing the back-end system, resulting in a one-to-one ratio. In production, where the big budget gets allocated, the ratio could be ten to one or worse.

Should you make QA an exact scale replica of the entire enterprise? It would be nice, wouldn't it? Of course, you can't do that. You can apply a test har-nesses, though. (See *Test Harness*, on page 110.) By mimicking a back-end system wilting under load, the test harness helps you verify that your front-end system degrades gracefully.

On the flip side, if you provide the back-end system, you probably expect a "normal" workload. That is, you reasonably expect that today's distribution of demand and transaction types will closely match yesterday's workload. If all else remains unchanged, then that is a reasonable assumption. Many factors can change the workload coming at your system, though: marketing campaigns; publicity; new code releases in the front-end systems; and even links on "funnel" sites such as Slashdot, Fark, and Digg. As a back-end system provider, you're even further removed from the marketers who would deliber-ately cause these traffic changes. Surges in publicity are even less predictable.

So, what can you do if your system serves such unpredictable callers? Be ready for anything. First, use capacity modeling to make sure you're at least in the ballpark. Three thousand threads calling into seventy-five threads is *not* in the ballpark. Second, don't just test your system with normal workloads. See what happens if you take the number of calls the front end could possibly make, double it, and direct it all against your most expensive transaction. If your system is resilient, it might slow down—even start to Fail Fast if it can't process transactions within the allowed time—but it should recover once the load goes down. Crashing, hung threads, empty responses, or nonsense replies indicate your system won't survive and might just start a cascading failure.

Remember This

Examine server and thread counts

In development and QA, your system probably looks like one or two servers, and so do all the QA versions of the other systems you call. In production, the ratio might be more like ten to one instead of one to one. Check the ratio of front-end to back-end servers, along with the number of threads each side can handle, in production compared to QA.

Observe near scaling effects and users

Unbalanced Capacities is a special case of Scaling Effects: one side of a relationship scales up much more than the other side. A change in traffic patterns—seasonal, market-driven, or publicity-driven—can cause a usually benign front-end system to suddenly flood a back-end system, in much the same way as a Slashdot or Digg post causes traffic to suddenly flood websites.

Stress both sides of the interface

If you provide the back-end system, see what happens if it suddenly gets ten times the highest ever demand, hitting the most expensive transaction. Does it fail completely? Does it slow down and recover? If you provide the front-end system, see what happens if calls to the back end stop responding or get very slow.

4.9 Slow Responses

As you saw in *Socket-Based Protocols*, on page 33, generating a slow response is worse than refusing a connection or returning an error, particularly in the context of middle-layer services in an SOA.

A quick failure allows the calling system to finish processing the transaction rapidly. Whether that is ultimately a success or a failure depends on the application logic. A slow response, on the other hand, ties up resources in the calling system and the called system.

Slow responses usually result from excessive demand. When all available request handlers are already working, there is no slack to accept new requests. They can also happen as a symptom of some underlying problem. Memory leaks often manifest via Slow Responses, as the virtual machine works harder and harder to reclaim enough space to process a transaction. This will appear as a high CPU utilization, but it is all due to garbage collection, not work on the transactions themselves. I have occasionally seen Slow Responses resulting from network congestion. This is relatively rare inside a

LAN but can definitely happen across a WAN—especially if the protocol is too chatty. More frequently, however, I see applications letting their socket's send buffers get drained and their receive buffers get full, causing a TCP stall. This usually happens in a hand-rolled, low-level socket protocol, in which the read() routine does not loop until the receive buffer is drained.

Slow responses tend to propagate upward from layer to layer in a gradual form of cascading failure.

If you give your system the ability to monitor its own performance (see Chapter 17, *Transparency*, on page 231), then it can also tell when it isn't meeting its service-level agreement. Suppose that your system is a service provider that is required to respond within one hundred milliseconds. When a moving average over the last twenty transactions exceeds one hundred milliseconds, your system could start refusing requests. This could be at the application layer, in which the system would return an error response within the defined protocol. Or, it could be at the connection layer, by refusing new socket connections. Of course, any such refusal to provide service must be well-documented and expected by the callers. (Since the developers of that system will surely have read this book, they will already be prepared for failures, and their system will handle them gracefully.)

 ## Remember This

Slow Responses triggers Cascading Failures

Upstream systems experiencing Slow Responses will themselves slow down and might be vulnerable to stability problems when the response times exceed their own timeouts.

For websites, Slow Responses causes more traffic

Users waiting for pages frequently hit the Reload button, generating even more traffic to your already overloaded system.

Consider Fail Fast

If your system tracks its own responsiveness,[21] then it can tell when it is getting slow. Consider sending an immediate error response when the average response time exceeds the system's allowed time (or at the very least, when the average response time exceeds the caller's timeout!).

Hunt for memory leaks or resource contention

Contention for an inadequate supply of database connections produces Slow Responses. Slow Responses also aggravates that contention, leading

---

21. See Chapter 17, *Transparency*, on page 231.

to a self-reinforcing cycle. Memory leaks cause excessive effort in the garbage collector, resulting in slow response. Inefficient low-level protocols can cause network stalls, also resulting in slow response.

4.10 SLA Inversion

 A service-level agreement (SLA) is a contractual agreement about how well the organization must deliver its services. These are quantitative measures of service delivery with financial penalties if the service provider does not meet them. A number of trends are combining to make SLAs increasingly important. Outsourcing—of people, infrastructure, and operations—is a major driver. Increased awareness of the IT Infrastructure Library (ITIL, soon to be ratified as ISO 20000)[22] and the IT Service Management Framework (itSMF)[23] also drives interest in SLAs. Beyond those, however, there is a general trend in IT operations toward higher degrees of professionalism. IT managers regard themselves as providers of a critical service, necessary for their organizations to continue functioning. They need quantitative SLAs so they can allocate resources according to business need rather than responding to the generic complaint, "My application is too slow; make it faster."

In the Figure 14, *Project Frammitz Architecture*, on page 82, a company's new website—Project Frammitz—is built for high availability. It's mission critical, so redundancy is built in at every level: power, network, storage, server hardware, and applications. It uses a shared-nothing (see ``*Shared Nothing*'', on page 75) architecture to allow maximum horizontal scalability without bottlenecks. Frammitz is required to meet a 99.99% availability SLA. That's slightly more than four minutes of downtime allowed per month.

Despite the careful engineering, Frammitz can meet that SLA only through sheer luck.

The system itself is designed for high availability, but it relies on numerous other services. A stand-alone web system with no links to settlement, accounting, fulfillment, or inventory systems probably can't sell much. Add fraud detection, channel partner integration, outsourcing of key services, spam cannons, geocoding services, address verification, and credit card authorization, and you've got a real spiderweb. Each of those dependencies is vulnerable to the SLAs on the other end of the connection. Figure 15, *Project*

---

22. See http://www.itil.co.uk/.
23. See http://www.itsmf.com/.

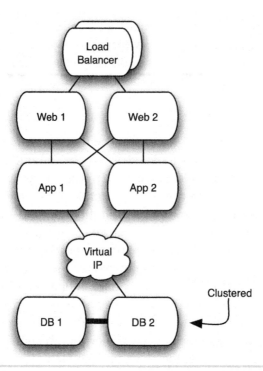

Figure 14—Project Frammitz Architecture

Frammitz External Dependencies, on page 83 shows the systems that Frammitz depends upon, and their respective SLAs.

For every service, inside your company or outside, your system depends on transport layer availability, naming services (DNS), and application-level protocols. Any one of those layers for any one of the external connections can fail. Unless every one of your dependencies is engineered for the same SLA you must provide, then the best you can possibly do is the SLA of the worst of your service providers. In the case of Project Frammitz, because it depends on partner 1 and pricing and promotions, neither of which offer any SLA at all, then strictly speaking, Project Frammitz cannot offer an availability SLA.

According to the laws of probability, the situation is even worse. If built naively, the probability of failure in Project Frammitz is the joint probability of a failure in any component or service. That is, a single failure in a dependency is enough to make Frammitz fail; therefore:

P(frammitz up) = (1 - P(internal failure)) * P(partner 1 up) * P(inventory up) ...]

If Frammitz requires five external services that each have a 99.9% availability, then the *best* Frammitz can possibly do is 99.5%.

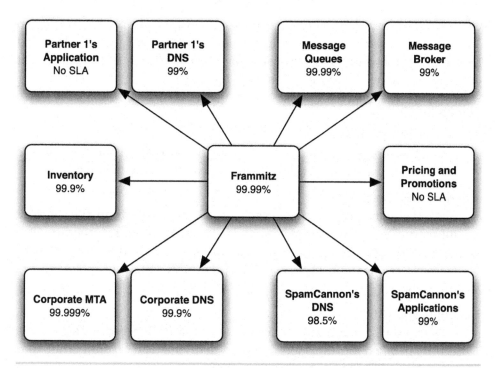

Figure 15—Project Frammitz External Dependencies

If Frammitz were perfectly decoupled from all external systems, then the probability of failure is just P(internal failure). Most systems will fall somewhere in between.

When calling third parties, service levels only decrease.

This is an SLA inversion: a system that must meet a high-availability SLA depends on systems of lower availability. You have to operate on wishful thinking to commit to that high-availability SLA. There are two basic responses to an SLA inversion. First, you can decouple from the lower-SLA system. Make sure your application can continue to function without the remote system. Degrade gracefully. Decoupling middleware is an excellent approach to decoupling, but depending on the nature of the remote service, it might not be an option. At the least, employ circuit breakers to protect your application from each of the allies/potential enemies. Second, be careful when crafting your service-level agreements. Do not simply state "99.99% availability." (See Chapter 13, *Availability*, on page 197.)

Instead, reorient the discussion around the availability of specific functions or features in the system. Features that do not depend on any external parties can have your maximum SLA. Features that require third-party services can have only whatever service-level agreement the third party offers, degraded by the probability of a failure in your own system. This is the IT equivalent of the Second Law of Thermodynamics:[24] service levels only go down.

Remember This

Don't make empty promises

An SLA inversion means you are operating on wishful thinking: you've committed to a service level that you can achieve only through luck.

Examine every dependency

SLA Inversion lurks in unexpected places, particularly in the network infrastructure. For example, what is the SLA on your corporate DNS cluster? (I hope it's a cluster, anyway.) How about on the SMTP service? Message queues and brokers? Enterprise SAN? SLA dependencies are everywhere.

Decouple your SLAs

Be sure you can maintain service even when your dependencies go down. If you fail whenever they do, then it's a mathematical certainty that your availability will *always* be less than theirs.

4.11 Unbounded Result Sets

Design with skepticism, and you will achieve resilience. Ask, "What can system X do to hurt me?" and then design a way to dodge, duck, dip, dive, and dodge whatever wrench your supposed ally throws.

If your application is like most, it probably treats its database server with far too much trust. I'm going to try to convince you that a healthy dose of skepticism will help your application dodge a bullet or two.

A common structure in the code goes like this: send a query to the database, and then loop over the result set, processing each row. Often, processing a row means adding a new data object to a collection. What happens when the database suddenly returns five million rows instead of the usual hundred or so? Unless your application explicitly limits the number of results it is willing to process, it can end up exhausting its memory or spinning in a while loop long after the user loses interest.

---

24. Entropy always increases.

Black Monday

Have you ever had a surprising discovery about an old friend? You know, like the most boring guy in the office suddenly tells you he's into BASE jumping? That happened to me about my favorite commerce server. One day, with no warning, every instance in the farm—more than a hundred individual, load-balanced instances—started behaving badly. It seemed almost random. An instance would be fine, but then a few minutes later it would start using 100% of the CPU. Three or four minutes later, it would crash with a HotSpot memory error. The operations team was restarting them as fast as they could, but it took a few minutes to start up and preload cache. Sometimes, they would start crashing before they were even finished starting. We could not keep more than 25% of our capacity up and running.

Imagine (or recall, if you've been there) trying to debug a totally novel failure mode while also participating in a 5 a.m. (with no coffee) conference call with about twenty people. Some of them are reporting the current status, some are trying to devise a short-term response to restore service, others are digging into root cause, and some of them are just spreading disinformation.

We sent a system admin and a network engineer to go looking for denial-of-service attacks. Our DBA reported that the database was healthy but under heavy load. That made sense, because at start-up, each instance would issue hundreds of queries to warm up its caches before accepting requests. Some of the instances would crash before they started accepting requests, which told me it was not related to incoming requests. The high CPU condition looked like garbage collection to me, so I told the team I would start looking for memory problems. Sure enough, when I watched the "heap available" on one instance, I saw it heading toward zero. Shortly after it hit zero, the JVM got a HotSpot error.

Usually, when a JVM runs out of memory, it throws an OutOfMemoryError. It crashes only if it is executing some native code that doesn't check for NULL after calling malloc(). The only native code I knew of was in the Type 2 JDBC driver.[25] Type 2 drivers use a thin layer of Java to call out to the database vendor's native API library. Sure enough, dumping the stack showed execution deep inside the database driver.

But what was the server doing with the database? For that, I asked our DBA to trace queries from the application servers. Soon enough, we had another

---

25. For non-Java programmers, *native code* just means fully compiled instructions for the host processor. Typically, this is C or C++ code in dynamically linked libraries. Native code is notorious as a source of crashes under stress.

instance crash, so we could see what a doomed server did before it went into the twilight zone. The queries all looked totally innocuous, though. Routine stuff. None of the hand-coded SQL monsters that I had seen elsewhere (eight-way unions with five joins in each subquery, and so on). The last query I saw was just hitting a message table that the server used for its database-backed implementation of JMS. The instances mainly used it to tell each other when to flush their caches. This table should never have more than 1,000 rows, but our DBA saw that it topped the list of most expensive queries.

For some reason, that usually tiny table had more than ten million rows. Because the app server was written to just select all the rows from the table, each instance would try to receive all ten-million-plus messages. This put a lock on the rows, since the app server issued a "select for update" query. As it tried to make objects out of the messages, it would use up all available memory, eventually crashing. Once the app server crashed, the database would roll back the transaction, releasing the lock. Then the next app server would step off the cliff by querying the table. We did an extraordinary amount of hand-holding and manual work to compensate for the lack of a LIMIT clause on the app server's query. By the time we had stabilized the system, Black Monday was done...it was Tuesday.

We did eventually find out why there were more than ten million messages in that table, but that's a different story.

This failure mode can occur when querying databases, access distributed objects, or web services. It can also occur via AJAX requests to web servers. A common form of this happens when traversing master/detail links. Because datasets in development tend to be small, the application developers may never experience negative outcomes. After a system is in production for a year, however, even a traversal such as "fetch customer's orders" can return huge result sets.

In the abstract, an unbounded result set occurs when the caller allows the other system to dictate terms. It is a failure in handshaking. In any API or protocol, the caller should always indicate how much of a response it is prepared to accept. TCP does this in the "window" header field. Search engine APIs allow the caller to specify how many results to return and what the starting offset should be. There is no standard SQL syntax to specify result set limits. ORM tools (such as Hibernate and iBatis) support query parameters that can limit results returned from a query but do not usually limit results when following an association (such as container to contents). Therefore, beware any relationship that can accumulate unlimited children, such as orders to order lines or user profiles to site visits. Entities that keep an audit trail of changes are also suspect.

If you are handcrafting your own SQL, use one of these recipes to limit the number of rows to fetch:

```
-- Microsoft SQL Server
SELECT TOP 15 colspec FROM tablespec


-- Oracle (since 8i)
SELECT colspec FROM tablespec
WHERE rownum <= 15


-- MySQL and PostgreSQL
SELECT colspec FROM tablespec
LIMIT 15
```

An incomplete solution (but better than nothing) would be to query for the full results but break out of the processing loop after reaching the maximum number of rows. Although this does provide some added stability on the application server, it does so at the expense of wasted database capacity.

Unbounded result sets are a common cause of slow responses. They can result from violation of steady state.

 ## Remember This

Use realistic data volumes

Typical development and test data sets are too small to exhibit this problem. You need production-sized data sets to see what happens when your query returns a million rows that you turn into objects. As a side benefit, you'll also get better information from your performance testing when you use production-sized test data.

Don't rely on the data producers

Even if you think a query will never have more than a handful of results, beware: it could change without warning because of some other part of the system. The only sensible numbers are "zero," "one," and "lots," so unless your query selects exactly one row, it has the potential to return too many. Don't rely on the data producers to create a limited amount of data. Sooner or later, they'll go berserk and fill up a table for no reason, and then where will you be?

Put limits into other application-level protocols

Web service calls, RMI, DCOM, XML-RPC: all are vulnerable to returning huge collections of objects, thereby consuming too much memory.

CHAPTER 5

Stability Patterns

Now that you've seen some antipatterns to avoid, you'll look at the flip side. In this chapter, you'll examine some patterns that are the inverse of the killers from the last chapter. These eight healthy patterns provide architecture and design guidance to reduce, eliminate, or mitigate the effects of cracks in the system. Not one of these will help your software pass QA, but they *will* help you get a full night's sleep, or an uninterrupted dinner with your family, once your software launches.

Don't make the mistake of assuming that a system that includes more of these patterns is superior to one with less of them. "Count of patterns applied" is never a good quality metric. Instead, I want you to develop a recovery-oriented mind-set. At the risk of sounding like a broken record, I'll say it again: expect failures. Apply these patterns wisely to reduce the damage done by an individual failure.

5.1 Use Timeouts

 In the early days, networking issues affected only programmers working on low-level software: operating systems, network protocols, remote filesystems, and so on. Today, all but the most trivial applications deal with networks, in some form or another, thus exposing every application to the fundamental rule of networks: networks are fallible. The wire could be broken, some switch or router along the way could be broken, or the computer you are addressing could be broken. Even if you've already established communication, any of these elements could become broken at any time. When that happens, your code can't just wait forever for a response that might never come; sooner or later, it needs to give up. Hope is not a design method.

The timeout is a simple mechanism allowing you to stop waiting for an answer once you think it will not come. I once had a project to port the BSD sockets library to a mainframe-based UNIX environment. I attacked the project with a stack of RFCs and a dusty pile of source code for UNIX System V Release 4. Two issues nagged at me throughout the entire project. First, heavy use of "#ifdef" blocks for different architectures made it look less like a portable operating system than twenty different operating systems intermingled. Second, the networking code was absolutely riddled with error handling for different flavors of timeouts. By the project's end, I had grown to understand and appreciate the significance of timeouts.

Now and forever, networks will always be unreliable.

Request for comments: the Internet Engineering Task Force's version of a standard.

Well-placed timeouts provide fault isolation; a problem in some other system, subsystem, or device does not have to become your problem. Unfortunately, at higher and higher levels of abstraction, away from the dirty world of hardware, good placement of timeouts becomes increasingly rare. Indeed, many high-level APIs have few or no explicit timeout settings. Vendor-provided client libraries are notoriously devoid of timeouts. API libraries often handle socket communication on behalf of the application. When these libraries hide the actual socket from the application, they also prevent the application from setting vital timeouts.

Timeouts can also be relevant within a single application. Any resource pool can be exhausted. Conventional usage dictates that the calling thread should be blocked until one of the resources is checked in. (See *Blocked Threads*, on page 62.)

It is essential that any resource pool that blocks threads must have a timeout to ensure threads are eventually unblocked whether resources become available or not.

Also beware of java.lang.Object.wait(). Use the form that takes a timeout argument, instead of the simpler no-argument form. The same goes for classes in the new[1] java.util.concurrent library. Always use the form of poll(), offer(), or tryLock() that can take a timeout argument. If you don't, you might end up waiting forever.

An approach to dealing with pervasive timeouts is to organize long-running operations into a set of primitives that you can reuse in many places. For example, suppose you need to check out a database connection from a resource pool, run a query, turn the ResultSet into objects, and then check the

---

1. Added in Java 5. In earlier versions of Java, you can download the "util-concurrent" library. Substitute package names appropriately.

> **Joe asks:**
> ## Is All This Clutter Really Necessary?
>
> You may think, as I did when porting the sockets library, that handling all the possible timeouts creates undue complexity in your code. It certainly adds complexity. You may find that half your code is devoted to error handling instead of providing features. I argue, however, that the essence of aiming for production—instead of aiming for QA—is handling the slings and arrows of outrageous fortune. That error-handling code, if done well, adds resilience. Your users may not thank you for it, because nobody notices when a system *doesn't* go down, but you will sleep better at night.

database connection back into the pool. At least three points in that interaction could hang indefinitely. Instead of coding that sequence of interactions dozens of places, with all the associated handling of timeouts (not to mention other kinds of errors), create a QueryObject (see *Patterns of Enterprise Application Architecture [Fow03]*) to represent the part of the interaction that changes.

Use a generic Gateway to provide the template for connection handling, error handling, query execution, and result processing. (See Spring's JdbcTemplate.[2]) Collecting this common interaction pattern into a single class also makes it easier to apply the Circuit Breaker pattern.

Timeouts are often observed together with retries. Under the philosophy of "best effort," the software attempts to repeat an operation that timed out. Immediately retrying an operation after a failure has a number of consequences, but only some of them are beneficial. If the operation failed because of any significant problem, it is likely to fail again if retried immediately. Some kinds of transient failures might be overcome with a retry (for example, dropped packets over a wireless WAN). Within the walls of a data center, however, the failure is probably because of something wrong with the other end of a connection. Despite Cisco's advertisements about "self-healing networks," my experience has been that problems on the network, or with other servers, tend to last for a while. Thus, fast retries are very likely to fail again.

From the client's perspective, making me wait longer is a very bad thing. If you cannot complete an operation because of some timeout, it is better for you to return a result. It can be a failure, a success, or a note that you've queued the work for later execution (if I should care about the distinction). In any case, just come back with an answer. Making me wait while you retry the operation might push your response time past *my* timeout.

---

2.   See http://static.springframework.org/spring/docs/1.2.x/api/org/springframework/jdbc/core/JdbcTemplate.html.

On the other hand, queuing the work for a slow retry later is a very good thing, making the system much more robust. Imagine if every mail server between the sender and receiver had to be online, ready to process your mail, and had to respond within sixty seconds in order for email to make it through. The store-and-forward approach obviously makes much more sense. In the case of failure in a remote server, queue-and-retry ensures that once the remote server is healthy again, the overall system will recover. Work does not need to be lost completely just because part of the larger system is not functioning. How fast is fast enough? It depends on your application and your users. For a website using service-oriented architectures, "fast enough" is probably anything less than 250 milliseconds. Beyond that, you will start to lose capacity and customers.

Timeouts have natural synergy with circuit breakers. A circuit breaker can tabulate timeouts, tripping to the "off" state if too many occur.

The Timeouts and Fail Fast patterns both address latency problems. The Timeouts pattern is useful when you need to protect your system from someone else's failure. Fail Fast is useful when you need to report why you won't be able to process some transaction. Fail Fast applies to incoming requests, whereas the Timeouts pattern applies primarily to outbound requests. They're two sides of the same coin.

Timeouts can also help with unbounded result sets by preventing the client from processing the entire result set, but they aren't the most effective approach to that particular problem. I'd consider that a stopgap but not much more than that.

Timeouts apply to a general class of problems. As such, they help systems recover from unanticipated events.

 Remember This

Apply to Integration Points, Blocked Threads, and Slow Responses

The Timeouts pattern prevents calls to Integration Points from becoming Blocked Threads. Thus, they avert Cascading Failures.

Apply to recover from unexpected failures

When an operation is taking too long, sometimes we don't care why…we just need to give up and keep moving. The Timeouts pattern lets us do that.

Consider delayed retries

Most of the explanations for a timeout involve problems in the network or the remote system that won't be resolved right away. Immediate retries are liable to hit the same problem and result in another timeout. That just makes the user wait even longer for his error message. Most of the time, you should queue the operation and retry it later.

5.2 Circuit Breaker

 Not too long ago, when electrical wiring was first being built into houses, many people fell victim to physics. The unfortunates would plug too many appliances into their circuit. Each appliance drew a certain amount of current. When current is resisted, it produces heat proportional to the square of the current times the resistance (I^2R). Because they lacked superconducting home wiring, this hidden coupling between electronic gizmos made the wires in the walls get hot, sometimes hot enough to catch fire. Pfft. No more house.

The fledgling energy industry found a partial solution to the problem of resistive heating, in the form of fuses. The entire purpose of an electrical fuse is to burn up before the house does. It is a component designed to fail first, thereby controlling the overall failure mode. This brilliant device worked well, except for two flaws. First, a fuse is a disposable, one-time use item; therefore, it is possible to run out of them. Second, residential fuses (in the United States) were about the same diameter as copper pennies. Together, these two flaws led many people to conduct experiments with homemade, high-current, low-resistance fuses (that is, a 3/4-inch disk of copper). Pfft. No more house.

Residential fuses have gone the way of the rotary dial telephone. Now, circuit breakers protect overeager gadget hounds from burning their houses down. The principle is the same: detect excess usage, fail first, and open the circuit. More abstractly, the circuit breaker exists to allow one subsystem (an electrical circuit) to fail (excessive current draw, possibly from a short-circuit) without destroying the entire system (the house). Furthermore, once the danger has passed, the circuit breaker can be reset to restore full function to the system.

You can apply the same technique to software by wrapping dangerous operations with a component that can circumvent calls when the system is not healthy. This differs from retries, in that circuit breakers exist to prevent operations rather than reexecute them.

In the normal "closed" state, the circuit breaker executes operations as usual. These can be calls out to another system, or they can be internal operations that are subject to timeout or other execution failure. If the call succeeds, nothing extraordinary happens. If it fails, however, the circuit breaker makes a note of the failure. Once the number of failures (or frequency of failures, in

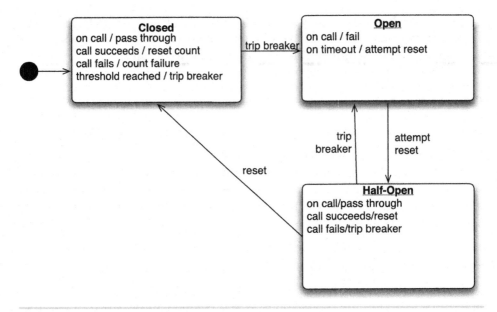

Figure 16—Circuit Breaker State Transitions

more sophisticated cases) exceeds a threshold, the circuit breaker trips and "opens" the circuit, as shown in Figure 16, *Circuit Breaker State Transitions*, on page 94.[3] When the circuit is "open," calls to the circuit breaker fail immediately, without any attempt to execute the real operation. After a suitable amount of time, the circuit breaker decides that the operation has a chance of succeeding, so it goes into the "half-open" state. In this state, the next call to the circuit breaker is allowed to execute the dangerous operation. Should the call succeed, the circuit breaker resets and returns to the "closed" state, ready for more routine operation. If this trial call fails, however, the circuit breaker returns to the "open" state until another timeout elapses.

When the circuit breaker is open, all calls will immediately fail. This should probably be indicated by some type of exception. To provide good feedback to the user, it is useful to throw a different exception when the circuit is open. This allows the calling code to handle this type of exception differently.

Depending on the details of the system, the circuit breaker may track different types of failures separately. For example, you may choose to have a lower threshold for "timeout calling remote system" failures than "connection refused" errors.

---

3. The Leaky Bucket pattern from *Pattern Languages of Program Design 2 [VCK96]* provides a wonderful implementation for this type of counter.

Circuit breakers are a way to automatically degrade functionality when the system is under stress. This can have an impact on the business of the system. Therefore, it is essential to involve the system's stakeholders when deciding how to handle calls made when the circuit is open. For example, should a retail system accept an order if it cannot confirm availability of the customer's items? What about if it cannot verify the customer's credit card or shipping address? Of course, this conversation is not unique to the use of a circuit breaker, but discussing the circuit breaker can be a more effective way of broaching the topic than asking for a requirements document.

The state of the circuit breakers in a system is important to another set of stakeholders: operations. Changes in a circuit breaker's state should always be logged, and the current state should be exposed for querying and monitoring. (See Chapter 17, *Transparency*, on page 231 for more detail.) In fact, the frequency of state changes is a useful metric to chart over time; it is a leading indicator of problems elsewhere in the enterprise. Likewise, operations needs some way to directly trip or reset the circuit breaker.

Circuit breakers are effective at guarding against integration points, cascading failures, unbalanced capacities, and slow responses. They work so closely with timeouts that they often track timeout failures separately from execution failures.

 Remember This

Don't do it if it hurts

Circuit Breaker is the fundamental pattern for protecting your system from all manner of Integration Points problems. When there's a difficulty with Integration Points, stop calling it!

Use together with Timeouts

Circuit Breaker is good at avoiding calls when Integration Points has a problem. The Timeouts pattern indicates that there is a problem in Integration Points.

Expose, track, and report state changes

Popping a Circuit Breaker *always* indicates there is a serious problem. It should be visible to operations.[4] It should be reported, recorded, trended, and correlated.

---

4. See Chapter 17, *Transparency*, on page 231.

5.3   Bulkheads

 In a ship, *bulkheads* are metal partitions that can be sealed to divide the ship into separate, watertight compartments. Once hatches are closed, the bulkhead prevents water from moving from one section to another. In this way, a single penetration of the hull does not irrevocably sink the ship. The bulkhead enforces a principle of damage containment.

You can employ the same technique. By partitioning your systems, you can keep a failure in one part of the system from destroying everything. Physical redundancy is the most common form of bulkheads. If there are four independent servers, then a hardware failure in one can't affect the others. Likewise, if there are two application instances running on a server and one crashes, the other will still be running (unless, of course, the first one crashed because of some external influence that would also affect the second).

At the largest scale, a mission-critical service might be implemented as several independent farms of servers, with certain farms reserved for use by critical applications and others available for noncritical uses. For example, a ticketing system could provide dedicated servers for customer check-in. These would not be affected if other, shared servers are overwhelmed with "flight status" queries (as sometimes happens during severe weather). Such a partitioning would have allowed the airline in Chapter 2, *Case Study: The Exception That Grounded An Airline*, on page 9 to keep checking passengers at airports, even if channel partners could not look up fares for that day's flights.

> Protect critical clients by giving them their own pool to call.

In Figure 17, *Hidden Linkages*, on page 97, Foo and Bar both use the enterprise service Baz. Because both depend on a common service, each system has some vulnerability to the other. If Foo suddenly gets crushed under user load, goes rogue because of some defect, or triggers a bug in Baz, Bar—and its users—also suffer. This kind of unseen coupling makes diagnosing problems (particularly performance problems) in Bar very difficult. Scheduling maintenance windows for Baz also requires coordination with both Foo and Bar, and it may be difficult to find a window that works for both clients.

Assuming both Foo and Bar are critical systems with strict SLAs, it'd be safer to partition Baz, as shown in Figure 18, *Partitioned System*, on page 97.

Dedicating some capacity to each critical client removes most of the hidden linkage. They probably still share a database and are, therefore, subject to deadlocks across instances, but that's another antipattern.

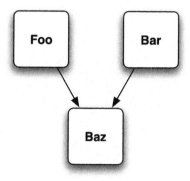

Figure 17—Hidden Linkages

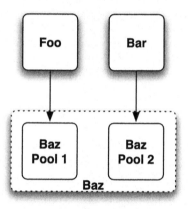

Figure 18—Partitioned System

Of course, it would be better to preserve all capabilities. Assuming that failures will occur, however, you must consider how to minimize the damage caused by a failure. It is not an easy effort, and one rule cannot apply in every case. Instead, you must examine the impact to the business of each loss of capability and cross-reference those impacts against the architecture of the systems. The goal is to identify the natural boundaries that let you partition the system in a way that is both technically feasible and financially beneficial. The boundaries of this partitioning may be aligned with the callers, with functionality, or with the topology of the system.

At smaller scales, CPU binding is an example of partitioning via bulkheads. Binding a process to a CPU or CPU group ensures that the operating system schedules that process' threads on only the designated CPU or CPU group. Because it reduces the cache bashing that happens when processes migrate

Bulkheads vs. Capacity

With a pool of servers for each client, Baz requires much more accurate demand projections. Foo and Bar must be more accurate about their needs, because each one has strictly limited resources available to it. If the server pool were combined, then excess demand from one client could be compensated by surplus capacity from the other. There is more overall tolerance.

If Foo and Bar have different peak seasons—or even just different peak hours—then the shared pool needs less total capacity than the sum of the individual capacities would be. This efficiency is one of the major motivators for IT to move toward service-oriented architectures in the first place. How can we keep that efficiency while gaining the safety of bulkheads?

One way to get both is with virtualization. Baz can use the same pool of physical hardware to create virtual servers dedicated to Foo and Bar. Then, shifting capacity between the clients becomes an administrative change to the virtual machines. Booting an additional virtual machine takes just a few minutes. The latest versions of VMware ESX can even move the virtual machines automatically, based on their service-level policies. Migrating a live virtual machine typically takes less than ten seconds.

Virtual servers provide an excellent mechanism for implementing bulkheads.

from one CPU to another, CPU binding is often regarded as a performance tweak. If a process goes berserk and starts using all CPU cycles, it can usually drag down an entire host machine. I've seen eight CPU servers consumed by a single process. If that process is bound to a CPU, however, it can use all available cycles only on that one CPU.

You can partition the threads inside a single process, with separate thread groups dedicated to different functions.[5] For example, it is often helpful to reserve a pool of request-handling threads for administrative use. That way, even if all request-handling threads on the application server are hung, it can still respond to admin requests—perhaps to collect data for post-mortem analysis or a request to shut down.

Bulkheads are effective at maintaining service, or partial service, even in the face of failures. They are especially useful in service-oriented architectures, where the loss of a single service could have repercussions throughout the enterprise. In effect, a service inside an SOA represents a single point of failure for the enterprise.

---

5. For example, prior to version 9, WebLogic allowed you to allocate a set of threads to a particular activity by creating a custom activity queue. (In version 9.x, this is now called a *constraint* on a *work manager*.)

> ## Bulkheads vs. Performance
>
> Binding a multithreaded application server to one CPU may decrease its performance, particularly if it is tested in isolation. When there are multiple instances of the application server running on the host, the situation is less clear. If each application server's threads can be scheduled across all CPUs, then context switching and cache flushing may reduce overall throughput. Optimizing performance here is a multivariate problem; it requires balancing the right number of server instances, the right number of threads per server, the amount of memory dedicated, and the probability of contention inside the application itself. Be sure to test for the maximum *overall* throughput, not just the best response time from an individual server.

 Remember This

Save part of the ship

The Bulkheads pattern partitions capacity to preserve partial functionality when bad things happen.

Decide whether to accept less efficient use of resources

When the system is not in jeopardy, partitioning the servers means each partition needs more reserve capacity. If all servers are pooled, then less total reserve capacity is needed.

Pick a useful granularity

You can partition thread pools inside an application, CPUs in a server, or servers in a cluster.

Very important with shared services models

In a service-oriented architecture, there may be many enterprise systems dependent on your application. If your application goes down because of Chain Reactions, does the entire company come to a halt? Then you'd better put in some Bulkheads.

5.4   Steady State

 Roget's Thesaurus (3rd ed.) offers the following definition for the word *fiddling*: "To handle something idly, ignorantly, or destructively." It offers helpful synonyms such as *fool*, *meddle*, *tamper*, *tinker*, and *monkey*. Fiddling is often followed by the "ohnosecond": that very short moment in time during which you realize that you have pressed the wrong key and brought down a server, deleted vital data, or otherwise damaged the peace and harmony of stable operations.

Every single time a human touches a server is an opportunity for unforced errors.[6]

It's best to keep people off of production systems to the greatest extent possible. If the system needs a lot of crank-turning and hand-holding to keep running, then administrators develop the habit of staying logged in all the time. This inevitably leads to fiddling. To that end, the system should be able to run indefinitely without human intervention.

Unless the system is crashing every day (in which case, look for the presence of the stability antipatterns), the most common reason for logging in will probably be cleaning up log files or purging data.

> Don't encourage fiddling. Systems should run indefinitely without intervention.

Any mechanism that accumulates resources (whether it is log files in the filesystem, rows in the database, or caches in memory) is like the bucket from those high-school calculus problems. The bucket fills up at a certain rate, based on the accumulation of data. It must be drained at the same rate, or greater, or it will eventually overflow. When this bucket overflows, bad things happen: servers go down, databases get slow or throw errors, response times head for the stars. The Steady State pattern says, for every mechanism that accumulates a resource, some other mechanism must recycle that resource. You'll look at several types of sludge that can accumulate and how to avoid the need for fiddling.

Data Purging

It certainly seems like a simple enough principle. Computing resources are always finite; therefore, you cannot continually increase consumption without limit. Still, in the rush of excitement about rolling out a new killer application, the next great mission-critical, bet-the-company whatever, data purging always gets the short end of the stick. It certainly doesn't demo as well as...well, anything else in the world demos better than purging, really. It sometimes seems that you'll be lucky if the system ever runs at all in the real world. The notion that it will run long enough to accumulate too much data to handle seems like a "high-class problem"—the kind of problem you'd love to have.

---

6. I know of one incident in which an engineer, attempting to be helpful, observed that a server's root disk mirror was out of sync. He executed a command to "resilver" the mirror, bringing them back into synchronization. Unfortunately, he made a typo and synced the good root disk from the new, totally empty drive that had just been swapped in to replace a bad disk, thereby instantly annihilating the operating system on that server.

Data purging never makes it into the first release, but it should.

Nevertheless, someday your little database will grow up. When it hits the teenage years—about two in human years —it will get moody, sullen, and resentful. In the worst case, it will start undermining the whole system (and it will probably complain that nobody understands it, too).

The most obvious symptom of data growth will be steadily increasing I/O rates on the database servers. You may also see increasing latency at constant loads.

Data purging is nasty, detail-oriented work. Referential integrity constraints in the database are half the battle. It can be very difficult to cleanly remove obsolete data without leaving orphaned rows. The other half of the battle is ensuring that applications still work once the data is gone.

For example, will the applications work if items are missing from the middle of collections? (Hint: under Hibernate, they won't!) As a consequence, data purging always gets left until after the first release is out the door. The thin rationale is, "We've got six months after launch to implement purging." (Somehow, they always say "six months." It's kind of like a programmer's estimate of "two weeks.")

Of course, after launch, there are always emergency releases to fix critical defects or add "must-have" features from marketers tired of waiting for the software to be done. The first six months can slip away pretty quickly, but when that first release launches, a fuse is lit.

Purging in Practice

I gave a talk at OTUG[7] that eventually led to this book. I was thrilled to see most of my project's team in attendance, including the sponsor. When I was presenting this very issue about the importance of data purging and its usual neglect, I could see everyone from my project nodding along (with their eyes open!). So you can imagine my chagrin when we launched our first release without data purging!

We eventually implemented a very thorough purge process, based on measuring our shortest fuse to see how long we had. It ended up being a very close thing when we rolled out the first iteration of purging, which took care of the highest-volume data items. That bought us time. Subsequent releases rolled out more rigorous routines for lower-volume accumulations.

Another type of sludge you will commonly encounter is old log files.

---

7. The Object Technology Users' Group in the Twin Cities of Minneapolis and St. Paul, Minnesota. See http://www.otug.org/.

Log Files

Last week's log files are about as interesting as a book full of actuarial tables. A few rare, special people would be delighted to pore through them. The rest of us regard them as warmly as the dumpster behind a sushi restaurant. Last month's log files are even worse. The main thing these old log files do is take up valuable disk space.

Left unchecked, however, they become more than just a meaningless pile of uninterpreted bytes. When log files grow without bound, they will eventually fill up their containing filesystem. Whether that's a volume set aside for logs, the root disk, or the application installation directory (I hope not), it means trouble. When log files fill up the filesystem, they jeopardize stability. That's because of the different negative effects that can occur when the filesystem is full. On a UNIX system, the last 5% to 10% percent (depending on the configuration of the filesystem) of space is reserved for root. That means an application will start getting I/O errors when the filesystem is 90% or 95% full. Of course, if the application is running as root, then it can consume the very last byte of space. On a Windows system, an application can always use the very last byte. In either case, the operating system will report errors back to the application. For a Java-based system, that means java.io.IOException. For .NET, it's a System.IO.IOException. For C, it's an errno value of ENOSPC. (Show of hands, please: Who checks errno for ENOSPC after *every* call to write()?) In almost every case, logging libraries do not handle the I/O exception themselves. Instead, they wrap it or translate it and then throw a new exception at the application code.[8]

What happens next is anyone's guess. In the best-case scenario, the logging filesystem is separate from any critical data storage (such as transactions), and the application code protects itself well enough that users never realize anything is amiss. Significantly less pleasant, but still tolerable, is a nicely worded error message asking the users to have patience with us and please come back when we've got our act together. Several rungs down the ladder is serving a stack trace to the user.

Worse yet, I saw one system where the developers had added a "universal exception handler" to the servlet pipeline. This handler would log any kind of exception. It was reentrant, so if an exception occurred while logging an exception, it would log *both* the original and the new exception. As soon as the filesystem got full, this poor exception handler went nuts, trying to log

---

8. Log4J is a pleasant exception in this regard. It uses a pluggable ErrorHandler policy to dispose of exceptions in any of the "appenders."

an ever-increasing stack of exceptions. Because there were multiple threads, each trying to log its own Sisyphean exception, this application server was able to consume eight entire UltraSPARC III CPUs—for a little while, anyway. The exceptions, multiplying like Leonardo da Pisa's rabbits, rapidly consumed all available memory. This was followed shortly by a JVM crash.

> Don't leave log files on production systems. Copy them to a staging area for analysis.

A less dramatic problem with large log files is their poor signal-to-noise ratio. Consider access logs from a web server. Other than WebTrends-type analysis, it's very unlikely that you will find value in last month's access logs. With eight million requests, which corresponds to 800,000 to 4,000,000 page views, depending on the number of assets per page, Apache's common log format produces more than a 1GB a day in access logs. No human being can find an event of interest in that volume of data. And by the way, there's no reason to leave those log files on production systems. Copy them off to a staging area for analysis.

Of course, it's always better to avoid filling up the filesystem in the first place. Log file rotation requires just a few minutes of configuration.

The various translations of Log4J, including Log4R (Ruby) and Log4Net (any .NET language), all support a RollingFileAppender, which can be configured to rotate log files based on size. You should always use RollingFileAppender in place of the default FileAppender. In java.util.logging, the default FileHandler can also be configured to rotate logs based on size by setting its limit property to the maximum number of bytes to write to the current file. The count variable controls how many old files to keep. The product of limit and count obviously determines how much space the log files can possibly consume.

In the case of legacy code, third-party code, or code that doesn't use one of the excellent logging frameworks available, the logrotate utility is ubiquitous on UNIX. For Windows, you can try building logrotate under Cygwin, or you can hand roll a .vbs or .bat script to do the job. Logging can be a wonderful aid to transparency. Make sure that all log files will get rotated out and eventually purged, though, or you will eventually spend time fixing the tool that's supposed to help you fix the system.

Between data in the database and log files on the disk, there are plenty of ways for persistent data to clog up your system. Like jingles from old commercials, sludge stuck in memory can clog up your application.

> **Joe asks:**
> ## What About Sarbanes-Oxley? Don't We Have to Keep All Our Log Files Forever?
>
> You will sometimes hear people talking about logging in terms of Sarbanes-Oxley (SOX) requirements. SOX makes many heavy demands on IT infrastructure and operations. One of these demands is that the company must be able to demonstrate adequate controls on any system that produces financially significant information. In other words, if a billing system feeds into the company's financial reports, the company must be able to demonstrate that nobody can monkey with the billing system's data.
>
> For most customer-facing websites, this is irrelevant in reality but often perceived as necessary. Financials come from order management systems or credit card settlement systems, not from web and application servers. The website cannot possibly retain web server logs for the years required by SOX, not even on tape or DVD. Further, could web server access logs actually prove anything about the integrity of the financial controls? Not likely. That comes from tracking administrator login sessions.
>
> Unfortunately, legal issues are not always decided based on rational probability analysis, particularly in an area as fuzzy and ill-defined as SOX compliance. Your best bet is to work with your company's CIO or compliance staff. (Many companies have dedicated SOX consultants.) They will help define how your system can stay in compliance. Start these discussions early. They involve legal, IT, and finance departments, so you should not expect speedy resolution.

In-Memory Caching

Use Caching Carefully, on page 176 has much more to say on the subject of caching. To a long-running server, memory is like oxygen. Cache, left untended, will suck up all the oxygen. Low memory conditions are a threat to both stability and capacity. Therefore, when building any sort of cache, it's vital to ask two questions:

- Is the space of possible keys finite or infinite?
- Do the cached items ever change?

If there is no upper bound on the number of possible keys, then cache size limits must be enforced. Unless the key space is finite and the items are static, then the cache needs some form of cache invalidation. The simplest mechanism is a time-based cache flush. You can also investigate least recently used (LRU) or working-set algorithms, but nine times out of ten, a periodic flush will do.

Improper use of caching is the major cause of memory leaks, which in turn lead to horrors like daily server restarts. Nothing gets administrators in the habit of being logged on to production like daily (or nightly) chores.

Sludge buildup is a major cause of slow responses, so steady state helps avoid that antipattern. Steady state also encourages better operational discipline by limiting system administrators' need to log on to the production servers.

Remember This

Avoid fiddling

Human intervention leads to problems. Eliminate the need for recurring human intervention. Your system should run at least for a typical deployment cycle without manual disk cleanups or nightly restarts.

Purge data with application logic

DBAs can create scripts to purge data, but they don't always know how the application behaves when data is removed. Maintaining logical integrity, especially if you use an ORM tool, requires the application to purge its own data.

Limit caching

In-memory caching speeds up applications, until it slows them down. Limit the amount of memory a cache can consume.

Roll the logs

Don't keep an unlimited amount of log files. Configure log file rotation based on size. If you need to retain them for compliance, do it on a non-production server.

5.5 Fail Fast

If slow responses are worse than no response, the worst must surely be a slow *failure* response. It's like waiting through the interminable line at the DMV, only to be told you need to fill out a different form and go back to the end of the line. Can there be any bigger waste of system resources than burning cycles and clock time only to throw away the result?

If the system can determine in advance that it will fail at an operation, it's always better to fail fast. That way, the caller doesn't have to tie up any of its capacity waiting; it can get on with other work.

How can the system tell whether it will fail? What kind of secret heuristics am I about to reveal? Is this the application-level equivalent of Intel's branch-prediction algorithms?

It's actually much more mundane than that. There is a large class of "resource unavailable" failures. For example, when a load balancer gets a connection request but not one of the servers in its service pool is functioning, it should immediately refuse the connection. Some configurations have the load balancer queue the connection request for a while, in the hopes that a server will become available in a short period of time. This violates the Fail Fast pattern.

In any service-oriented architecture, the application can tell from the service requested roughly what database connections and external integration points will be needed. The service can very quickly check out the connections it will need and verify the state of the circuit breakers around the

> Check resource availability at the start of a transaction.

integration points. It can tell the transaction manager to start a transaction. This is sort of the software equivalent of the cook's *mise en place*—gathering all the ingredients it will need to service the request before it begins. If any of the resources are not available, it can fail immediately, rather than getting partway through the work.

> **Black**
>
> One of my more interesting projects was for a studio photography company. Part of the project involved working on the software that rendered images for high-resolution printing. The previous generation of this software had a problem that generated more work for humans downstream: if color profiles, images, backgrounds, or alpha masks weren't available, it "rendered" a black image full of zero-valued pixels. This black image went into the printing pipeline and was printed, wasting paper, chemicals, and time. Quality checkers would pull the black image and send it back to the people at the beginning of the process for diagnosis, debugging, and correction. Ultimately, they would fix the problem (usually by calling developers to the printing facility) and remake the bad print. Since the order was already late getting out the door, they would expedite the remake—meaning it interrupted the pipeline of work and went to the head of the line.
>
> When my team started on the rendering software, we applied the Fail Fast pattern. As soon as the print job arrived, the renderer would check for the presence of every font (missing fonts caused a similar remake, but not because of black images), image, background, and alpha mask. It preallocated memory, so it couldn't fail an allocation later. The renderer reported any such failure to the job control system immediately, before it wasted several minutes of compute time. Best of all, "broken" orders would be pulled from the pipeline, avoiding the case of having partial orders waiting at the end of the process. Once we launched the new renderer, software-induced remake rate[9] dropped to zero.

---

9.   Orders could still be remade because of other quality problems: dust in the camera, poor exposure, bad cropping, and so on.

The only thing we didn't preallocate was disk space for the final image. We violated "steady state" under the direction of the customer, who indicated that they had their own rock-solid purging process. Turns out the "purging process" was one guy who occasionally deleted a bunch of files. A little less than one year after we launched, the drives filled up. Sure enough, the one place we broke the Fail Fast principle was the one place our renderer failed to report errors before wasting effort. It would render images—several minutes of compute time—and then throw an IOException in the log file.

Another way to fail fast in a web application is to perform basic parameter-checking in the servlet or controller that receives the request, before loading EJBs or domain objects. Be cautious, however, that you do not violate encapsulation of the domain objects. If you are checking for more than null/not-null or number formatting, you should move those validity checks into the domain objects or an application facade.

Even when failing fast, be sure to report a system failure (resources not available) differently than an application failure (parameter violations or invalid state). Reporting a generic "error" message may cause an upstream system to trip a circuit breaker just because some user entered bad data and hit Reload three or four times.

The Fail Fast pattern improves overall system stability by avoiding slow responses. Together with timeouts, failing fast can help avert impending cascading failures. It also helps maintain capacity when the system is under stress because of partial failures.

 Remember This

Avoid Slow Responses and Fail Fast

If your system cannot meet its SLA, inform callers quickly. Don't make them wait for an error message, and don't make them wait until they time out. That just makes your problem into their problem.

Reserve resources, verify Integration Points early

In the theme of "don't do useless work," make sure you will be able to complete the transaction before you start. If critical resources aren't available—for example, a popped Circuit Breaker on a required call out —then don't waste work by getting to that point. The odds of it changing between the beginning and the middle of the transaction are slim.

Use for input validation

Do basic user input validation even before you reserve resources. Don't bother checking out a database connection, fetching domain objects, populating them, and calling validate() just to find out that a required parameter wasn't entered.

5.6   Handshaking

Handshaking refers to signaling between devices that regulate communication between them. Serial protocols such as RS-232 (now EIA-232C) rely on the receiver to indicate when it is ready to receive data. Analog modems used a form of handshaking to negotiate a speed and a signal encoding that both devices would agree upon. And, as illustrated earlier, TCP uses a three-phase handshake to establish a socket connection. TCP handshaking also allows the receiver to signal the sender to stop sending data until the receiver is ready. Handshaking is ubiquitous in low-level communications protocols but is almost nonexistent at the application level.

The sad truth is that HTTP doesn't handshake well. HTTP-based protocols, such as XML-RPC or WS-I Basic, have few options available for handshaking. HTTP provides a response code of "503 Service Unavailable," which is defined to indicate a temporary condition.[10] Most clients, however, will not distinguish between different response codes. If the code is not a "200 OK,"[11] "403 Authentication Required," or "302 Found (redirect)," the client probably treats the response as a fatal error.

Similarly, the protocols beneath CORBA, DCOM, and Java RMI are equally bad at signaling their readiness to do business.

Handshaking is all about letting the server protect itself by throttling its own workload. Instead of being victim to whatever demands are made upon it, the server should have a way to reject incoming work. The closest approximation I've been able to achieve with HTTP-based servers relies on partnership between a load balancer and the web or application servers. The web server notifies the load balancer—which is pinging a "health check" page on the web server periodically—that it is busy by returning either an error page (HTTP response code 503 "Not Available" works) or an HTML page with an error message. The load balancer then knows not to send any additional work to that particular web server.

Of course, this helps only for web services and still breaks down if all the web servers are too busy to serve another page.

In a service-oriented architecture, the server can provide a "health check" query for use by clients. The client would then check the health of the server before making a request. This provides good handshaking at the expense of

---

10.   See http://www.w3.org/Protocols/rfc2616/rfc2616-sec10.html.

11.   Many clients even treat other 200 series codes as errors!

doubling the number of connections and requests the server must process. On the downside, most of the time for a typical web service call is spent just setting up and tearing down the TCP connection, so making a health check call before the actual call just doubles that connection overhead.

Handshaking can be most valuable when unbalanced capacities are leading to slow responses. If the server can detect that it will not be able to meet its SLAs, then it should have some means to ask the caller to back off. If the servers are sitting behind a load balancer, then they have the binary on/off control of stopping responses to the load balancer, which would in turn take the unresponsive server out of the pool. This is a crude mechanism, though. Your best bet is to build handshaking into any custom protocols that you implement.

Circuit breakers are a stopgap you can use when calling services that cannot handshake. In that case, instead of asking politely whether the server can handle the request, you just make the call and track whether it works.

Overall, handshaking is an underused technique that could be applied to great advantage in application-layer protocols. It is an effective way to stop cracks from jumping layers, as in the case of a cascading failure.

 ### Remember This

Create cooperative demand control

Handshaking between client and server permits demand throttling to serviceable levels. Both client and server must be built to perform Handshaking. Most common application-level protocols—such as HTTP, JRMP, IIOP, and DCOM—do not perform Handshaking.

Consider health checks

Health-check requests are an application-level workaround for the lack of Handshaking in the protocols. Consider using them when the cost of the added call is much less than the cost of calling and failing.

Build Handshaking into your own low-level protocols

If you create your own socket-based protocol, build Handshaking into it, so the endpoints can each inform the other when they are not ready to accept work.

5.7 Test Harness

As you've seen in previous chapters, distributed systems have failure modes that are extraordinarily difficult to provoke in development or QA environments. To be more thorough about testing various components together, we often resort to an "integration testing" environment. In this environment, our system is fully integrated to all the other systems it must interact with.

Integration testing presents problems of its own, however. What version should we test against? For greatest assurance, we'd like to test against the versions of our dependencies that will be current when we release our system. I could construct a mathematical proof, using set theory, that shows this approach constrains *the entire company* to testing only one new piece of software at a time, but I'll leave that as "an exercise for the reader." Furthermore, the interdependencies of today's systems create such an interlocking web of systems that the integration testing environment really becomes unitary—one global integration test that shadows the real production systems of the entire enterprise. Such a unitary environment would need change control just as rigorous—or perhaps more so—than the actual production environments.

There is a more abstract difficulty. ("More abstract than set theory?" you may ask.) Integration test environments can verify only what the system does when its dependencies are working correctly. Although it may be possible to provoke the remote system into returning errors, it's still functioning more or less within specifications. If the specifications say, "The system shall return an error code 14916 unless the request includes the date of the last telephone sanitization," then the caller can force that error condition to occur. Nevertheless, the remote system is still operating within specifications.

The main theme of this book, however, is that every system will eventually end up operating outside of spec; therefore, it's vital to test the local system's behavior when the remote system goes wonky. Unless the designers of the remote system built in modes that simulate the whole range of out-of-spec failures that can occur naturally in production, there will be behaviors that integration testing does not verify.

A better approach to integration testing would allow you to test most or all of these failure modes. It should preserve or enhance system isolation to avoid the version-locking problem and allow testing in many locations instead of the unitary enterprise-wide integration testing environment I described earlier.

To do that, you can create test harnesses to emulate the remote system on the other end of each integration point. Hardware and mechanical engineers have used test harnesses for a long time. Software engineers have used test harnesses, but not as maliciously as they should. A good test harness should be devious. It should be as nasty and vicious as real-world systems will be. The test harness should leave scars on the system under test. Its job is to make the system under test cynical.

Consider building a test harness that substitutes for the remote end of every web services call. Because the remote call uses the network, the socket connection is susceptible to the following failures:

- It can be refused.

- It can sit in a listen queue until the caller times out.

- The remote end can reply with a SYN/ACK and then never send any data.

- The remote end can send nothing but RESET packets.

- The remote end can report a full receive window and never drain the data.

- The connection can be established, but the remote end never sends a byte of data.

- The connection can be established, but packets could be lost causing retransmit delays.

- The connection can be established, but the remote end never acknowledges receiving a packet, causing endless retransmits.

- The service can accept a request, send response headers (supposing HTTP), and never send the response body.

- The service can send one byte of the response every thirty seconds.

- The service can send a response of HTML instead of the expected XML.

- The service can send megabytes when kilobytes are expected.

- The service can refuse all authentication credentials.

These failures fall into distinct categories: network transport problems, network protocol problems, application protocol problems, and application logic problems. With a little mental exercise, you can find failure modes in every layer of the seven-layer OSI model. It would be costly and bizarre to add switches and flags to applications that would allow them to simulate all of these failures. Who would want to risk turning on a "simulated failure" once the system is promoted into production? Integration testing environments are good at examining failures only in the seventh layer—the application layer—and not even all of those.

Joe asks:
Why Not Mock Objects?

Mock objects are a technique commonly applied with unit testing.[a] A *mock object* supplies an alternative implementation—to be used by the object under test—that can be controlled by the unit test itself. For example, suppose an application uses a DataGateway object as a layer facade for the entire persistence layer. The real implementation of DataGateway would deal with connection parameters, a database server, and a bunch of test data. That's a lot of coupling for a single test, which often results in irreproducible test results or hidden dependencies between tests. A mock object improves the isolation of a unit test by cutting off all the external connections. Mock objects are often used at the boundaries between layers.

Some mock objects can be set up to throw exceptions when the object under test invokes their methods. This does permit the unit test to simulate some kinds of failures, especially those that map to exceptions (assuming that the underlying code in the real implementation would generate exceptions).

A test harnesses differs from mock objects, in that a mock object can be trained to produce behavior that conforms only to the defined interface. A test harnesses runs as a separate server, so it is not obliged to conform to any interface. It can provoke network errors, protocol errors, or application-level errors. If all low-level errors were guaranteed to be recognized, caught, and thrown as the right type of exception, there would be no need for test harnesses.

---

a.   See http://www.junit.org.

A test harness "knows" that it is meant for testing; it has no other role to play. Whereas the real application would not be written to call the low-level network APIs directly, the test harness can. Therefore, it is able to send bytes too quickly,

> Make your test harness act like a hacker.

or very slowly. It can set up extremely deep listen queues. It can bind to a socket and then never service a single connection attempt. The test harness should act like a little hacker, trying all kinds of bad behavior to break callers.

Many kinds of bad behavior will be similar for different applications and protocols. For example, refusing connections, connecting slowly, and accepting requests without reply would apply to any socket protocol: HTTP, RMI, or RPC. For these, a single test harness can simulate many types of bad network behavior. One trick I like is to have different port numbers indicate different kinds of misbehavior. On port 10200, it would accept connections but never reply. Port 10201 gets a connection and a reply, but the reply will be copied from /dev/random. Port 10202 will open a connection, then drop it immediately, and so on. That way, I don't need to change modes on the test harness, and a single test harness can break many applications. It can even help with functional testing in the development environment by letting multiple developers hit the test harness from their workstations. (Of course, it's also worthwhile to let the developers run their own instances of the killer test harness.)

Bear in mind that your test harness might be really, really good at breaking, even killing applications. It's not a bad idea to have the test harness log requests, in case your application dies without so much as a whimper to indicate what killed it.

The test harness can be designed like an application server; it can have pluggable behavior for the tests that are related to the real application. A single framework for the test harness can be subclassed to implement any application-level protocol, or any perversion of the application-level protocol, necessary.

 ## Remember This

Emulate out-of-spec failures

Calling real applications lets you test only those errors that the real application can deliberately produce. A good Test Harness lets you simulate all sorts of messy, real-world failure modes.

Stress the caller

The Test Harness can produce slow responses, no responses, or garbage responses. Then you can see how your application reacts.

Leverage shared harnesses for common failures

You don't necessarily need a separate Test Harness for each integration point. A "killer" server can listen to several ports, creating different failure modes depending on which port to which you connect.

Supplement, don't replace, other testing methods

The Test Harness pattern augments other testing methods. It does not replace unit tests, acceptance test, FIT tests, and so on. Each of those techniques help verify functional behavior. Test Harness helps verify "nonfunctional" behavior while maintaining isolation from the remote systems.

5.8   Decoupling Middleware

Middleware is a graceless name for tools that inhabit a singularly messy space —integrating systems that were never meant to work together. Rebranded as *enterprise application integration*, middleware became a hot property for a few years in the early 2000s and then faded back into its shadowy, thankless realm. Middleware occupies the essential interstices between enterprise systems. It is the connective tissue that bridges gaps between different islands of automation. (How's that for a mixed metaphor?)

Often described as "plumbing"—with all the connotations—middleware will always remain inherently messy, since it must work with different business processes, different technologies, and even different definitions of the same logical concept. This "unsexiness" must be part of the reason why service-oriented architectures are currently stealing attention from the less glamorous, but more necessary, job of middleware.

Done well, middleware simultaneously integrates and decouples systems. It integrates them by passing data and events back and forth between the systems. It decouples them by letting the participating systems removing specific knowledge of and calls to the other systems. Since integration points are the number-one cause of instability, this looks like a good thing.

Any kind of synchronous call-and-response or request/reply method forces the calling system to stop what it's doing and wait. In this model, the calling system and the receiving system must both be active at the same time—they are synchronous in time—though they may be in different places. This category covers remote procedure calls (RPC), HTTP, XML-RPC, RMI, CORBA, DCOM, and any other analog of local method calls. Tightly coupled middleware amplifies shocks to the system. Synchronous calls are particularly vicious amplifiers that facilitate cascading failures.

Less tightly coupled forms of middleware allow the calling and receiving systems to process messages in different places and at different times. The venerable IBM MQseries and any of the publish/subscribe messaging systems fall into this category, as do system-to-system messaging via SMTP or SMS. (These latter two protocols frequently have message brokers implemented with carbon, hydrogen, oxygen, and nitrogen rather than silicon. Latency also tends to be high.)

Figure 19, *Coupling Spectrum of Middleware*, on page 115 depicts the spectrum of coupling exhibited by different middleware technologies.

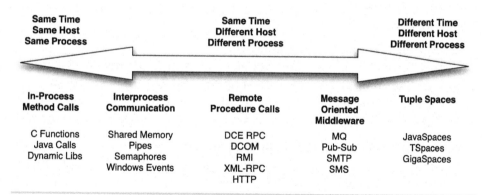

Figure 19—Coupling Spectrum of Middleware

Message-oriented middleware decouples the endpoints in both space and time. Because the requesting system doesn't just sit around waiting for a reply, this form of middleware cannot produce a cascading failure.

The main advantage of synchronous (tightly coupled) middleware lies in its logical simplicity. Suppose a customer's proposed credit card purchase needs to be authorized. If this authorization is implemented using a remote procedure call or XML-RPC, the application can clearly decide whether to proceed with the next step of the checkout process or to send the user back to the payment methods page. By comparison, if the system just sends a message asking for credit card authorization, without waiting for a reply, then it must somehow decide what to do if the authorization request ultimately fails or, worse, remains unanswered. Designing asynchronous processes is inherently harder. The process must deal with exception queues, late responses, callbacks (computer-to-computer as well as human-to-human), and assumptions. These decisions even involve the business sponsors of the calling system, who will occasionally have to decide what the acceptable level of financial risk is.

You can apply most of the patterns in this chapter without greatly affecting the implementation cost of the system. Middleware decisions are not the same. First, the products are expensive. Second, different styles of middleware necessitate very different designs. That makes the cost of changing your mind very high. Switching from a request/reply RPC model to a tuplespace requires different thinking at all levels.

Finally, middleware is often purchased at an enterprise level, so these decisions will often be made for you, before you even start architecture or design work on your project.

Remember This

Decide at the last responsible moment

Other stability patterns can be implemented without large-scale changes to the design or architecture. Decoupling Middleware is an architecture decision. It ripples into every part of the system. This is one of those nearly irreversible decisions that should be made early rather than late.

Avoid many failure modes through total decoupling

The more fully you decouple individual servers, layers, and applications, the fewer problems you will observe with Integration Points, Cascading Failures, Slow Responses, and Blocked Threads. You'll find that decoupled applications are also more adaptable, since you can change any of the participants independently of the others.

Learn many architectures, and choose among them

Not every system needs to look like a three-tier application with an Oracle database. Learn many architectural styles, and select the best architecture for the problem at hand.

CHAPTER 6

Stability Summary

In time, even shockingly unlikely combinations of circumstances will eventually occur. If you ever catch yourself saying, "The odds of that happening are astronomical," or some similar utterance, consider this: ten million page views per day over three years (assuming fifty assets per page) gives your system 547,500,000,000 chances for something to go wrong. That's more than *five hundred billion* opportunities for bad things to happen. Recent astronomical observations indicate there are four hundred billion stars in the Milky Way galaxy. Astronomically unlikely coincidences happen daily.

> Astronomically unlikely coincidences happen daily.

Failures are inevitable. Our systems, and those we depend on, will fail in ways large and small. Stability antipatterns amplify transient events. They accelerate cracks in the system. Avoiding the antipatterns does not prevent bad things from happening, but it will help minimize the damage when bad things do occur.

Judiciously applying these stability patterns result in software that stays up, come hell or high water. The key to applying these patterns successfully is judgment. Examine the software's requirements cynically. View other enterprise systems with suspicion and distrust—any of them can stab you in the back. Identify the threats, and apply stability patterns appropriate to each threat. Paranoia is just good thinking.

Staying up is more than half the battle. Consider the odds against your system. Approximately half of all projects are canceled in development. Of the survivors, another half are late, overbudget, and do not meet requirements. Of the remainder (less than 25% of all projects) that make it to production, the majority incur major costs through downtime, lost revenue, and maintenance costs.

You've already stepped over the decaying carcasses of other systems on your way to production. Be proud!

Sadly, the absence of a problem is not usually noted. You might be salvaging a badly botched implementation in which case you now have an opportunity to look like a hero. On the other hand, if you've done a great job of designing a stable system from the beginning, it's unlikely that anyone will notice your system's *lack* of downtime. That's just the way it is. Deliver an unbreakable system, and users will surely go on to complain about something else. That's just what users do.

In fact, with a system that never goes down, the users will most likely complain that it's slow. Next, you'll look at capacity and performance and how to get the most out of your resources.

Part II

Capacity

CHAPTER 7

Case Study: Trampled by Your Own Customers

7.1 Countdown and Launch

After years of work, the day of launch finally arrived. I had joined this huge team (more than three hundred in total) nine months earlier to help build a complete replacement for this retailer's online store, content management, customer service, and order-processing systems. Destined to be the company's backbone for the next seven years, it was already more than a year late when I joined the team. For the previous nine months, I had been in crunch mode: taking lunches at my desk and working late into the night. Minnesota winter will test your soul even under the best of times. Dawn rises late, and dusk falls early. None of us had seen the sun for months. It often felt like an inescapable Orwellian nightmare. We had crunched through spring, the only season worth living here for. One night I went to sleep in winter, and the next time I looked around, I realized summer had arrived.

After nine months, I was still one of the new guys. Some of the development teams had crunched for more than a year. They had eaten lunches and dinners brought in by the client every day of the week. Even today, some of them still shiver visibly remembering turkey tacos.

Today, however, was the day of triumph. All the toil and frustration, the forgotten friends, and the divorces were going to fade away after we launched.

The marketing team—many of whom hadn't been seen since the requirements-gathering meetings two years earlier—gathered in a grand conference room for the launch ceremony, with champagne to follow. The technologists who had turned their vague and ill-specified dreams into reality gathered around a wall full of laptops and monitors that we set up to watch the health of the site.

At 9 a.m., the program manager hit the big red button. (He actually had a big red button, which was wired to an LED in the next room where a techie clicked Reload on the browser being projected on the big screen.) The new site appeared like magic on the big screen in the grand conference room. Where we lurked in our lair on the other side of the floor, we heard the marketers give a great cheer. Corks popped. The new site was live and in production.

CDN: Content Delivery Network, also known as an "edge network". An accelerator that caches images and static content near the browser. This removes up to 80% of requests from your site's web servers.

Of course, the real change had been initiated by the CDN.[1] They had a scheduled update to their metadata set to roll out across their network at 9 a.m. Central time. The change would propagate across the CDN's network of servers, taking about eight minutes to be effective worldwide. We expected to see traffic ramping up on the new servers starting at about 9:05 a.m. (The browser in the conference room was configured to bypass the CDN and hit the site directly, going straight to what the CDN calls the "origin servers." Marketing people aren't the only ones who know how to engage in smoke and mirrors.) In fact, we could immediately see the new traffic coming in to the site.

By 9:05 a.m., we already had 10,000 sessions active on the servers.

At 9:10 a.m., more than 50,000 sessions were active on the site.

By 9:30 a.m., there were 250,000 sessions active on the site. Then, the site crashed.

7.2 Aiming for QA

To understand why the site crashed so badly, so quickly, we must take a brief look back at the three years leading up to that point.

It's rare to see such a greenfield project these days, for a number of good reasons. For starters, there's no such thing as a website project. Every one

---

1. In fact, the CDN had given the world a sneak preview of the new site the Saturday before our Monday launch. Somehow, the metadata change was entered incorrectly, and the origin server switch took place on Saturday afternoon. From the time when an executive at the client noticed the new site was visible (and taking orders!) with its partially loaded content until we identified the CDN as the cause of the problem took about an hour. It was then another hour to get the change reversed and propagated across the CDN's network. Oops!

is really an enterprise integration project with an HTML interface. Most projects have at least some kind of back end with which they must integrate.

> Every website project is really an enterprise integration project.

When the back end is being developed along with the front end, you might think the result would be a cleaner, better, tighter integration. It's possible that could happen, but it doesn't come automatically; it depends on Conway's law. The more common result is that both sides of the integration end up aiming at a moving target.

Replacing the entire commerce stack at once also brings a significant amount of technical risk. If the system is not built with the stability patterns, it probably follows a typical tightly coupled architecture. In such a system, the overall probability of system failure is the joint probability that any one component fails.

Even if the system is built with the stability patterns (this one wasn't), a completely new stack means that nobody can be sure how it will run in production. Capacity, stability, control, and adaptability are all giant question marks.

Early in my time on the project, I realized that the development teams were building everything to pass testing, not to run in production. Across the fifteen applications and more than five hundred integration points, every single configuration file was written for the integration-testing environment. Hostnames, port numbers, database passwords: all were scattered across thousands of configuration files. Worse yet, some of the components in the applications assumed the QA topology, which we knew would not match the production environment. For example, production would have additional firewalls not present in QA. (This is a common "penny-wise, pound-foolish" decision that saves a few thousand dollars on network gear but costs more in downtime and failed deployments.) Furthermore, in QA, some applications had just one instance that would have several clustered instances in production. In many ways, the testing environment also reflected outdated ideas about the system architecture that everyone "just knew" would be different in production. The barrier to change in the test environment was high enough, however, that most of the development team chose to ignore the discrepancies rather than lose one or two weeks of their daily build-deploy-test cycles.

When I started asking about production configurations, I thought it was just a problem of finding the person or people who had already figured these issues out. I asked the question, "What source control repository are the production

Conway's Law

In a Datamation article in 1968, Melvin Conway described a sociological phenomenon: "Organizations which design systems are constrained to produce designs whose structure are copies of the communication structures of these organizations." It is sometimes stated colloquially as, "If you have four teams working on a compiler, you will get a four-pass compiler."

Although this sounds like a Dilbert cartoon, it actually stems from a serious, cogent analysis of a particular dynamic that occurs during software design. For an interface to be built within or between systems, Conway argues, two people must—in some fashion—communicate about the specification for that interface. If the communication does not occur, the interface cannot be built.

Note that Conway refers to the "communication structure" of the organization. This is usually not the same as the formal structure of the organization. If two developers embedded in different departments are able to communicate directly, that communication will be mirrored in one or more interfaces within the system.

I've found Conway's law useful in a proscriptive mode—creating the communication structure that I wanted the software to embody—and in a descriptive mode—mapping the structure of the software to help understand the real communication structure of the organization.

Conway's original article is available on the web at the author's site http://www.melconway.com/research/committees.html.

---

configurations checked into?" and "Who can tell me what properties need to be overridden in production?"

Sometimes when you ask questions but don't get answers, it means nobody knows the answers. At other times, though, it means nobody wants to be seen answering the questions. On this project, it was some of both.

I decided to compile a list of properties that looked as if they might need to change for production: hostnames, port numbers, URLs, database connection parameters, log file locations, and so on. Then I hounded developers for answers. A property named "host" is ambiguous, especially when the host in QA has five applications on it. It could mean "my own hostname," it could mean "the host that is allowed to call me," or it could mean "the host I use to launder money." Before I could figure out what it should be in production, I had to know which it was.

Once I had a map of which properties needed to change in production, it was time to start defining the production deployment structure. Thousands of files would need changes to run in production. All of them would be overwritten with each new software release. The idea of manually editing thousands of files, in the middle of the night, for each new release was a nonstarter. In addition, some properties were repeated many, many times. Just changing a database password looked as if it would necessitate editing more than a hundred files across twenty servers, and that problem would only get worse as the site grew.

Faced with an intractable problem, I did what any good developer does: I added a level of indirection. The key was to create a structure of overrides that would remain separate from the application code base. The overrides would be structured such that each property that varied from one environment to the next existed in exactly one place. Then each new release could be deployed without overwriting the production configuration. These overrides also had the benefit of keeping production database passwords out of the QA environment (which developers could access) and out of the source control system (which anyone in the company could access), thereby protecting our customers' privacy.

In setting up the production environment, I had inadvertently volunteered to assist with the load test.

7.3 Load Testing

With a new, untried system, the client knew that load testing would be critical to a successful launch. The client had budgeted a full month for load testing, longer than I had ever seen. Before the site could launch, marketing had declared that it must support 25,000 concurrent users.

Load testing is usually a pretty hands-off process. You define a test plan, create some scripts (or let your vendor create the scripts), configure the load generators and test dispatcher, and fire off a test run during the small hours of the night. The next day, after the test is done, you can analyze all the data collected during the test run. You analyze the results, make some code or configuration changes, and schedule another test run. Time elapsed before the next test: about three or four days.

We knew that we would need much more rapid turnaround. So, we got a bunch of people on a conference call: the test manager, an engineer from the load test service, an architect from the development team, a DBA to watch database usage, and me (monitoring and analyzing applications and servers).

Load testing is both art and science. It is impossible to duplicate real production traffic, so you use traffic analysis, experience, and intuition to achieve as close a simulation of reality as possible. Traffic analysis gives you nothing

What Is a Concurrent User?

Load testing companies often talk about "concurrent users," when they really mean "bots." Some business sponsors have picked up on the term and use it when they really mean "sessions." There is no such thing as a "concurrent user." Unless you are building a pure two-tier client/server system where users connect directly to the database, the concurrent user is fiction.

Counting concurrent users is a misleading way of judging the capacity of the system. If 100% of the users are viewing the front page and then leaving, your capacity will be much, much higher than if 100% of the users are actually buying something.

You cannot measure the concurrent users. There is no long-standing connection, just a series of discrete impulses. The servers receive this sequence of requests that they tie together by some identifier. This series of requests gets identified with a session —an abstraction to make programming applications easier.

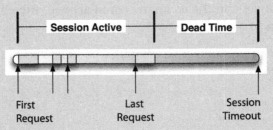

Notice that the user actually goes away at the start of the dead time. The server cannot tell the difference between a user who is never going to click again and one who just has not clicked yet. Therefore, the server applies a timeout. It keeps the session alive for some number of minutes after the user last clicked.

That means the session is absolutely guaranteed to last longer than the user. Counting sessions overestimates the number of users.

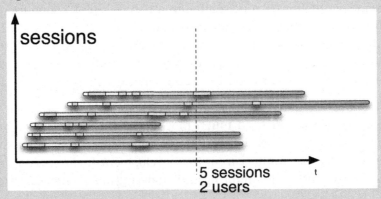

When you look at all of the active sessions, some of them are destined to expire without another request. The number of active sessions is one of the most important measurements about a web system, but don't confuse it with counting users.

but variables: browsing patterns, number of pages per session, conversion rates, think time distributions, connection speeds, catalog access patterns, and so on. Experience and intuition help you assign importance to different variables. We expected think time, conversion rate, session duration, and catalog access to be the most important drivers. Our first scripts provided a mix of "grazers," "searchers," and "buyers." More than 90% of the scripts would view the home page and one product detail page. These represented bargain hunters who hit the site nearly every day. We optimistically assigned 4% of the virtual users to go all the way through checkout. On this site, as with most ecommerce sites, checkout is one of the most expensive things you can do. It involves external integrations (CCVS, address normalization, inventory checks, and available-to-purchase checks) and requires more pages than almost any other session. A user who checks out often accesses twelve pages during the session, whereas a user who just scans the site and goes away typically hits no more than seven pages. We believed this mix of virtual users would be slightly harsher on the systems than real-world traffic.

On the first test run, the test had ramped up to only 1,200 concurrent users when the site got completely locked up. Every single application server had to be restarted. Somehow, we needed to improve capacity by twenty times.

We were on that conference call twelve hours a day for the next three months, with many interesting adventures along the way. During one memorable evening, the engineer from the load-testing vendor saw all the Windows machines in their load farm start to download and install some piece of software. The machines were being hacked while we were on the call using them to generate load! On another occasion, it appeared that we were hitting a bandwidth ceiling. Sure enough, some AT&T engineer had noticed that one particular subnet was using "too much" bandwidth, so he capped the link that was generating 80% of our load. But, aside from the potholes and pitfalls, we also made huge improvements to the site. Every day, we found new bottlenecks and capacity limits. We were able to turn configuration changes around during a single day. Code changes took a little longer, but they still got turned around in two or three days.

We even accomplished a few major architecture changes in less than a week. I'll discuss these improvements in the next chapter.

This early preview of operating the site in production also gave us an opportunity to create scripts, tools, and reports that would soon prove to be vital.

After three months of this testing effort and more than sixty new application builds, we had achieved a tenfold increase in site capacity. It could handle

12,000 active sessions, which we estimated to represent about 10,000 customers at a time (subject to all the caveats about counting customers). Furthermore, when stressed over the 12,000 sessions, the site didn't crash anymore, although it did get a little "flaky." During these three months, marketing had also reassessed their target for launch. They decided they would rather have a slow site than no site. Instead of requiring 25,000 concurrent users, they thought 12,000 sessions would suffice for launch during the slow part of the year. Everyone expected that we would need to make major improvements before the holiday season.

7.4 Murder by the Masses

So after all that load testing, what happened on the day of the launch? How could the site crash so badly and *so fast*? Our first thought was that marketing was just way off on their demand estimates. Perhaps the customers had built up anticipation for the new site. That theory died quickly when we found out that customers had never been told the launch date. Maybe there was some misconfiguration or mismatch between production and the test environment?

The session counts led us almost straight to the problem. It was the number of sessions that killed the site. Sessions are the Achilles heel of every application server. Each session consumes resources, mainly RAM. With session replication enabled (it was), each session gets serialized and transmitted to a session backup server after each page request. That meant the sessions were consuming RAM, CPU, and network bandwidth. Where could all the sessions have come from?

> Sessions are the Achilles heel of every application server.

Eventually, we realized noise was our biggest problem. All of our load testing was done with scripts that mimicked real users with real browsers. They went from one page to another linked page. The scripts all used cookies to track sessions. They were *polite* to the system. In fact, the real world can be rude, crude, and vile.

Things happen in production—bad things that you can't always predict. One of the difficulties we faced came from search engines. Search engines drove something like 40% of visits to the site. Unfortunately, on the day of the switch, they drove customers to old-style URLs. The web servers were configured to send all requests for .html to the application servers (because of the application servers' ability to track and report on sessions). That meant that each customer coming from a search engine was guaranteed to create a session on the app servers, just to serve up a 404 page.

Another huge issue we found was with the search engines spidering the site. Some of the spiders (particularly for the lesser-known search engines) do not keep track of cookies, for legitimate reasons. They do not want to influence marketing data or advertising revenue. The spiders generally expect the site to support session tracking via URL rewriting. Without the cookies, however, they were creating a new session on each page request. That session was then going resident in memory until it expired (thirty minutes). We found one search engine that was creating up to ten sessions per second.

Then there were the scrapers and shopbots. We found nearly a dozen high-volume page scrapers. Some of them were very clever about hiding their origins. One in particular sent page requests from a variety of small subnets to disguise the fact that they were all originating at the same source. In fact, even consecutive requests from the same IP address would use different User-Agent strings to mask the true origin.

ARIN[2] can still identify the source IP addresses as belonging to the same entity, though. These commercial scrapers actually sell a subscription service. A retailer wanting to keep track of a competitor's prices can subscribe to a report from one of these outfits. It delivers a weekly or daily report of the competitor's items and prices. That's one reason why some sites won't show you a sale price until you put the item in your cart. Of course, none of these scrapers properly handled cookies, so each of them was creating additional sessions.

User-Agent: an HTTP header sent by the browser to identify itself. Nearly all browsers claim to be some form of Mozilla, even Microsoft's Internet Explorer.

We also had the amateur shopbots to handle. Several source IPs hit the same product detail page URL from the old site once per minute. It took us a while to identify the product, which ultimately turned out to be a PlayStation 2. Three years after PS2's famous shortages, scripts were still running to look for the quantity available on the console, which created even *more* sessions.

Finally, there were the sources that we just called "random weird stuff."[3] For example, one computer on a Navy base would show up as a regular browsing session, and then about fifteen minutes after the last legitimate page request, we'd see the last URL get requested again and again. More sessions.

7.5   The Testing Gap

Despite the massive load-testing effort, the site still crashed when it confronted the real world. Two things were missing in our testing.

---

2.   See http://www.arin.net.

3.   OK, we didn't really use the word *stuff*.

First, we tested the application *the way it was meant to be used*. Test scripts would request one URL, wait for the response, and then request another URL that was present on the response page. None of the load-testing scripts tried hitting the same URL, without using cookies, 100 times per second. If they had, we probably would have called the test "unrealistic" and ignored that the servers crashed. Since the site used only cookies for session tracking, not URL rewriting, all of our load test scripts used cookies.

In short, all the test scripts obeyed the rules. It would be like an application tester who only ever clicked buttons in the right order. Most testers I've known are perverse enough that if you tell them the "happy path" through the application, that's the *last* thing they'll do. It should be the same with load testing. "Noise" might just bleed away some amount of your capacity, but it could bring your site down.

Second, the application developers did not build in the kind of safety devices that would cut off bad things. When something was going wrong, the application would keep sending threads into the danger zone. Like a car crash on a foggy freeway, the new request threads would just pile up into the ones that were already broken or hung.

> Don't just follow the "happy path."

7.6 Aftermath

The grim march in the days and weeks following launch produced impressive improvements. The CDN's engineers redeemed themselves for their "sneak preview" error before launch. In one day, they used their edge server scripting to help shield the site from some of the worst offenders. They added a gateway page that served three critical capabilities. First, if the requester did not handle cookies properly, the page redirected the browser to a separate page that explained how to enable cookies. Second, we could set a throttle to determine what percentage of new sessions would be allowed. If we set the throttle to 25%, then only 25% of requests for this gateway page would serve the real home page. The rest of the requests would receive a very politely worded message asking them to come back later. Over the next three weeks, we would have an engineer watching the session counts at all times, ready to pull back on the throttle anytime the volume appeared to be getting out of hand. If the servers got completely overloaded, it would take nearly an hour to get back to serving pages, so it was vital to use the throttle to keep them from getting saturated. By the third week, we were able to keep the throttle at 100% all day long. Third, we could block specific IP addresses from hitting the site. Whenever we observed one of the shopbots or request floods, we would add them to the blocked list.

All those things could have been done as part of the application, but in the mad scramble following launch, it was easier and faster to have the CDN handle them for us. We had our own set of rapid changes to pursue.

The home page was completely dynamically generated, from the JavaScript for the drop-down category menus to the product details and even to the link on the bottom of the page for "terms of use." One of the application platform's key selling points was personalization. Marketing was extremely keen on that feature but had not decided how to use it. So, this home page being generated and served up five million times a day was exactly the same every single time it got served. It required more than 1,000 database transactions to build the page. (Even if the data was already cached in memory, a transaction was still created because of the way the platform works.) The JavaScript drop-down menus with nice rollover effects required traversal of eighty-odd categories. Also, traffic analysis showed that a significant percentage of visits per day just hit the main page. Most of them did not present an identification cookie, so personalization wasn't even possible. Still, if the application server got involved in sending the home page, it would take time and create a session that would occupy memory for the next thirty minutes. So, we quickly built some scripts that would make a static copy of the home page and serve that for any unidentified customers.

Have you ever looked at the legal conditions posted on most commerce sites? They say wonderful things like "By viewing this page you have already agreed to the following conditions...." It turns out that those conditions exist for one reason. When the retailer discovers a screen scraper or shopbot, they can sic the lawyers on the offending party. We kept the legal team busy those first few days. After we identified another set of illicit bots hitting the site to scrape content or prices, the lawyers would send cease-and-desist notices; most of the time, the bots would stop. (Like shooing a dog away from the dinner table, though, they always come back—sometimes even in disguise.)

One of the most heroic efforts in that chaotic time happened the week of launch. The IT operations manager identified six extra servers that matched our configuration. They had been requisitioned by a different department but were not in use yet. The manager reallocated them for the commerce site (and presumably ordered replacements) as extra application servers. One of our sysadmins spent a marathon 36-hour shift provisioning them: operating system install, network configuration, filesystem configuration, SAN access, and monitoring. Once he got to that point, we had someone drive him back to his hotel room where he could crash. I was then able to get the application server and applications installed and configured the same day. We doubled the capacity of the application server layer in two days, from bare metal to serving requests.

This particular application server's session failover mechanism is based on serialization. The user's session remains bound to the original server instance, so all new requests go back to the instance that already has the user's session in memory. After every page request, the user's session is serialized and sent over the wire to a "session backup server." The session backup server keeps the sessions in memory. Should the user's original instance go down—deliberately or otherwise—the next request gets directed to a new instance, chosen by the load manager. The new instance then attempts to load the user's session from the session backup server. This mechanism works well (and scales surprisingly well), considering that the sessions are all kept in memory rather than in a database or on disk; that is, it scales well so long as the session data is kept small. For instance, it is common to include the user's ID, her shopping cart ID, and maybe some information about her current search, such as keywords and results page index. It would not be typical to put the entire shopping cart in the session in serialized form or the entire search results (up to 2,000 results). Sadly, that is exactly what we found in the sessions. We had no choice but to turn off session failover.

All these rapid response actions share some common themes. First, nothing is as permanent as a temporary fix. Most of these remained in place for the next year or two. Second, they all cost a tremendous amount of money, mainly in terms of lost revenue. Clearly, customers who get throttled away from the site are less likely to place an order. (At least, they are less likely to place an order at *this* site.) Disabling session failover meant that any user in the checkout process on an instance would not be able to finish checking out when that instance went down. Instead of getting an order confirmation page, for example, they would get sent back to their shopping cart page. Most customers who got sent back to their cart page, when they had been partway through the checkout process, just went away. Making the home page static made personalization difficult, even though it had been one of the original goals of the whole rearchitecture project. The direct cost of doubling the application server hardware is obvious, but it also brought added operational cost. Finally, there is the opportunity cost of spending the next year in remediation projects instead of rolling out new, revenue-generating features.

The worst part is that no amount of those losses were necessary. It is now more than two years since that site launched. Today, the site handles more than four times the load, on fewer servers, without having gone through a hardware refresh. The software has improved that much. If the site had originally been built the way it is now, the engineers would have been able to join marketing's party and pop a few champagne corks instead of popping fuses.

CHAPTER 8

Introducing Capacity

Back before the dot-com crash, one IBM commercial perfectly captured the paradox of deploying systems. A group of anxious entrepreneurs gathered around a screen to observe the launch of their new site. The "orders received" counter ticked upward a few clicks, and the group cheered. Their cheers turned into uncomfortable silence when the counter started to zoom toward the stratosphere.

I know the feeling. It is the same sinking, helpless feeling that the launch team had on the ecommerce site from the previous chapter. On the other hand, I've seen a system improve over eighteen months to handle four times the demand with two-thirds of the original hardware. The improved capacity came entirely from software design changes.

This chapter presents a way of thinking about capacity and some specific patterns and antipatterns that will affect your system's capacity. The next chapter will examine the financial aspects of capacity planning.

8.1 Defining Capacity

Marketers and managers toss words such as *performance* and *capacity* around with casual abandon. Architecture and development requires more precision. At the risk of being pedantic, let me define some terms.

Performance measures how fast the system processes a single transaction. This can be measured in isolation or under load. The system's performance has a major impact on its throughput. Even if using the word *performance*, the customer does not really care about performance. Customers are interested in either throughput or capacity. End users, on the other hand, don't care about overall capacity; they care only about the performance of their own transactions. They can't log in to the servers to see whether the applications are running. As far as they know, when the response time exceeds their expectation, the system is down.

Throughput describes the number of transactions the system can process in a given time span. The system's performance clearly affects its throughput but not necessarily in a linear way. Throughput is always limited by a constraint in the system—a bottleneck. Optimizing performance of any non-bottleneck part of the system will not increase throughput.

Scalability is commonly used two different ways. First, it can describe how throughput changes under varying loads. A graph of requests per second versus response time measures scalability. In the second sense, it refers to the modes of scaling supported by a system. I will use the word *scalability* in the sense of adding capacity to the system.

Finally, the maximum throughput a system can sustain, for a given workload, while maintaining an acceptable response time for each individual transaction is its *capacity*.

Notice that the definition of capacity includes several important variables. There is no single fixed number that you can regard as your capacity. If the workload changes—perhaps because users are interested in different services around the holidays—then your capacity might be dramatically different.

This definition also requires a judgment. What constitutes an "acceptable response time?" For an ecommerce retailer, any response time longer than two seconds will cause customers to walk away. For a financial exchange, it could be shorter—on the order of milliseconds. A travel reservation system, on the other hand, might be allowed five hundred milliseconds for any availability search but thirty seconds to confirm a reservation.

8.2 Constraints

The hardest thing about dealing with capacity is working with nonlinear effects. Our brains can subconsciously integrate differential equations fast enough to drive a car or catch a baseball. Somehow, though, whenever we start talking about capacity, everybody wants to fall back to linear projection. Have you ever been asked, "So, if we can handle 10,000 users at 50% CPU usage, we should be able to handle 20,000 users total, right?"

In every system, exactly one constraint determines the system's capacity.[1] This constraint is whatever limiting factor hits its ceiling first. Once the

---

1. See *The Goal [Gol04]* for more information about the Theory of Constraints.

constraint is reached, all other parts of the system will begin to either queue up work or drop it on the floor. For example, suppose that the constraint is your database server. If you are using Oracle with the multithreaded server option (MTS) enabled, then the server can process as many simultaneous requests as there are daemon processes configured. Let's say that it's a small database server, with just fifty processes handling all the incoming requests. The fifty-first request just has to wait its turn. The application server that issued the fifty-first request could probably serve more pages, if it could just get its data back. Likewise, the web server's worker is certainly idling, waiting for the application server to respond.

Suppose instead that the application servers' RAM is the constraint. Each user session consumes a certain amount of RAM. Once all available RAM is consumed, any new sessions cause the application server to start paging. Again, the web server is probably just waiting for a response from the application server. The database server will actually be happier once the application server starts thrashing—it gets to kick back and relax for a change.

Any nonconstraint metric is useless for projecting or increasing capacity. If smoke is trickling out of your database, it does no good to look at your web server's CPU usage to project the total number of sessions your system can handle. This also means that once you have found the constraint, you can reliably predict capacity improvements based on changes to that constraint. If memory is the constraint, then increasing the memory will increase capacity, until, of course, something else becomes the constraint.

Understanding the capacity of any system requires *systems thinking*, as described by Peter Senge in *The Fifth Discipline [Sen94]*—the ability to think in terms of dynamic variables, change over time, and interrelated connections. No one simple formula will produce an all-encompassing "capacity number."

Start by considering the system as a whole. Find the driving variables. A driving variable is something like "page requests per second." At the "whole-system" level, an easy way to find the driving variables is to look for things that are outside your control, such as user demand, the clock, the calendar, and so on.

Driving variables are causally correlated to following variables. Following variables move in response to driving variables. All directly measurable performance statistics are following variables: CPU usage, free memory, I/O rates, page-swapping rates, network bandwidth, and so on. Load testing, stress testing, observations of production systems, and data analysis will help you determine following variables correlated to each driving variable.[2] Be aware that a single following variable might have significant correlation to more than one driving variable.

From the whole-system view, you can begin decomposing into layers or subsystems, again looking for driving variables and following variables. These will often change their nature from one layer to the next. For example, database I/O drives application server response time, which drives web server memory usage. In this way, a following variable in one relationship can be a driving variable in another relationship. This web of interrelations shows you how changes in the primary driving variables ripple through the entire system.

The constraint in your system will be a limit in one of the following variables. When the constraining variable approaches its limit, it can no longer satisfy the demands of the driving variable. In a correlation analysis with variable windows, you will see a strong correlation between the constraining variable and the primary driving variables up until the constraint is reached. At that point, the correlation breaks down, because the demand continues to rise, but servicing of that demand must fall off. This produces the well-known knee in load-testing charts. The rapid falloff at the knee indicates that a constraint has already been reached.

Once you have identified the constraint, the rest is easy. To improve capacity, you must elevate the constraint by increasing the resource needed for the constraining variable or decreasing your usage of the resource.

8.3 Interrelations

You will often see effects in one layer surface as causes in another layer. For example, if demand on one layer exceeds its capacity, then that layer's performance degrades. It responds slowly or not at all. Slow response is actually worse than no response. When that happens, the slowdown in one layer can trigger a cascading failure in another layer. This can make it difficult to separate capacity questions from stability questions. During the launch of the retail site described in Chapter 7, *Case Study: Trampled by Your Own Customers*, on page 121, the team experienced a severe capacity problem that led directly to a stability problem.

---

2. You're looking for a high correlation coefficient, somewhere between 0.8 (highly correlated) and 1.0 (perfect correlation).

8.4 Scalability

Successful systems get more demand placed on them over time. At some point, the system will need more capacity, which often requires additional hardware. A horizontally scalable system can grow by adding more servers. A vertically scalable system requires upgrades to the existing servers. These are sometimes described as "getting wide" or "getting big."

Any server that can be placed in a homogeneous pool of resources, behind a load balancer or virtual IP address, allows horizontal scaling, as shown in Figure 20, *Horizontal Scaling*, on page 140. You get perfect horizontal scaling when each server can run without knowing anything about any other server. These "shared-nothing" architectures provide nearly linear growth in capacity. Doubling the number of servers should almost double the capacity (unless the added load pummels some other service into submission). Cluster architectures also allow horizontal scaling, though they usually have somewhat less than linear benefit, because of the overhead of cluster management.

Web servers are perfectly horizontally scalable. So are Ruby on Rails servers. J2EE application servers such as WebSphere, WebLogic, and JBoss are horizontally scalable via clustering.

Sometimes, it's impractical or impossible to add more servers in parallel. When that happens, each individual server needs to be as large as possible. Database servers, for example, get very unwieldy when you try to cluster three or more redundant servers. It's better to run a beefy pair with failover.

Scaling vertically requires enough headroom in the server chassis to allow more CPUs and RAM to be added. See Figure 21, *Vertical Scaling*, on page 140. Once the chassis is maxed out, it's a *forklift upgrade* to add more horsepower to the individual machines. Since boxes that can grow to large numbers of CPUs tend to be the most expensive end of the product line, a vertically scalable architecture has a higher initial cost than a horizontally scalable one. A horizontally scalable architecture lets you spend your infrastructure dollars more flexibly; you won't have so much capital tied up in a few huge chassis. Instead, you can start with the smallest number of servers you need and spend incrementally. (This also helps you take advantage of the time value of money, instead of forcing you to put your largest expenditures up front.)

Forklift upgrade: replacing the entire chassis of a server. Large database servers can weigh hundreds of pounds.

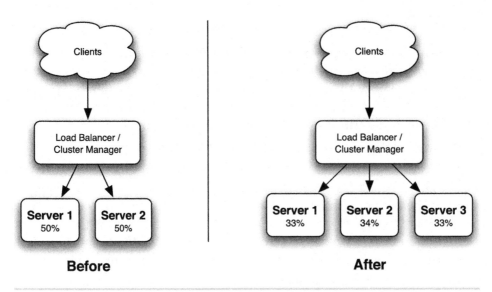

Figure 20—Horizontal Scaling

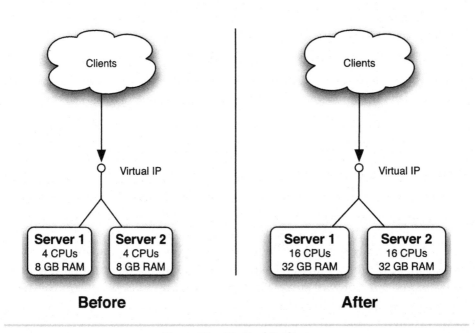

Figure 21—Vertical Scaling

8.5   Myths About Capacity

People have been known to believe some strange things, such as the medieval notion that witches would float like a duck or that linear projection of CPU usage can tell you the capacity of a system. Some of these beliefs are harmless. If the operations manager thinks that the system crashes whenever he wears his Hawaiian shirt, you might actually be better off *not* disabusing him of his superstition. On the other hand, some fallacious beliefs cost the company millions of dollars.

CPU Is Cheap

I've seen terrible offenses committed by bad developers justifying their sloppiness with a glib assertion that CPU is cheap. It would be like saying, "Peanut butter is cheap, so I'll use three times the usual amount to make this sandwich." In the 1960s, a computer cost several years worth of a programmer's salary. It was natural to spend hours or days of a programmer's time squeezing every last cycle out of a program. That's a case of using the cheap resource to maximize usage of the expensive resource. Today, however, a CPU typically costs less than half a days worth of programmer time. So, why bother spending the programmers' time optimizing for CPU usage?

The silicon microchips themselves might be cheap (relative to times past, anyway), but CPU cycles are not cheap. Every CPU cycle consumes clock time. Clock time is latency. A wasteful application makes its users wait longer than they need to, and if there's anything users hate, it's waiting. For web systems, latency in the application has a dual effect. The added processing directly increases the burden on the application servers themselves. Suppose that an application takes just 250 milliseconds of extra processing per transaction. If the system processes a million transactions a day, that extra 250 milliseconds per transaction makes for an extra 69.4 *hours* of compute time every day. Assuming an 80% load factor on each server, you'll need four additional servers to handle this load.

> In reality, 250 milliseconds per transaction adds up to 69.4 hours of CPU time every day.

Since most application servers process transactions on threads from a pool, there's a nonlinear effect on the throughput lurking here. The longer a request-handling thread is checked out from the pool, the higher the probability that an incoming request must be queued instead of executing immediately.

Latency in the application servers harms the web servers, too. While a web server is waiting for the application server to respond, it's holding certain idle resources: at least two sockets (one for the incoming HTTP request and one to the application server), some memory for the request state, and some memory for a partially buffered response. Even if the web server does nothing at all to service that connection, those resources are scarce. Application server CPU usage directly drives web server memory usage.

Finally, some CPUs cost more than others. I don't just mean that PA-RISC chips cost more than Intel x86 chips. I mean that only so many chips fit into a single machine. If you are building with four-way boxes, then the fifth CPU has a disproportionate cost because you have to buy a new chassis. The extra chassis requires its own RAM, probably some local disk, NICs, possibly a Fibre Channel adapter, cooling fans, and so on. It needs its own rack space, or floor space if it is large enough. Your software might be licensed per host, rather than per CPU. Monitoring/managing an extra box costs more. The extra box puts more burden on the data center's cooling system.

These charts show the marginal cost per CPU vs. the CPU count. These assume no disk space, software cost, or management costs. This is just the cost of the CPU chips, the chassis, and RAM. For these entry-level servers in Figure 22, *Cost per CPU for Sun 440 Servers*, on page 143, the cost differential is not large, because the chassis itself does not cost much. The differential comes mostly from the extra RAM and disk space needed. Still, the multiplier for a "breaking" CPU vs. a "nonbreaking" CPU is about 1.2. That is, the cost of the third CPU is about 1.2 times the cost of the second CPU.

On a bigger iron, this picture changes radically. More advanced systems have a much higher cost when you cross that threshold. The chassis for a Sun Fire 6900—shown in Figure 23, *Cost per CPU for Sun Fire 6900*, on page 143 —costs more than $200,000. A new chassis for an Sun E25K, with just the minimal configuration, costs more than a million dollars. The breakpoint comes at a much higher CPU count, of course—the E25K can take 72 processors—but a million dollars will pay for a lot of profiling and optimization in the application stack. You want to be sure that there are no wasted cycles before laying down a million dollars. You definitely want to make sure you need it before committing to that 73rd CPU!

Storage Is Cheap

It is common to hear people assert that disk space is cheap. Who could argue with that? After all, ten years ago storage cost around a dollar per megabyte; now it is less than fifty cents per gigabyte.[3] True, there's still the SCSI

---

3. Source: Pricewatch (http://www.pricewatch.com), Jan. 13, 2007; 500GB SATA drive for $147.

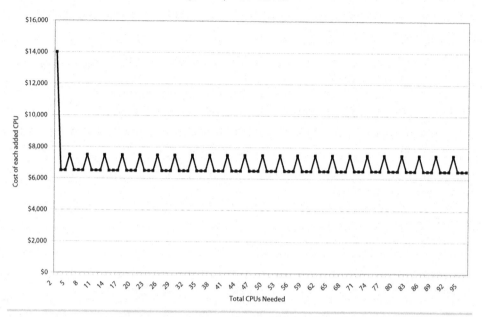

Figure 22—Cost per CPU for Sun 440 Servers

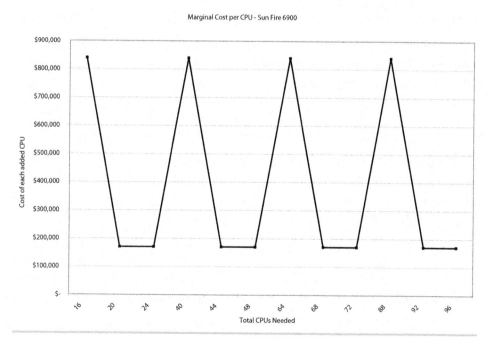

Figure 23—Cost per CPU for Sun Fire 6900

premium, if that's the direction you are going, but drives are cheap enough that a laptop can carry every picture you've ever taken. (You professional photographers are excluded.)

The trouble is that the modern definition of *storage* is much more than just individual drives. *Storage* is the entire managed system of drives, interconnects, allocation, redundancy, and backups needed to deliver high levels of service at efficient costs. Storage is more of a service than a piece of commodity hardware in today's large enterprise. It begins with drives, but it does not end there.

Storage is a service, not a device.

Disks might be local to a server. In that case, each server has to have space enough for the following:

- The operating system
- The applications
- The local configurations or data
- The log files
- The temporary working space needed by the applications

Every single server needs that much space. Here is another multiplier effect: 1GB of disk might be cheap to purchase, but you actually have to purchase that 1GB of disk *n* times over, once for each server. Twenty servers makes 20GB, not 1GB.

Also, don't forget to consider the effects of RAID. Almost all data center class servers boot from RAID 1 volumes. RAID 1 mirrors drives, which requires 100% overhead, or double the number of disks. Data tends to get stored on RAID 5 volumes, which has 20% overhead. Either way, there's another multiplier effect. If you're using mirrored drives, double the space required. That 1GB now looks like 40GB (1GB, mirrored, for each of the twenty servers).

It gets even worse when you consider backups. An extra gigabyte of data across twenty servers could be the added data that pushes your backups out of their window. That would force you to get more tape drives running in parallel to finish the backups in time. More tapes might also be needed.

Managed storage: space on disk drives plus such high-availability features as RAID striping or mirroring plus backups.

A gigabyte of data on local storage costs less than one dollar. In the enterprise, however, *managed storage* can be charged back at rates of up to $7 per gigabyte. It's very important to discuss storage and storage management with your company's IT group when designing for production.

Joe asks:
What Are SAN and NAS, and What's the Difference?

Don't you just love when vendors work so hard to brand themselves and position themselves differently that they end up sounding almost exactly the same? SAN and NAS are radically different under the covers, but those differences get masked by palindromic acronyms.

Network-attached storage (NAS) refers to a storage appliance that plugs into your IP network that provides space via NFS or CIFS (Windows shares). NAS devices often support multiple ancillary protocols such as HTTP and FTP, all from one set of disks and their filesystems. NAS devices are commonly built on top of Linux or embedded Windows, though some are available with other flavors of UNIX on them. Most NAS appliances have multiple drives that can be configured as RAID 0, 1, or 5.

Storage area networks (SANs) are a completely different animal. A SAN is really a completely separate network from your existing IP network. SANs use Fibre Channel (FC) networks that run at 2GB per second. If you are using a SAN, then somewhere there is a large frame with many disk drives plugged into it. SAN management software allows the administrators to create logical volumes—with any RAID level—out of the physical drive. To the client operating system, the SAN host bus adapter (HBA) makes the remote drives appear just like local, physical drives.

Because a SAN is really an entirely new and separate network, it requires lots of costly infrastructure. Because the SAN will immediately become business-critical, that infrastructure must be fast, reliable, and redundant. SAN reliability comes from multipathing; every server should have multiple paths to each of its volumes. That means dual-channel cards on the server, dual switches, and dual controllers on the storage frame.

NAS has very low start-up costs; 500GB NAS units are available for less than $700 today. Terabyte NAS units can be had for less than $1,000. By contrast, you should expect to pay at least a million dollars for an enterprise SAN. SAN also requires ongoing systems management, whereas a NAS generally turns into a dumping ground with little structure or ongoing management. NAS is a choice that a department or even a project team can make, but a SAN is a CIO-level decision.

Bandwidth Is Cheap

This myth is less frequently said but is just as often assumed. In today's market an OC3 connection costs from $7,500 to $12,000 per month. A serious business will have at least a pair of connections, preferably from different carriers. Load balancing both connections gets you a theoretical maximum of 310Mb per second of bandwidth for $15,000 to $24,000 per month.

Based on the shape of your traffic, you might find it advantageous to get a burstable connection instead of a dedicated one. A dedicated connection offers the most predictable pricing. You have the same bandwidth available every second of every day for a flat rate. With a burstable connection, you pay a flat rate, usually much less than the dedicated rate charge, for the "committed" bandwidth. As long as you stay below that committed level, you pay nothing extra.

If your transfer rate exceeds the committed bandwidth, you get charged per megabit minute.[4] Burstable connections can be cheaper than dedicated. The costs can mount quickly, however, if your daily peak always goes over your committed bandwidth. If you get Slashdotted, hang on to your wallet!

So, how many concurrent requests can you get out of that pair of OC3s? Let's look at some of the variables. Ironically, the more users you have on broadband, the worse your bandwidth looks. TCP/IP handshaking guarantees that they will try to pull data as fast as they can receive it. Because they can receive data faster than dial-up users, broadband users will each use a larger share of your available bandwidth. A typical dial-up user is still connecting at 44Kbps. Once you factor in the overhead of PPP, they are probably pulling data from your site at only 38Kbps or 39Kbps. Some cable-modem customers these days are getting download rates of 6Mbps. Back-of-the-envelope calculations say you could service thirteen times as many dial-up users as cable-modem users.

If most of your users will be connecting from other businesses, the picture is about the same as home broadband users. Corporate networks generally limit their employee's computers to 10Mbps (though you'll see a move toward 100Mbps connections to the desktop in the next few years). Even though many corporate networks now have gigabit Ethernet backbones, they still try to prevent bandwidth hogs from monopolizing the network. Plus, corporate firewall/proxy servers tend to be saturated during prime time anyway. So, the time when users are most likely to hit your site (the key post-lunch email and web hour) is also when they are most likely to be slowed by an overburdened proxy server. Therefore, corporate users end up at about the same bandwidth as DSL or cable-modem users.

When you consider the cost of bandwidth, just as with CPU and storage, you must look at the multiplier effects. Dynamically generated pages tend to have a lot of junk characters in them. Suppose each page has just 1,024 bytes of

---

4. Like kilowatt hours for electricity: the product of the excess transfer rate in megabits times the number of minutes at that level.

junk in it. For a million pages per day, you are sending 1,024,000,000 excess bytes. That's just short of one *gigabyte* of unnecessary transfers. Most pages have far more than 1,024 unnecessary bytes. I'll discuss page-building techniques that eliminate this waste in the next chapter.

8.6 Summary

Capacity management is an ongoing process of monitoring and optimization. It involves many dimensions and opposing dynamics. Software changes, traffic changes, and even marketing campaigns can all cause different forces to dominate your capacity. Working with capacity requires a big-picture view of the system as a whole. Overly simplistic or linear models for capacity will mislead you and can cost your company a great deal of money in excess spending or lost revenue.

Capacity is fundamentally a measure of how much revenue the system can generate during a given period of time. Therefore, bad design choices that reduce capacity directly reduce the company's top-line revenue numbers. Offsetting those bad choices requires additional capital expenditure and ongoing operational expense. To get the most from your investments, you should always do the following:

- Always look for the multiplier effects. These will dominate your costs.

- Understand the effects that one layer has on another.

- Improving nonconstraint metrics will not improve capacity.

- Try to do the most work when nobody is waiting for it.

- Place safety limits on everything: timeouts, maximum memory consumption, maximum number of connections, and so on.

- Protect request-handling threads.

- Monitor capacity continuously. Each application release can affect scalability and performance. Changes in user demand or traffic patterns change the system's workload.

CHAPTER 9

Capacity Antipatterns

As you saw in the previous chapter, if CPU, disk, and bandwidth are actually expensive, then it behooves you to maximize the value you get from them. In this chapter, you'll take a look at the antipatterns that harm your system's capacity.

These capacity antipatterns make your applications do more work than necessary, turning electricity into heat instead of revenue. Hardware is expensive, so we need to get as much out of it as possible.

9.1 Resource Pool Contention

I have a love/hate relationship with database connection pools. I view them as a necessary evil. Because it takes up to 250 milliseconds to establish a new database connection, it is worth reusing database connections when possible. Used well, connection pools, like all resource pools, can improve capacity by improving throughput. Left untended, however, resource pools can quickly become the biggest bottleneck in an application.

The bottleneck arises when there is contention for the resources. More threads require one of the resources than are available. In this case, most connection pools will simply block the requesting thread indefinitely until a resource becomes available. This clearly cannot help throughput. Figure 24, *Contention Among Threads*, on page 150, illustrates the percentage of processing time spent in resource pool contention for threads using pools of various sizes. In each case, the contention is zero until the number of threads exceeds the number of resources available. The uppermost curve shows what happens when the threads fight over just four database connections. By the time thirty requests are active, more than 80% of CPU time is spent uselessly waiting for one of the connections to become available.

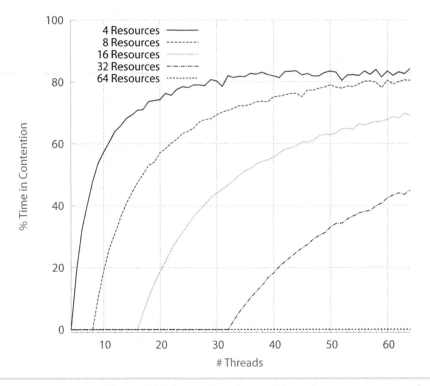

Figure 24—Contention Among Threads

If the request-handling threads spend most of their time blocked, waiting for resources, they are obviously not processing requests. Indeed, Figure 25, *Effects of Contention on Throughput*, on page 151, shows the throughput (in "tasks per minute") of various numbers of request-handling threads with resource pools of different sizes. The lines represent resource pools of different sizes. In the left side of the graph, each curve appears to be more or less linear, and all curves have a similar slope. Each curve begins to flatten out when the number of threads exceeds the number of resources. This is the "knee"— that artifact familiar to everyone who has ever run load tests. To a substantial degree, additional request-handling threads do nothing for throughput, once resource contention begins.

Ideally, every thread immediately gets the resource it needs. To guarantee this, make the resource pool size equal to the number of threads. Although this alleviates the contention in the application server, it might shift the problem to the database server. With Oracle, for example, each connection spawns a process on the database server. Depending on configuration, this

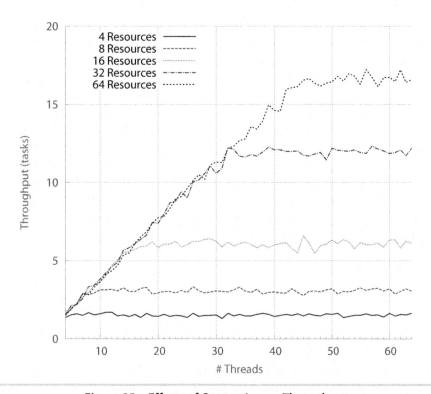

Figure 25—Effects of Contention on Throughput

process will use a few megabytes of RAM. If there are many application servers, then the database server is on the wrong end of another multiplier effect.

For example, with a server farm with twenty machines, each running five application server instances and each instance using a pool of fifty database connections, the database server must bear 5,000 connections. If each connection uses just 1MB of RAM, then the database server requires 5GB of RAM just for these connections. Worse yet, some proportion of the connections will be idle most of the time. (If they were all busy 100% of the time, then the database would be the constraint.) Other databases do not spawn processes for each connection,[1] but they must all devote some resources to each connection.

Blocking indefinitely when resources are exhausted ensures a stability problem. (See *Blocked Threads*, on page 62.) The system will be better served if

---

1. Oracle also supports the more complex multithreaded server (MTS) configuration, which multiplexes connections to processes. DBAs who can properly configure MTS occupy the highest tier of the Oracle priesthood.

the resource pool is configured to block for a limited time only. Each application server is configured differently, so it pays to become expert in your particular resource pool's behavior.[2] When the time expires with no available resource, the pool will either return null or throw an exception. The application code must also be prepared for this to happen.

The common resource pool classes all suffer from some degree of poor transparency. At runtime, you want to know how often callers are blocking, what's the highest number of resources checked out since start-up is (the high-water mark), and how many resources have been created and destroyed. All these metrics can highlight capacity problems. JBoss and WebLogic allow access to some of this information through JMX, but it is up to you to poll the metrics on some periodic basis for offline analysis.

 ## Remember This

Eliminate contention under normal loads

During "regular peak" operation, there should be no contention for resources. Regular peak load would occur on a typical day outside your company's peak season.

If possible, size resource pools to the request thread pool

If there's always a resource ready when a request-handling thread needs it, then you have no efficiency loss to overhead. For database connections, the added connections mainly consume RAM on the database server, which, while expensive, is less costly than lost revenue. Be careful, however, that a single database server can handle the maximum number of connections. During a failover situation, one node of a database cluster must serve all the queries—and all the connections.

Prevent vicious cycles

Resource contention causes transactions to take longer. Slower transactions cause more resource contention. If you have more than one resource pool, this cycle can cause throughput to drop exponentially as response time goes up.

Watch for the Blocked Threads pattern

The capacity problem of resource pool contention can quickly turn into a stability problem if threads block forever when a resource is not available.

---

2. The Jakarta Commons' BasicDataSource supports this via the maxWait property. JBoss uses the <blocking-timeout-millis> element in its data source configuration files. Check your documentation.

9.2　Excessive JSP Fragments

In the Java realm, JSP is the standard page-templating language. JSP files are compiled in two passes. First, the application server generates a .java file with application server–specific servlet code. Second, the application server compiles that source file into bytecode. After the second compilation step, the new class file is loaded into the JVM. Like all Java classes, compiled JSPs are loaded into the JVMs permanent generation. The permanent generation is exactly what it says. The objects in the permanent generation are the actual class and method definitions.

J2EE application servers almost always come with start-up scripts that use the -noclassgc JVM argument. This option tells the JVM to not unload classes from the permanent generation. It's usually billed as a performance improvement, and sometimes it is. The problem arises when you have large numbers of JSP classes being loaded during one execution of the application server. In that situation, the default permanent generation size might not be large enough. If there is no limit to the number of JSPs that your JVM might have to load, then there is no upper bound on the permanent generation size you need. Because each JSP gets compiled and loaded into the permanent generation, without class garbage collection, the permanent generation will eventually fill up. When that is happening, enabling class garbage collection by removing the -noclassgc option will alleviate some of the pain. Essentially, you would move from a deteriorating performance that will eventually be indistinguishable from a crash to consistently lower, but not degeneration, performance.

 Remember This

Don't use code for content

> Loading JSP classes into memory is a kind of caching. If you have enough JSP files, you will fill the permanent generation. Even if you don't, it's a waste of otherwise useful memory to keep a class in memory when it might not be accessed again before you restart the application server.

9.3　AJAX Overkill

AJAX (Asynchronous JavaScript plus XML) has become synonymous with "Web 2.0" sites like Google Maps and del.icio.us. An AJAX application embeds JavaScript in its web pages that will send requests to the website in the background, typically while the user is doing something else. The server's

JSPs as Content

I've seen this happen when JSPs are treated like content rather than code. One site I worked on had more than 25,000 JSP fragments. The vast majority of them were chunks of content for product promotions or category-level pages. The trouble was that none of them ever got retired. As a server ran through the day, more and more of the content JSPs got loaded as classes into the permanent generation. This can lead to serious garbage collection issues, because the JVM tries harder and harder to fit all of the classes into the permanent generation (especially if you've used the -XX:MaxPermSize option to limit that portion of the heap). In this case, the JSPs did not even need to be executable code. They presented only static content. It would have been better to use HTML fragments with a caching content repository to manage those 25,000 page fragments. (See *Use Caching Carefully*, on page 176, for other warnings about the proper use of caching.)

response is used to update a portion of the current browser page, instead of the "Web 1.0" technique of loading a new page for each content update.

Although the pieces of the AJAX technique have been around for several years, Google brought them into the spotlight with Gmail and Google Maps. These applications got everyone's attention more for what they didn't do rather than what they did. Gmail can autocomplete addresses or expand and collapse sections of a conversion without reloading the page. Google Maps takes it even further. You can pan and zoom a map without ever reloading a page. New map tiles get loaded asynchronously and just pop into view as they become available.

Unfortunately, not everyone has a server farm the size of Google's. For many sites, AJAX applications mean many more requests coming from the browser to the web servers. They will also come more rapidly. An average user has a five- to ten-second "think time" between page clicks on a typical site. (It is likely that part of the "think time" is really "wait time" as the user waits for the page to finish downloading and rendering.) With an AJAX-based site, the time between HTTP requests is more like one to three seconds. The individual requests will tend to be smaller, and since the response typically consists of a partial page instead of a full page, the responses will be smaller as well. The combined effect depends greatly on the way you employ AJAX techniques. Used well, it can reduce your bandwidth costs. Used poorly, AJAX techniques will place more burden on the web server and application server layers.

A full treatment of AJAX is beyond the scope of this book (see *Pragmatic Ajax* *[GGA06]* for a wealth of detail), but since it can be such a double-edged sword, here are some ways to apply it without cutting yourself.

Interaction Design

AJAX is a technique, not a goal. The user experience should be primary, so apply AJAX only where it actually makes the user interaction smoother. For example, I've seen a site built on an "AJAX home page"—a single master page that contained the only HTML for the site. All interactions for the site went through AJAX requests and were displayed within the same page. It was awful. The site seemed to break the browser! The Back button caused the browser to leave the site, instead of backing up a page. Worse yet, since updates happened some short time after the user's action but that time varied depending on the complexity of the request, the page seemed to change randomly without any of the browser's usual feedback.

The best places to apply AJAX are those interactions that represent a single task in the user's mind. In Gmail's case, that task is "send an email." It could be any multistep interaction that would ordinarily take a few pages to complete. If you have "wireframes" for your site, look for a linear chain of pages that eventually returns to the home page or some other nexus.

Request Timing

Some of the early AJAX libraries' tutorials show autocomplete requests happening every quarter second, which will obviously increase the demand on the site's servers. Newer libraries support configurable delays, so they send only an autocomplete request some length of time (often 500 milliseconds) after the user stops typing. Of course, that's the delay before the request is *sent*. The user will experience that delay plus the latency involved in sending the request, waiting for the server to process it, and receiving the results.

Session Thrashing

Be sure to configure session affinity so the AJAX requests go to the same application server that the user's session resides on. Avoid unnecessary session failover.

Response Formatting

Do not return HTML pages or fragments. HTML is needlessly verbose; it wastes bandwidth. Instead, return just the data—without formatting—that the client can use to dynamically update the elements on the page.

Use JavaScript object notation (JSON) for data,[3] rather than XML. I know XML is in the name, but that's mainly because it makes a catchier buzzword

---

3.   See http://www.json.org/.

than "AJAS" would. JSON is much easier to parse in the browser and can be a lot less verbose (reducing bandwidth consumption). See http://www.json.org/example.html for some examples of JSON's brevity compared with XML.

Remember This

Avoid needless requests

Don't use polling requests for fizzy features such as autocompletion. If you must have autocompletion—for an address book, part number, department name, or whatever—send a request only when the input field actually changes. (Some of the online tutorials send the request every quarter second!)

Respect your session architecture

Make sure your AJAX requests include a session ID cookie or query parameter. (This is much easier with session cookies than query parameters!) If you don't, your application server will create a new, wasted session for every AJAX request.

Minimize the size of replies

Return the least amount of data necessary. Reply with XML or JSON, not HTML.

Increase the size of your web tier

Your web servers will be dealing with more requests. Be sure to increase the maximum number of connections your web tier can handle, either by adding servers or by increasing the number of clients each server will handle.[4]

9.4   Overstaying Sessions

Somewhere back in the dim reaches when the original Java Servlet specification was being created, it was decided that the default session timeout should be thirty minutes. That is the length of time a session will stay resident in memory *after* the user's last request. As discussed in Chapter 7, *Case Study: Trampled by Your Own Customers*, on page 121, the user actually goes away at the beginning of the session timeout period. The trouble is that you cannot predict which request will be the user's last. (Sounds ominous, doesn't it?) All you can say for certain is that the session resides in memory after the user is long gone.

---

4.   For Apache, this is the MaxClients configuration parameter.

JSON Goes to the Dark Side

One note of caution regarding JSON: some examples use the JavaScript eval() function to execute the JSON string, thereby putting objects directly into the interpreter's scope. This is a terrible idea! Even if you've used SSL and strong certificates to verify the site to the browser, how are you verifying the application code to the site? It takes only one rogue programmer to craft a nasty bit of JSON to be executed on the user's machine. A malicious JSON script can do a lot of damage, from sending private data to a third party to submitting phony orders. It is certainly true that a "black hat" developer can do tremendous damage in other areas, but why make it easy for them to attack your users, too?

As long as the session is active, it consumes resources—mainly memory. Java application servers are perpetually memory constrained. (Many would say they are memory pigs, too.) Abundant free memory is critical to the stability and performance of Java-based applications. Therefore, sessions residing in memory are a direct threat to the health and well-being of the system. They are a threat to the system in direct proportion to their tenure in memory.

Your system's goal should be to expunge these sessions at the earliest opportunity. The common default timeout of thirty minutes is overkill. For a live site, examine your traffic patterns to find the average and standard deviation of the time between page requests that you would still call a session. In other words, two visits in the same day but hours apart are not the same workflow. Likewise, two visits from the same user, both starting at the home page one hour apart are *probably* not the same session either. On the other hand, two requests twenty-nine minutes apart but from one deep page to another deep page, probably are the same activity in the user's eyes. A good bet is to set the session timeout to one standard deviation past the average of that delay. In practice, this will be about ten minutes for a retail site, five for a media gateway, and up to twenty for travel-industry sites.

> Set the session timeout to one standard deviation past the average think time.

An even better bet is to make the session itself unnecessary. If the session holds a bunch of transient state that goes away when the user does, then it is important to keep the session around longer. On the other hand, if everything in the session is just an in-memory copy of persistent state, then the session can be discarded and re-created anytime. Under that approach, the session is purely an in-memory cache. I strongly endorse this model, both for its benefits to capacity and stability and for its benefits to the user. Only developers get the idea behind sessions. Users do not appreciate being put on the clock. Getting kicked back to the starting line just because a new episode of *24* came on is intensely frustrating. A user expects to come and go at will and pick up an interaction where it left off.

This means there should be no such thing as a transient shopping cart and that the user's search results should still be available later—whether that's using a search engine or just database queries. The user's identity and preferences should still be active. (However, the user should be able to dissociate his identity from the particular *device* he is using, such as a terminal in a library or airport.)

The only exception is financially sensitive data such as credit cards or Social Security numbers.[5]

 ## Remember This

Curtail session retention

Keep sessions in memory for as short a time as reasonable. This time will vary from one domain to another.

Remember that users don't understand sessions

Users understand automatic logout for security reasons. They won't understand why their shopping cart disappears because they spent twenty minutes researching a product on another website. Things shouldn't disappear just because the user goes away for a while.

Keep keys, not whole objects

If you keep whole objects in the session, do it with soft references. Keep keys to persistent objects instead. You will get better capacity, and your users will have a better experience: they can come back in an hour or a week and pick up where they left off.

9.5 Wasted Space in HTML

 I've seen a lot of bad things justified with arguments that "bandwidth is cheap" and "CPU is cheap." As you saw in Section 8.5, *Myths About Capacity*, on page 141, neither statement is true. You should not excuse inefficiency.

Web applications harbor a lot of inefficiency that makes users suffer every day. Suppose a page could be reduced from 200KB to 150KB—not an uncommon reduction, by the way. That's 25% fewer bytes the user has to download. Those 50KB take ten seconds on an average dial-up connection. The extra bytes matter for broadband users, too. Here's why.

---

5.   Social Security numbers are the U.S. equivalent of a national identification number.

The application server uses CPU cycles to generate those 50KB of wasted space. As they stream out of the application server's NIC, they use bandwidth. They go into a network switch, get checksummed, buffered, routed, rechecksummed, and serialized out some other port on the switch. That port might be connected to a firewall—a special-purpose router—that does the same network operations as the switch, plus some security checks. The same 50KB now goes back to a switch—maybe the same one, maybe not—and goes through the same low-level network rigamarole and then heads out to a web server. The web server buffers the 50KB in memory, along with the meaningful part of the page. If each request uses 200KB instead of 150KB of web server memory, then the web servers need 33% more RAM to handle their users. Once the whole page is done being generated, the web server sends it down to the browser...through another firewall, switch, and at least one router.

Those 50KB cover a lot of ground! At each step, they either use more RAM or more network bandwidth than necessary.

There's another effect at work here. The larger the page, the longer the browser and web server keep their connection open. While that connection is open, obviously no other request can use it. But, the web server can handle only a finite number of connections! The same way that threads can contend for database connections,[6] end users can contend for web server connections. When a user can't get a web server connection, your site might as well be down.

It's in your best interest to see to it that those connections are serviced and released as quickly as possible.

So, if they're so pernicious, then who sets out to make bloated HTML pages? Nobody, of course. Bloat is never invited; it sneaks in where nobody looks. Designers create stylish page layouts in Dreamweaver. Application programmers carve those into ASP, JSP, or .rhtml templates. Then application servers generate full pages from the templates. Each step of that process allows inefficiency to creep in. We'll look at some of the most common types.

Whitespace

Web applications are built of page fragments, whether they are JSPs, JHTMLs, tiles, or .rhtmls. These fragments make life easier for the programmer by allowing bits and bobs of HTML to be reused from one page to another and by separating them from the superstructure of the pages. The flip side is that stitching together those page fragments can lead to extremely large pages.

---

6. See *Resource Pool Contention*, on page 149.

The easiest way for waste to creep in is as whitespace. All the custom tags used by these various templating languages get replaced with their generated content, but the whitespace used to format the files in a readable way gets preserved. This includes newlines after template tags, even when the template tag "expands" to nothing, such as a conditional tag with a false condition.

One particularly egregious site had a front page that consisted of more than 100 separate JSP fragments. The generated HTML was more than *600KB*, with one-third of that consisting entirely of newline characters on lines full of spaces.

It sounds trivial, but think of the dial-up user waiting an extra five seconds to download nothing but spaces! The effect on the systems was profound as well. The whitespace was eating an extra 200KB per page request on the web servers, because they buffered the response page before sending it to the browser. Since the web servers tended to be memory bound instead of CPU bound, this reduced the site's overall capacity. That excess whitespace would have cost the company more than $15,000 a year just in bandwidth costs, without considering the cost of extra web servers.

> Whitespace would have cost $15,000 a year.

You can add an interceptor to the application server that filtered out the excess whitespace. I've often seen that the CPU cost of filtering was less than the RAM and bandwidth cost of not filtering.

Expensive Spacer Images

Almost every dynamically generated HTML page has one or more spacer images on it. These little transparent GIFs, or 1-pixel images, of various colors (sometimes called *shims*) are ubiquitous. They turn out to be bad for bandwidth and bad for the user's experience.

Suppose you have a table cell that needs to be a certain size to make the layout work. You can already set the width and height of the cell itself, but it is common to see a spacer image as the cell's contents. For example:

```
<img src="/images/spacer.gif" width="17" height="23">
```

That's 53 bytes for the image reference. It could be replaced with this:

```
 
```

Those 5 bytes take the place of 53, saving 48 bytes. Forty-eight bytes doesn't sound like much, except that a typical page will have anywhere from twelve to forty spacers in various places.

Don't forget to consider the multiplier effect either. Forty-eight bytes saved in twelve places on a page times a million page requests per day equals 576,000,000 bytes. Will your switches and routers notice an extra 576,000,000 bytes a day in traffic?

For the user, each different spacer image (not the reference from the page but the actual URL) means an extra request to the server. Even if the user's browser already has the image in cache, the browser often asks, "Is the image I have still current?" This is especially true for dynamically generated pages that usually tell the browser not to cache the page content.

Each one of those requests for spacer images—or checking the cache status of the spacers—eats up a web server connection for some small amount of time. Although the web server sends the spacer image for the umpteenth time, it could have been processing a revenue-generating transaction for some other user.

Excess HTML Tables

While we're putting HTML pages on a diet, let's examine the use of tables for formatting. All current browser versions support Cascading Style Sheets (CSS). Clever use of CSS and styles can provide every bit as much control over formatting as tables. The capacity difference is striking. Table structures must be sent on every page, every time the page is served. A style sheet has to be downloaded only once.

Even if the style sheet is larger than a typical HTML page, the net savings is more important. I've seen side-by-side comparisons of CSS-formatted pages vs. HTML-formatted pages where the CSS version was less than one half of the HTML version. For fantastic examples of the designs possible with pure CSS and HTML, spend some time looking at http://www.csszengarden.com/. I have at least one "I didn't know you could do that!" moment every time I look at that site.

 ## Remember This

Omit needless characters

Omit wasted characters in HTML. Generating it takes CPU cycles on the application server. It takes bandwidth on the application servers' network cards, bandwidth on the network switches, bandwidth on the web servers, and bandwidth on the users' connections. Downloading it takes time, particularly for users on slow connections. Eliminate whitespace to save your users' time and your company's money.

Remove whitespace

Whitespace sneaks into generated pages near loops, conditionals, and includes. The directive gets replaced, maybe by a zero-length string, but the coder's nice formatting remains. I've seen pages with 400KB of tabs, spaces, and newlines.

Replace spacer images with nonbreaking spaces or CSS

Web design programs leave spacer images such as mouse droppings in a page. Tiny but noisome. When turning a page design into code, eliminate every image possible.

Replace HTML tables with CSS layout

Aside from being more "Web 2.0," CSS style sheets don't have to be downloaded on every page the way a table-based superstructure does. HTML files with styles and classes can be much smaller than their table-driven counterparts.

9.6 The Reload Button

I swear, sometimes users are the worst thing that can happen to a system. That's never more true than when the system is already under stress. Suppose your site is getting slow. If it's a J2EE site, then some user sometime will hit a full garbage collector and have a fifteen-second response time. (I've always found it ironic that because most garbage collections happen because of a failed memory allocation, they are virtually guaranteed to happen while processing some user's request.) A user sitting in front of a web browser has no idea how much work is or is not going on at the other end of the network. If the user doesn't see a page within ten seconds, he or she is likely to hit Reload. When that happens, the browser abandons its connection from the previous request, opens a new socket, and fires a new HTTP request at you.

Nobody tells the application server to stop processing the previous request. In fact, if the connector between the web server and the application server buffers responses, it might not even be possible to find out that the previous connection was dropped until the entire page has been built and buffered into the web server's memory. At best, the application server might get an IOException when trying to send the response, which is still hardly ideal.

If the page request causes something transactional to happen, such as updating a user's profile or logging some tracking data, then the second request could actually block waiting on the first one to complete. In really bad cases, it could deadlock with the first request.

There is no good answer about what to do with the Reload button. Just make sure your site is fast enough that users don't click it.

Remember This

Make the Reload button irrelevant

Fast sites don't provoke the user into hitting the Reload button. You want your site to serve pages so fast that the Reload button never comes into it. Reload requests hurt your site when it's already suffering.

9.7 Handcrafted SQL

Essentially every application today must work with a relational database. Many applications rely on object/relational mapping to bridge the gap. Whether you're using Ruby on Rails' ActiveRecord, Hibernate, or any of the three EJB persistence models, some form of object/relational mapping is in play. ORM packages generate very predictable, repetitive SQL. Predictable access patterns of SQL are good for capacity, because a competent DBA can tune the database to make those queries perform well.[7]

Each of these ORM layers allows the developer to get down to direct SQL access in one way or another. Hibernate, for example, allows you to embed a named SQL query directly in your mapping files, which you can then reference by name in your application. Even if it's just getting access to a database connection and issuing a query directly, it's always possible to send handcrafted SQL directly to the database. This capability is usually described as a way to improve performance, so why do I call it a capacity killer? Well, it's mainly because object-oriented developers do weird, wonderful, and torturous things to a perfectly innocent database.

The problem is that developer-crafted SQL tends to be idiomatic and unpredictable. Database tuning for the rest of the application won't help for these beastly one-offs, and it might actually harm them. Likewise, tuning for these oddities does no good to the rest of the application and might harm it.

What makes these handcrafted SQL queries so bad? They usually suffer from a handful of common mistakes. First, they often join on nonindexed columns. Second, they usually join too many tables. If it were a simple relationship,

---

7. Watch out, though, for the "N+1" problem with ORM tools. This problem arises when accessing the members of a collection. Some ORM frameworks send one query to find the membership of the collection and then send one query per member to populate the individual objects.

Serialize on Source Address

I've seen some application servers try to ensure that they process just one request from a source IP address at a time. This fails in two ways. First, if you use a caching network such as Akamai, then all requests appear with the same source IP address. This also occurs if the user is on a corporate network with a single "gateway" proxy server. Second, once the user hits Reload, the user's browser is no longer waiting for a response to the first request. Serializing requests just exacerbates the problem, because now the user's second request won't even process until the first one completes. This means the frustrated user will still be looking at a spinning logo instead of a page and may well hit Reload two or three more times before leaving your site for a competitor.

Depending on your load balancing and session affinity configuration, the second request might not even go to the same application server as the first. Therefore, your application code should be prepared for a single user to be executing the same transaction several times without causing deadlocks.

then the developer would just use the ORM package to follow the relations. Since they're already dropping down into handwritten SQL, you know there's some unusual access pattern going on. Third, developers try to treat SQL as if it were either a procedural language or an object-oriented language instead of the set-based relational language it really is. They will issue some query that joins five tables to select exactly the one row they're looking for, and then they'll issue that query 100 more times to find other individual rows. Fourth, developers like to exercise features of SQL that they shouldn't. I once saw an eight-way union, where each subselect in the union was joining five tables by nonindexed columns. It took a full page just to print the thing out. The query plan had about forty table scans in it.

Table scan: the slowest way to find something in a large table. The database server iterates over every row in the table to find matching rows.

Properly tuned databases are important for production use, to a degree that is sometimes hard to believe. Every DBA has stories about some process that was reduced from eighteen hours to three minutes, just by adding an index here or analyzing table statistics there. An order-of-magnitude gain is common. Developers do not see these effects because they work with such unrealistically small data sets during development and QA. Characterizing performance requires realistic data volumes. Sometimes, data is available from the existing production system. It will probably need "scrubbing" before it can be used in nonproduction environments. Scrubbing usually involves replacing private data with a random scramble of characters to protect confidential customer data—particularly since test data is often sent outside the company or offshore altogether. For new development, there might not be any existing data sets available. In that case, an hour or two of development time spent creating a data generator will pay off many times over.

Handcrafted SQL is closely related to dynamically generated SQL. Dynamically generated SQL from an ORM tool is just fine, because it is predictable. That's not the kind of dynamically generated SQL I'm warning you about. The kind that keeps me awake at night is where some piece of code is doing query-by-example by looping over attributes and tacking on bits of a WHERE clause or where the tables and joins are being assembled dynamically. Save those for the reporting system. They don't belong in transactional systems.

Each query like this has a risk of hitting some very, very slow condition. You can tune the database to respond well only to certain predictable access patterns. You cannot make it respond well to every possible query.

 Remember This

Minimize handcrafted SQL

You might be tempted to roll your own SQL as a performance optimization. It's always a good idea to see whether there are ways to do the same in the database itself—through hinting, indexing, or views.

See whether the DBA laughs at the queries

If it doesn't pass the laugh test, it shouldn't go into production. Period.

Verify gains against real data

Try your handcrafted SQL against production-sized data. Gains observed in a development database sometimes evaporate when they hit radically different query plans in production.

9.8 Database Eutrophication

 In ecology, a lake "ages" through a process called *eutrophication*. This is the slow buildup of sludge from dead microbes, rotting fish, and algae. In advanced stages, the sludge removes enough oxygen from the water that nothing can live in the lake any more, and the lake dies. The same thing can happen to your database, only it will be your system that goes belly-up.

In development and QA, testing typically proceeds with data sets ranging from tiny to laughably miniscule. Combined with the short time systems typically spend in QA, it is easy for database schemas to slip into production without any serious high-volume testing. Once users start pouring through the doors (or load balancers), however, this can change rapidly.

Indexing

Object/relational mapping (ORM) tools make it easy to create and traverse relationships between tables. Connections defined in the ORM tool's mapping file don't trigger any DBA review. Thus, whereas a data architect defining referential integrity rules is likely to slap an index on any foreign key relationship, tables related via object properties probably do not get the same careful attention. Selecting a row—in other words, traversing an object relationship—by an unindexed column results in the dreaded "table scan." It's exactly what it sounds like, a linear search through all rows, looking for rows with a column that matches the query.

With the size of data set typically used in development, you can't even measure the time difference between querying by an indexed column and querying by an unindexed column. (Indeed, on the "laughably miniscule" end of the spectrum, a table scan might even be the fastest query plan! This is especially true if the whole table is already cached in memory, which it usually is for toy data.) Give it a year or two in production, though, and your users could end up waiting minutes for some simple operation to complete. In general, any column that is the target of an association in the ORM mapping should be indexed.

Database schemas are often designed well in advanced of the application code that will use the schema. As a result, indexes created during design might not match the actual access patterns implemented in the application. The database architect should remain involved during application development to ensure that the schema is continuously adapted to be as efficient as possible for the application's functionality. This is particularly true in the case of agile projects, wherein relationships between entities come and go far more often than in a traditional "big design up-front" project.

Partitioning

Another key design consideration relates to the ability to keep the database well-structured during production operations. Database architects always want to know as much as possible about table growth rates and the amount of churn to expect in each table. This information helps them lay out the tables on disk. Mapping the logical tables to physical storage well has a tremendous impact on the long-term performance of the database. Unfortunately, the early guesses about growth rates and retention often turns out to just be flat wrong. Sometimes, it also changes radically from one release to the next. For example, I saw an order management system go from generating 1GB of audit logs per year in one release to creating 1GB per *day* in the next release. When that happens, the storage layout for the database gets "spaghettified" as tables get spread across multiple physical extents. Response times suffer as the database performs excessive disk I/O. One solution would be to achieve perfect knowledge, with perfect specifications, before developing the application. Right.

Another solution would be to segment or partition the tables. (Exact terminology varies with the database vendor.) If there is some column that has a small finite set of values, where each value indicates a cluster of related rows, then that column is a good candidate for partitioning. For example, a table that holds orders while they are being processed will have a lot of churn. By adding a "day of the week" column, that table can be split into seven partitions. Each partition can be reorganized or moved to another physical extent separately, even while another partition of the table is in heavy use. This permits restructuring of the storage underneath the table without taking downtime.

Historical Data

The best answer to slowdowns due to data growth in the database is a rigorous routine of archival and elimination. We are dealing with transactional systems. The data should be only that needed to process the users' transactions. That means you don't need to keep all historical data online in the same database. In particular, reporting and ad hoc analysis should never be done in the production database. (A sneaky way to discourage this abusive practice is to ensure that the results would show only the last ninety days or six months of data!)

Data mining, reporting, or any other kind of analysis should be done in a true warehouse anyway. The OLTP schema is no good for data warehousing.

OLTP: online transaction processing. This is a schema optimized for fast inserts of transactional records. This is typically very bad for producing reports or performing ad-hoc queries.

Users might need, or just want, visibility into historical data. For example, Amazon now has almost ten years worth of my orders. (I wonder how many decades they plan to keep those orders online?) How often would an order from the spring of 1998 be needed? Multilevel storage allows you to keep historical data online, in a low-cost system, while keeping the most current transactional data in a higher-performance system.

Don't mix transactions and reporting.

This section can only scratch the surface of data and storage architecture. The subject merits an entire series of books. Over and above all else is this: a rigorous regimen of data purging is vital to the long-term stability and performance of your system.

Remember This

Create indexes; it's not just the DBA's responsibility

You know your application's intentions better than the DBA. You should know which columns will be used for lookups, which tables are read-mostly, and which are write-mostly. It's your responsibility to come up with the first iteration of indexes.

Purge sludge

Old data just slows down queries and inserts. Unless the user cares about it—such as an order history table—you should get it off the production servers.

Keep reports out of production

Reports can, and should, be served elsewhere. Don't jeopardize production operations by letting reports run expensive queries. Besides, reports are better served from a star schema than an OLTP schema anyway.

9.9 Integration Point Latency

Every communication with another system entails a certain amount of latency. A remote call takes at least 1,000 times as long as a local call. Whether that remote call is via DCOM, CORBA, web services, or a binary socket protocol, the caller will sit around doing nothing while waiting for a response. The caller must be processing some transaction, or it wouldn't be calling. Therefore, you know the caller takes at least as long to respond as the remote system.

Integration point latency can be a serious performance problem. The problem becomes acute when the integration point uses some flavor of remote object protocol. The "location transparency" philosophy for remote objects claims that a caller should be unaware of the difference between a local call and a remote call. This philosophy has been widely discredited for two major reasons. First, remote calls exhibit different failure modes than local calls. They are vulnerable to network failures, failure in the remote process, and version mismatch between the caller and server, to name a few. Second, location transparency leads developers to design remote object interfaces the same way they would design local objects, resulting in a chatty interface. Such designs use multiple method calls for a single interaction. Each method call incurs its own latency penalty. The cumulative effect is a very slow response time.

Performance problems for individual users become capacity problems for the entire system. Even if the thread processing a transaction is temporarily idle while it waits for a response, it still holds many resources. It certainly consumes memory and CPU time slices. It might also hold database connections that other threads need. Further down, the idle thread might have row or page locks in the database, causing contention at that level.

More abstractly, there is an opportunity cost to having a blocked thread wait for response from an integration point. It cannot do other work, even if other work is queued and waiting for a thread to process it.

 Remember This

Expose yourself to latency as seldom as possible
Integration point latency is like the house advantage in blackjack. The more often you play, the more often it works against you. Avoid chatty remote protocols. They take longer to execute, and they tie up those precious request-handling threads.

9.10 Cookie Monsters

 Some technologies just beg to be misused. Take bottle rockets. No matter how many warning labels manufacturers put on bottle rockets, it's still a firecracker with *a handle*. Ask Don Norman—handles are meant to be held.[8] You could take someone who had never seen fireworks in his life, and in ten minutes he'll be holding them in his hand, shooting them at his buddies. It might be a bad idea, but it still gets rediscovered by every generation.

HTTP cookies stand right there with bottle rockets in the "things that invite you to blow yourself up" category. They have legitimate uses, but some of their abuses will make your eyes bug out. On the surface, HTTP cookies appear to be a harmless, if somewhat inelegant, kluge around the stateless nature of web interactions. The server sends back an extra header or two with some data that it wants the client to send back at some point in the future.

The original authors of RFC 2109[9] clearly intended cookies to be used for session management. In fact, RFC 2109 is titled "HTTP State Management Mechanism." To their great credit, David Kristol and Lou Montulli did not just add a new HTTP header for a session identifier. Their invention, the HTTP cookie, applies far more generally. It can be used for session identification, but it can also be used for much more. (Giving credit where credit is due,

---

8. See *The Design of Everyday Things [Nor88]* about "affordances."
9. See http://www.ietf.org/rfc/rfc2109.txt.

RMI Across the Seas

I once worked on a fat-client Java system that used RMI to communicate with its server. The server provided a highly functional object-oriented view of the client's enterprise data warehouse. The client application allowed marketers to make connections between products from a hierarchy and media such as pictures, PDF files, and text documents.

Domestically, the system worked fine. Once we got a few users in the United Kingdom, however, they started clamoring for a local server and data warehouse, a multimillion-dollar investment. We found that expanding a node in the hierarchy (a tree control), which took less than a second for U.S. users, took *twenty minutes* from the United Kingdom!

Expanding a node in the tree control required the client to look up some details about the children of that node: its name, type, and number of children. The trouble was that the client would make one remote call to the parent node, asking it for a collection of children, and then the client would enumerate that list, calling each child three times. This is an example of a "1+N" problem: one call for the list plus one (or more) call for each element in the list.

We added a method to the parent that returned a collection of "Summary Objects" that contained the three bits of information needed for the tree control. Once we deployed that update, the U.K. users enjoyed the same subsecond response time as the U.S. users, without installing a replica of the entire data warehouse!

Tim Berners-Lee made the first set of good choices in making HTTP extensible via headers and requiring that agents ignore headers they do not understand, instead of throwing errors.)

Several developers have independently discovered the antipattern of storing anonymous persistent data via cookies. One group, for example, added an interceptor to the request-handling pipeline that would use Java serialization to persist anonymous users' shopping carts as cookies. The idea, of course, was to avoid creating database records for anonymous visitors who might never return. With the shopping cart cookie, then, a returning, anonymous visitor would have the items in her cart that were there when she was on the site before.

This idea has so many problems; it's hard to know where to begin. First, Java serialization presents some issues. Browsers keep cookies until their expiration date (or until the user upgrades computers, installs a different browser, or clears the browser's private data, and so on). As a result, the serialized form of the cart object could be months or years old. The odds are that a code change will make the serialized form invalid long before the user returns.

Errors in deserializing Java objects are thrown as IOExceptions, which most developers treat as very unlikely occurrences. Serialization makes IOException a routine part of doing business.

Even if the source code is the same, the products in the user's cart may well be different—or missing. Now the interceptor needs to handle referential integrity checking as well as code versioning problems.

And what if the browser just *lies*? HTTP, like any protocol, is nothing but an agreement about how two parties should interact. Either side of that interaction can be subversive or malicious. What would keep a malicious user from altering the cookie to set all prices to $0.01? Given a sophisticated enough attacker, armed with information about the company's software platform, it might be possible to use a serialized Cart object to subvert a lot of business rules about pricing and promotions. Even if the cookie is just data, don't trust it! Plenty of tools out there let users monkey around with HTTP requests and responses (Firefox extensions, smart HTTP proxies, session replay, and so on).

Then there's the capacity question. Cookies were meant to send small chunks of data, less than 100 bytes or so. That's all you need for a session identifier. With that little data, it does not matter much that the browser resends the cookie on each new HTTP request. Bump that up to a 4KB serialized object or XML fragment, and the bandwidth starts to add up. It's mostly wasted too. For something like the serialized cart idea, you need to deserialize the cart only once. After that, it is in memory in the user's session. Sending and resending the data on every request is a needless drain on your bandwidth.

On receiving a request, the web server must parse all the headers into its own internal structure. If there's an application server, then the web server resends the request parameters to the application server. All told, the extra cookies cross the wire twice (sometimes four times) and get parsed twice. Again, the extra time taken for a single request might not be much, but there's that multiplier effect to worry about.

It hurts the user too. Even broadband users typically have much less upstream bandwidth than downstream. Uploading the extra 4KB on each request adds up. (Hey, a few milliseconds here, a few milliseconds there, and pretty soon you're talking about real time!)

All of this extra processing adds up to an ongoing operational cost in production—day in and day out. The extra code to handle the cookie has an ongoing maintenance cost, all to avoid adding rows to the database for carts for anonymous visitors. The only argument against putting the carts in the database was the cost and complexity of writing a purge job to clean out unused carts periodically.

As a general mechanism, cookies produce some cool effects. Just remember that the client can lie, might send back stale or broken cookies, and might not send the cookies back at all.

 Remember This

Serve small cookies

Use cookies for identifiers, not entire objects. Keep session data on the server, where it can't be altered by a malicious client.

9.1 Summary

Statistics guarantee that the majority of programmers have never worked on really large, mission-critical software. First, salary surveys consistently show that most programmers have less than ten years of experience. Once they reach that ten-year mark, many programmers move into management or just out of programming. Second, the histogram of project sizes is heavily weighted toward the smaller end of the scale. So, take a young population with relatively few opportunities to work on giant projects, and it's no surprise that experience at that level is hard to find.

Without that experience, programmers are likely to re-create many of the capacity killers discussed in this section, either through ignorance or misguided intentions. These issues certainly aren't covered in colleges and universities, where *optimization* refers to tweaking up some search algorithm.

The capacity killers seem like obvious errors, and perhaps they are obvious when drawn out from a system and held up for examination. Nevertheless, I have seen them created and re-created by different development teams at different clients. Nobody deliberately selects a design with the purpose of harming the system's capacity; instead, they select a functional design without regard to its effect on capacity.

CHAPTER 10

Capacity Patterns

C.A.R. Hoare famously said, "Premature optimization is the root of all evil." This has often been misused as an excuse for sloppy design. Hoare's full quote said, "We should forget about small efficiencies, say about 97% of the time: premature optimization is the root of all evil." His true warning was against chasing small gains at the expense of complexity and development time.

The problem is that optimization happens late, which often means "not at all" when schedules are tight. (When aren't they tight?) Furthermore, optimization can increase the performance of individual routines by percentages, but it cannot lead you to fundamentally better designs. You would never optimize your way from a bubble-sort to a quicksort. Choosing a better design or an architecture optimized for scaling effects is the opposite of premature optimization; it obviates the need for optimization altogether.

Likewise, you ignore performance and capacity while designing your distributed system at your own peril. As I showed in Section 8.5, *Myths About Capacity*, on page 141, small changes in CPU, memory, and disk consumption get multiplied by some really big numbers when your system goes into production. I've seen poorly performing code cause an organization to budget ten million dollars for extra hardware to make it through one holiday season. Fixing a few of the antipatterns and implementing a couple of these capacity patterns[1] allowed them to avoid that ten-million-dollar expense. That was the equivalent of nearly one week of sales.

Avoiding the antipatterns is an important step, but there is more than just avoiding self-inflicted wounds. The capacity patterns in this chapter will take your application from *Fight Club* to *Rocky*.

---

1. Precompute Content and Use Caching Carefully, as it happens.

10.1 Pool Connections

As I mentioned in *Resource Pool Contention*, on page 149, resource pools can dramatically improve capacity. Resource pools eliminate connection setup time. Establishing a new database connection requires a TCP connection, database authentication, and database session setup. Taken together, this can easily take 400 to 500 milliseconds. Only starting a new thread is more expensive than creating a database connection.

In the early days of Perl CGI scripts, a script would open a connection, do some work, and then tear down the connection. This strategy was safe, clean, and easy to debug. Unfortunately, this approach hits the wall when the database server spends as much time managing connections as it does on processing transactions. To get past that point, individual page requests must share or reuse connections. These days, nearly every language and programming style permits connection pooling. There really is no excuse not to use it, except if you do it poorly.

Connection pooling does impose some considerations. Connections can get into a bad state. When that happens, every request that attempts to use the connection will get an error. The bad connection will get checked out, cause an error, and get thrown back into the pool. The good connections get used for actual work, so they stay checked out longer. As a result, the bad connection is more likely to be available when a request comes in. It therefore causes a disproportionate number of errors. One bad connection out of ten will cause more than 10% of requests to error out.

Connection pool sizing is a vital issue. An undersized connection pool leads to resource pool contention (again, see *Resource Pool Contention*, on page 149). An oversized connection pool can cause excess stress on the database servers.

A related issue is the design for checking connections out and in to the pool. For a web-based system, several strategies are possible. The simplest is the "per-page" model: a connection is checked out for the entire page. It is checked in when the page is completed. When multiple connection pools are involved, this model tends to be safer against deadlocks, since the same order of connection checkout and checkin can be enforced on all requests. On the other hand, this model does require a higher ratio of connections to request-handling threads, since each connection will be checked out for longer periods.

The "per-page" model is usually implemented with a transaction manager set to create a single transaction containing the entire page.

If individual pages are dynamically built from numerous fragments, it might not be possible to apply the "per-page" model. The "per-fragment" approach allows each fragment to check out its own connection, do some work, and check the connection back in to the pool. This model is more susceptible to deadlock but can achieve higher throughput than the "per-page" model. Fewer connections per request-handling thread are required, because the individual connections are checked in faster. The main advantage is individual fragments do not require global knowledge about the transaction context. Each can operate independently.

A hybrid approach allows each fragment to manage its own connections but creates a database transaction around the entire page. The connections then get attached to the transaction until it is rolled back or committed. This model combines the deadlock safety of the "per-page" model with the simplicity and isolation of the "per-fragment" model. It does require the larger connection pools of the "per-page" model. The hybrid approach can be hard to debug, since individual fragments might see uncommitted data that previous fragments have introduced in the transaction. The result will be a fragment that sees data you can't. It's very difficult to diagnose a fragment's behavior then.

No matter which strategy your application applies, you must monitor your connection pools for contention, or this capacity enhancer will quickly become a killer.

 Remember This

Pool connections

Connection pooling is basic. There's no excuse not to do it.

Protect request-handling threads

Do not allow callers to block forever. Make sure that any checkout call has a timeout and that the caller knows what to do when it doesn't get a connection back.

Size the pools for maximum throughput

Undersized resource pools lead to contention and increased latency. This defeats the purpose of pooling the connections in the first place. Monitor calls to the connection pools to see how long your threads are waiting to check out connections.

10.2 Use Caching Carefully

Caching can be a powerful response to a performance problem. It can reduce the load on the database server and cut response times to a fraction of what they would be without caching. When misused, however, caching can create new problems.

The maximum memory usage of all application-level caches should be configurable. Caches that do not limit maximum memory consumption will eventually eat away at the memory available for the system. When that happens, the garbage collector will spend more and more time attempting to recover enough memory to process requests. The cache, by consuming memory needed for other tasks, will actually cause a serious slowdown.

No matter what memory size you set on the cache, you need to monitor hit rates for the cached items to see whether most items are being used from cache. If hit rates are very low, then the cache is not buying any performance gains and might actually be slower than not using the cache. Keeping something in cache is a bet that the cost of generating it once, plus the cost of hashing and lookups, is less than the cost of generating it every time it is needed. If a particular cached object is used only once during the lifetime of a server, then caching it is of no help.

It's also wise to avoid caching things that are cheap to generate. I've seen content caches that had hundreds of cache entries that consisted of a single space character. A particular fragment of JSP had a conditional that checked to see whether a user was an employee by looking at a Boolean flag in the user's profile. It evaluated to false most of the time and rendered itself as nothing. Somehow, I doubt that a conditional on a Boolean was really expensive enough to warrant caching the outcome, especially when the cached object was relevant only for a single user.

In Java, caches should be built using SoftReference objects to hold the cached item itself. If memory gets low, the garbage collector is permitted to reap any object that is reachable only via soft references. As a result, caches that use soft references will help the garbage collector reclaim memory instead of preventing it.

In extreme cases, it might be necessary to move to a multilevel caching approach. In this approach, you keep the most frequently accessed data in memory but use disk storage for a secondary cache. This works well if the objects to cache are extremely large (such as images) or the working set is larger than what you can hold in memory. If fetching uncached data involves access over WAN connections, a multilevel cache is also helpful.

Precomputing results can reduce or eliminate the need for caching.

Finally, any cache presents a risk of stale data. Every cache should have an invalidation strategy to remove items from cache when their source data changes. The strategy you choose can have a major impact on your system's capacity. For example, a point-to-point notification might work well when there are ten or twelve application servers. If there are hundreds of application servers, then point-to-point unicast is not effective, and you need to look at either a message queue or some form of multicast notification. Of course, with multicast, it's a good idea to make sure that the application servers are not all going to hammer the database at the same time to reload the invalidated item.

 Remember This

Limit cache sizes

Unbounded caches consume memory that is better spent handling requests. Holding every object you've ever loaded in memory doesn't do the users any good.

Build a flush mechanism

Whether it's based on the clock, the calendar, or an event on the network, every cache needs to be flushed sooner or later. A cache flush can be expensive, though, so consider limiting how often a cache flush can be triggered, or you just might end up with attacks of self-denial.

Don't cache trivial objects

Not every domain object and HTML fragment is worth caching. Seldom-used, tiny, or inexpensive objects aren't worth caching: the cost of bookkeeping and reduced free memory outweighs the performance gain.

Compare access and change frequency

Don't cache things that are likely to change before they get used again.

10.3 Precompute Content

 As application architects and designers, we like dynamic content on the web. It's more interesting than static content, for one thing. For another, nobody needs programmers to put up static content. We even have a derogatory term for it—*brochureware*. When the requirements state that the content can change at any time, we tend to accept that and immediately jump to a database-driven, dynamically generated site. All of the common technologies drive us in that direction: JSP, ASP, Ruby on Rails, and so on.[2]

The trouble comes from that multiplier effect again. Consider a typical retail site. Almost every retail site allows shoppers to browse some kind of hierarchical structure of product categories. Whether the categories are represented as a single-rooted tree, a forest of trees, or a directed acyclic graph, they eventually deliver the user to some kind of product detail page. At least the top-level categories are shown on every page. Usually, a second level of categories is shown as well. The usual approach to generating the category menu is to query the database for the categories to show and then iterate over the categories in a page fragment, rendering HTML or JavaScript for each category. That chunk of code probably executes a million times a day. How often does the top-level categorization change? Once every three months? Small changes might happen once a week. But the code still runs a query and dynamically generates the HTML, just on the off chance that the categories have changed in the ten milliseconds since the HTML was generated last. Even if you cache the results of the database query, rendering HTML still takes a long time because of the sheer number of strings involved.

Why spend time rendering the HTML at all? If you can identify sections of the site where the content changes much less often than pages are generated, it's worth precomputing the rendered HTML fragments. This is especially valuable when you can identify the precise point in time when the content changes. Regenerate the precomputed content at that time, and then just serve that up as it is, instead of recomputing the same HTML millions of times.

News portal sites such as Slashdot and Fark precompute their main pages. Their stories change at least hourly, sometimes more often. Comment totals change every minute. Nevertheless, the main page of both of those sites is a template that pulls in a handful of large pieces of precomputed content. The sites get their "liveness" by recomputing the content every few minutes, but each version of the page still gets viewed hundreds or thousands of times before the next update.

The Profanity Master

One of the most egregious examples of excessively dynamic content I've ever seen came from the retail launch discussed in Chapter 7, *Case Study: Trampled by Your Own Customers*, on page 121. Tracing through garbage collection statistics showed that almost 10MB of garbage was being created for each page request. Now, the Java garbage collector has gotten a lot better in

---

2.   Not to mention Struts, Tiles, Tapestry, WebWork, WebObjects, SpringMVC, and so on.

the Java 2 and Java 5 virtual machines, but, really, 10MB? Something had to be seriously wrong in the code. When I found it, I couldn't decide whether to laugh, cry, or curse someone. I found the developer responsible and shouted "0x7f" at him. (I hexed him.)

Each product detail page, and each "product insert"—the little boxes on the home page and category pages—used a custom component called the Profanity Masker. This little gem was an ATG droplet, which is like a custom JSP tag. A droplet processes its contents and generates some output. Droplet input is buffered before the droplet is invoked, and the output is buffered before it gets included in the page. The Profanity Masker was being used around the product name, short description, long description, and specifications. For music, it was used once around each track name. For movies, it was used around each *actor's* name. A single product detail page could have twenty of these little buggers on it.

The Profanity Masker parsed its contents using StringTokenizer, and then compared each and every word in the content to its list of eleven dirty words. If the word was not in the list, it would append the word to the StringBuffer it was using to build the output. If the word was a match, it would replace the original, dirty word with its first letter, followed by the right number of asterisks so everyone could figure out what the original word was.

Think about that for a minute. Every single bit of textual content was being tokenized, compared word-for-word against a Vector (yes, a Vector not an ArrayList) of bad words, and then stitched back together. This was being done twenty times a page, with more than five million page views a day. That makes for somewhere around a gazillion string comparisons and 10MB of garbage for each and every page request. All that content was published nightly. Was there some chance that dirty words would spontaneously appear during the day? Why go to all that work on every single page view?

The funniest part of the story is the postscript. When we started asking whether it was OK to stop masking profanity (thus endangering young minds but protecting the site), the business sponsor in charge of content went ballistic. Product descriptions, album names, sample lyrics, and song titles are all copyrighted material. It's aggregated by a data vendor, but it ultimately comes from record companies and movie studios. By contract, you cannot just go altering the content, even if you're doing it for noble reasons. He was very upset to hear that the content was being changed when it got displayed on the site. We removed the Profanity Masker, but we never did find out why it was written in the first place.

Precomputing content does have some costs of its own. It requires storage space for each piece of computed content. There is some runtime cost to mapping an identifier to a file and reading the file. For commonly used content, this cost might motivate you to cache the content itself in memory. The cost of generating the content mainly occurs when the content changes. If the content gets used many times before it changes, then precomputing it is worthwhile.

Personalization works against precomputed content. If entire pages are personalized, then precomputed content is impossible. On the other hand, if just a few fragments or sections are personalized, then the majority of the page can be precomputed with a "punch out" for the personalized content.

Precomputing content is different from caching. Caching database results in memory is a trade-off, increasing stress in one variable (application server RAM) in order to relieve stress in another variable (either database CPU or database I/O, depending on which hurts worse in your system).

> Precompute most of a page. Use "punch outs" for personalized content.

Caching page fragments in memory is a similar trade-off, balancing application server response time against application server memory requirements. The first problem, though, is that caching page fragments in memory can ultimately hurt response time. If memory gets short or the cache size is less than the working set of fragments being served, then the application server will spend time thrashing the cache. Worse yet, it will be working with reduced memory for transient use while serving pages. Java application servers get very, very slow when you starve them for memory because you've got megabytes of cached content sitting in the old generation heap space. The second problem is that in-memory caches take time to "warm up." Whatever poor sap asks for the first page from a server with cold caches might end up waiting *minutes* to get a single page back. In-memory caching has its place, but storing rendered page fragments for large amounts of content is not the right way to employ caching.

Precomputed content does not need to be an all-or-nothing approach. Some high-traffic areas of the site can be precomputed, while less frequently visited pages can be fully dynamic. Except for Amazon, retailers decide what you will see on the home page, and everyone sees the same products on the home page. The site might greet customers by name, and it might show a saved shopping cart, so there are probably 100 or so bytes that are customer specific. The remaining 100KB (I'm being generous) are exactly the same for every single customer.

 Remember This

Precompute content that changes infrequently

Any content that you present many times before it changes could be precomputed to save time during request handling. Factor the cost of generating the content out of individual requests and into the deployment process.

10.4 Tune the Garbage Collector

In Java applications, garbage collection tuning is the quickest and easiest way to see some capacity improvements. An untuned application running at production volumes and traffic will probably spend 10% of its time collecting garbage. That should be reduced to 2% or less.

Modern garbage collectors are optimized for the typical bimodal distribution of object life spans. Most objects are ephemeral; they are created and discarded within microseconds. (Sun refers to this as *infant mortality*.) A much smaller population of objects are long-lived, often with life spans that match the program execution (singletons, service registries, server sockets, and so on). Objects are allocated in the eden space. If they survive a garbage collector pass, they get moved into a survivor space. Both the eden and survivor spaces are in the "young generation."

When the garbage collector runs, the first step it takes is to check the eden space for live objects. If no objects are live, then the entire eden space is recycled very quickly. Any live objects in that space will be moved into one of the survivor spaces. So, quickly disposing of objects is not a problem for the garbage collector. Different garbage collector phases can eventually move survivors into the tenured generation, which is examined by the garbage collector much less frequently than the young generation. (The third generation is the *permanent generation* that holds class and method definitions.)

You can get visibility into the garbage collector's behavior by passing the -verbosegc argument to the JVM at start-up time. Garbage collector reports go into the console output, so you need to ensure that standard out is directed somewhere. (For application servers, this usually requires changing a start-up script.) If you are using Java 5 or later, then you can use the jconsole tool that comes with the Java SDK. Figure 26, *JConsole Memory Tab*, on page 182 shows some of what jconsole can tell you. The Memory tab shows heap usage, broken down by generation and space, as well as the amount of time spent in garbage collection. This is a relatively idle calendar server that is clearly not suffering from excessive garbage collection.

Once you can see the garbage collection patterns, tuning the garbage collector is largely a matter of ensuring sufficient heap size and adjusting the ratios that control the relative sizes of the generations.

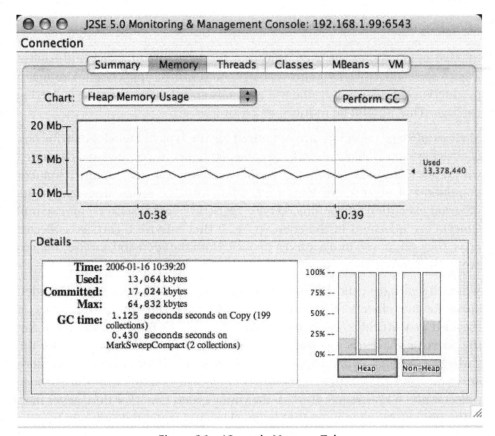

Figure 26—JConsole Memory Tab

Sun has excellent guides for garbage collection tuning available online.[3] As an added bonus, going through the exercise of tuning the garbage collector will often bring memory leaks to your attention!

Garbage collector tuning is part science, part art. Garbage collector behavior derives entirely from the application's behavior and demand patterns. Each code release changes the environment in some way. Even relatively small code releases can induce new behavior from users: promotions, ease of use changes, prominence of an expensive feature, and so on. Perfectly tuned (if there is such a thing) settings for one release can be totally wrong for the next release. As I will discuss in Chapter 17, *Transparency*, on page 231, you need a routine process to keep tuning and retuning settings.

---

3. For JDK 1.4.2, see http://java.sun.com/docs/hotspot/gc1.4.2/index.html. For Java 5, see http://java.sun.com/docs/hotspot/gc5.0/gc_tuning_5.html.

\\//   **Joe asks:**
ǯ   # What About Object Pooling?

In early versions of Java (around the 1.2 time frame), the idea that long-lived objects were good gained currency. I specifically remember being told that "creating an object is the second most expensive thing you can do in Java" (the first being creation of a new thread). The answer, supposedly, was to avoid creating objects whenever possible. Instead, you were supposed to keep objects around and reuse them.

Whether that was ever true is the subject of heated debate in the Java community. Either way, with current JVMs, object pooling is not the answer. Some systems have gone to ridiculous lengths to avoid creating new objects. They add so much complexity and bookkeeping that any possible performance gains will be wiped out.

The following table shows timing from a simple application that uses a NameFormatter to format 50,000 names. In the "pooled" configuration, the Jakarta "commons-pool" package is used to make an object pool to reuse the NameFormatter. In the "unpooled" configuration, 50,000 individual NameFormatters are created. The data clearly show that the bookkeeping overhead of the pool overwhelms the expense of constructing the objects. (All tests are against JDK 1.4.2.)

OS	CPU Speed	Overhead Pooled	Overhead Disposable
Windows XP Pro	1.86 GHz	20.30%	10.17%
Linux 2.6.14	2.66 GHz	31.46%	23.42%
Mac OS 10.4.4	1.67 GHz	24.69%	15.69%

Reserve object pooling for objects that really are expensive to create, such as network connections, database connections, and worker threads.

 ## Remember This

Tune the garbage collector in production

User access patterns make a huge difference in the optimal settings, so you can't tune the garbage collector in development or QA.

Keep it up

You will need to tune the garbage collector after each major application release. If you have an annual demand cycle, you will also need to tune it at different times during the year, as user traffic shifts between features.

Don't pool ordinary objects

The only objects worth pooling are external connections and threads. For everything else, rely on the garbage collector.

10.1 Summary

Resource pools can be a source of capacity-killing contention. Done well, however, they are a significant capacity enhancer. A connection pool eliminates up to 500 milliseconds from every transaction. Several strategies for connection management are available, each with benefits and drawbacks. These include the "per-page," "per-fragment," and hybrid models.

Caching is a double-edged sword. Done well, it will greatly increase a system's capacity to support users. As typically practiced, caches can grow too large, cached items never get flushed, and cheap objects are cached with no benefit. Limiting cache sizes is crucial. Java developers should make use of the SoftReference objects to collaborate with the garbage collector in managing cached objects.

Examine multiplier effects to find the right leverage points to make improvements. For example, dynamically rendered content a million times a day, when the content changes once a week, puts your system on the wrong side of a multiplier effect. The benefit is gained once a week, while the cost is borne a million times a day. The act of rendering that content once, whenever the underlying data changes, and storing the precomputed result provides a benefit a million times a day with the cost of managing the cache borne once a week.

Garbage collector tuning is vital to Java applications. It is not a one-time operation but rather an ongoing process. Each code release can change garbage collection patterns enough to merit retuning.

Part III

General Design Issues

CHAPTER 11

Networking

Networking in the data center goes far beyond the application-level sockets API. Data center network designs favor redundancy, security, and flexibility far more than networks to the desktop. An application requires some additional work to behave properly in this environment.

11.1 Multihomed Servers

Multihoming is the most striking difference between a machine in development or QA environments and the data center. Nearly every server in a data center will be *multihomed*. A server with more than one IP address is a multihomed server; it exists on several networks simultaneously. This architecture improves security by separating administration and monitoring onto its own highly secured network. It improves performance by segmenting high-volume traffic, such as backups, away from the production traffic. I'm sure you've experienced a network slowdown due to system backups. Backups can saturate any network, since they always run at full throttle. If you make a faster network, it just means the backups finish faster (up to a point, of course). These networks have very different security requirements, and an application that is not aware of the multiple network interfaces will easily end up accepting connections from the wrong networks. For example, it could accept administrative connections from the production network or offer production functionality over the backup network.

As shown in Figure 27, *Multiple Network Interfaces*, on page 188, this single server has four different network interfaces. In Linux, these would be eth0 through eth3. For Solaris, they could be ce0 through ce3 or qfe0 through qfe3, depending on the network card and driver version. Windows would give the interfaces incredibly long and unwieldy names by default.

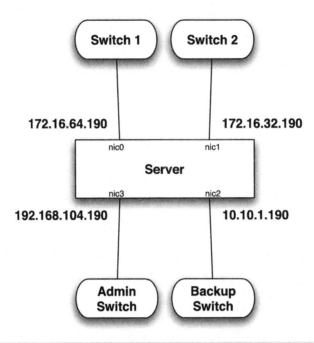

Figure 27—Multiple Network Interfaces

Of the four interfaces, two of them are dedicated to "production" traffic. These handle the application's functionality. If the server is a web server, then these handle the incoming requests and send the replies back. In this example, both interfaces are for production traffic. Because these are running to different switches, the server appears to be configured for high availability. These two interfaces might be load balanced, or they might be set up as a failover pair. As shown, two different IP addresses will get packets to this server. That means there are probably DNS entries for both addresses. In other words, this machine has more than one name! It has its own internal hostname—the string returned by the hostname command—but from the outside, more than one name reaches this host.

Another common configuration for multiple production interfaces is *bonding*, or *teaming*. In this configuration, both interfaces share a common IP address. The operating system ensures that an individual packet goes out over only one interface. Bonded interfaces can be configured to automatically balance outbound traffic or to prefer one link or the other. Bonding interfaces that connect to different switches requires some additional configuration on the switches, or else routing loops can result. You'll be very famous if you cause a routing loop in the data center, but not in a good way.

The two additional "back-end" interfaces are dedicated to special-purpose traffic. Because backups transfer huge volumes of data in bursts, they can clog up a production network. Therefore, good network design for the data center partitions the backup traffic onto its own network segment. These are sometimes handled by separate switches and sometimes just by separate VLANs on the production switches. With backup traffic partitioned off from the production network, application users do not necessarily suffer when the backups run. (They might, if the server doesn't have enough I/O bandwidth to process backups and application traffic at the same time. Nevertheless, users of *other* applications don't suffer when this server is being backed up.)

Finally, many data centers have a specific network for administrative access. This is an important security protection, because services such as SSH can be bound only to the administrative interface and are therefore not accessible from the production network. This can help if a firewall gets breached by an attacker or if the server handles an internal application and does not sit behind a firewall.

This multitude of interfaces affects the application software. By default, an application that listens on a socket will listen for connection attempts *on any interface.* For example, the Java ServerSocket class has four constructors as of Java 5. Three of these constructors bind to every interface on the server. Only the long form of the constructor can take a specific local address to define to which interface it should bind.

```
InetAddress addr = InetAddress.getByName("alpha.example.com");
ServerSocket socket = new ServerSocket(80, 50, addr);

Socket local = socket.accept();
...
```

Without the address, ServerSocket will bind to all interfaces, which would allow connections over the backup or administration networks to the production server. Or, conversely, it could allow connections over the production network to the administrative interface!

To determine which interfaces to bind to, the application must be told its own name or IP addresses. This is a big difference with multihomed servers. In development, the server can always call InetAddress.getLocalHost(), but on a multihomed machine, this simply returns the IP address associated with the server's internal hostname. This could be any of the interfaces, depending on local naming conventions. Therefore, server applications that need to listen on sockets must add configurable properties to define to which interfaces the server should bind.

11.2 Routing

Because servers in production usually have multiple network interfaces, questions will sometimes arise about which interfaces particular kinds of traffic should traverse. For example, it is relatively common to see an application server with a front-end network interface connected to one VLAN for communication to the web servers and with a back-end network interface connected to a different VLAN for communication to the database servers. In this case, the server must be told which interface to use in order to reach a particular destination IP address.

In the case of nearby servers, the routes are probably easy; they will just be based on the subnet addresses. In the example of the application server, the back-end interface probably shares a subnet with the database server, while the front-end interface probably shares a subnet with the web servers. Routing gets a bit more complicated when distant services—perhaps third-party services—are involved.

Spam cannon: a vendor doing high-volume email transmission, usually based on an XML feed of names and addresses. They fill in pretty, predefined HTML templates with personal data collected by the subscriber. They have high-bandwidth connections and, not often enough, algorithms to avoid crushing SMTP servers at small ISPs. Their hard work usually goes straight into "spam" folders.

Consider the case of a third-party *spam cannon* service. Data sent by application servers to the spam cannon should probably not go straight over the public Internet. Instead, it is probably routed over the back-end interface of the application servers through a VPN to the service.

Getting these routing issues right requires paying attention to each and every integration point. Getting them wrong risks reduced availability or, worse, exposure of customer data. For each connection to a remote system, I recommend keeping a record in a spreadsheet or a Microsoft Access database of the destination name, address, and desired route. Someday, somebody is going to need that information to write firewall rules anyway.

11.3 Virtual IP Addresses

Believe it or not, not every application is written to run across a cluster. For whatever reason, these applications can be active on only one server at a time. How can you get high availability out of an application, without the redundancy of running it on multiple servers?

Cluster servers are the answer. A cluster server is an application that acts like a controller for other applications. A cluster server such as Veritas Cluster Server, HP ServiceGuard, or Microsoft Cluster Server[1] runs on multiple

---

1. Now renamed to Microsoft Windows Server 2003 Clustering Services. Say that three times fast.

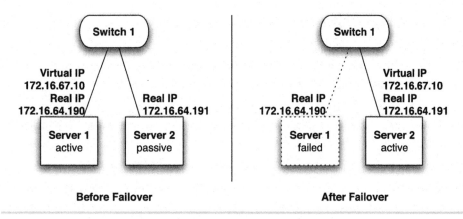

Figure 28—Virtual IP Address Migration

servers, collaborating across the servers to ensure that a specific "package" runs exactly once somewhere in the cluster. By configuring packages for applications, filesystems, and IP addresses, it is possible to have the cluster server orchestrate a clean shutdown on one server and startup on another server. Most of the time, the application is unaware it has been clustered.

Suppose the server hosting a critical—but not natively clustered—application goes down. The cluster server on its failover node will notice the lack of a regular heartbeat from the failed server. This cluster server then decides that the original server has failed.

It starts up the application on the secondary server, including mounting any required filesystems. It will also take over the virtual IP address assigned to the clustered network interface.

A *virtual IP address* is just an IP address that can be moved from one NIC to another as needed. At any given time, exactly one server claims the IP address. When the address needs to be moved, the cluster server and the operating systems collaborate to do some funny stuff in the lower layers of the TCP/IP stack. They associate the IP address with a new MAC address (hardware address) and advertise the new route (ARP). Figure 28, *Virtual IP Address Migration*, on page 191 depicts a virtual IP address before and after the active node fails.

Virtual IP addresses are often used for active/passive database clusters. Clients are instructed to connect only to the DNS name for the virtual IP address, not to the hostnames of either node in the cluster. That way, no matter which node currently holds the IP address, the client can connect to the same name.

Two Flavors of Virtual IP

Unfortunately, the term *virtual IP* is overloaded. Generally speaking, it means an IP address that is not strictly tied to an Ethernet MAC address. Cluster servers use it to migrate ownership of the address between the members of the cluster. Load balancers use virtual IPs to multiplex many services (each with its own IP address) onto a smaller number of physical interfaces. There is some overlap here, since load balancers typically come in pairs, so the virtual IP—as in "service address"—can also be a virtual IP as in "migrating address."

Of course, this approach cannot migrate the in-memory state of the application. As a result, any nonpersistent state about interactions will be lost. For databases, this includes uncommitted transactions. Some database drivers —such as a Oracle's JDBC and ODBC drivers—will automatically reexecute queries that are aborted because of a failover. Updates, inserts, or stored procedure calls cannot be automatically repeated. Therefore, any application calling a database through a virtual IP should be prepared to get a SQLException when such a failover occurs.

In general, if your application calls any other service through a virtual IP, it must be prepared for the possibility that the next TCP packet isn't going to the same interface as the last packet. This can cause IOExceptions in strange places. The application logic must be prepared to handle that error—and handle it differently than just a "destination unreachable" error. If at all possible, the application should retry its request against the new node (but see *Circuit Breaker*, on page 93 for some important safety limits on retries).

CHAPTER 12

Security

Full treatment of application security is way beyond the scope of this book. The topics covered in this chapter earned their place by sitting in the intersection of software architecture, operations, and security.

12.1 The Principle of Least Privilege

The principle of "least privilege" mandates that a process should have the lowest level of privilege needed to accomplish its task. For application software, this never includes running as root (UNIX/Linux) or Administrator (Windows). Anything these applications need to do, they can do as nonadministrative users.

I've seen Windows servers left logged in as Administrator for weeks at a time —with remote desktop access—because that's what some piece of software required. (This particular package also was not able to run as an NT service, so it was essentially just a Windows desktop application left running for a long time. That is *not* what I call data center ready!)

Software that requires execution as root is automatically a target for crackers. Any vulnerability in root-level software automatically becomes a critical issue. Once a cracker has gained root access, the only way to be sure the server is safe is to reformat and reinstall. Worse yet, for horizontally scalable applications, you might have to reinstall the entire cluster.

To further contain vulnerabilities, each major application should have its own user. The "apache" user should not have any access to the "websphere" user, for example.

Opening a socket on a port numbered less than 1024 would be the only thing for which a UNIX application might require root privilege. Web servers often want to open port 80 by default. Any web server sitting behind a load balancer (see Section 13.3, *Load Balancing*, on page 200) can use any port, including ones numbered 1024 or greater. Only the load balancer needs to listen to port 80.

A web server that is not behind a load balancer (I assume there's a good reason, though I can't think of one right now) will need to run as root in order to listen on port 80. Peel back the lid on Apache, however, and you'll find that it uses "privilege separation" to deliberately give up root access after it opens the socket. It uses low-level C functions to downgrade its own status to the configured user (usually "apache"). This is a one-way trip; the process cannot regain root privileges once it gives them up.

12.2 Configured Passwords

Passwords are the Achilles heel of application security. There's obviously no way that somebody can interactively key in passwords every time an application server starts up. Therefore, database passwords and credentials needed to authenticate to other systems must be configured in persistent files somewhere.

As soon as a password is in a text file, it is vulnerable. Any password that grants access to a database with customer information is worth thousands of dollars to an attacker and could cost the company thousands in bad publicity or extortion. These passwords must be protected with the highest level of security achievable.

At the absolute minimum, passwords to production databases should be kept separate from any other configuration files. They should especially be kept out of the installation directory for the software. (I've seen operations zip up the entire installation folder and ship it back to development for analysis. This happens most often when questions arise about the production configuration and whether the software was installed and configured correctly.) Files containing passwords should be made readable only to the owner, which should be the application user. If the application is written in a language that can execute privilege separation, then it is reasonable to have the application read the password files before downgrading its privileges. In that case, the password files can be owned by root. Beware! If the application keeps these files in memory, then memory dumps will also contain the passwords. For UNIX systems, core files are just memory dumps of the application. If an attacker can provoke a core dump and has access to a server's filesystem, then he can get the passwords. It's best to disable core dumps on production applications. For Windows systems, the "blue screen of death" indicates a kernel error, with an accompanying memory dump. This dump file can be analyzed with Microsoft kernel debugging tools, and depending on the configuration of the server, it can contain a copy of the entire physical memory of the machine—passwords and all.[1]

Password vaulting keeps passwords in encrypted files, which reduces the security problem to that of securing the single encryption key rather than securing multiple text files. This can assist in securing the passwords, but is not, by itself, a complete solution. Because it is easy to inadvertently change or overwrite file permissions, intrusion detection software such as Tripwire[2] or Open Source Tripwire[3] should be employed to monitor permissions on those vital files.

---

1. In fact, there's a registry edit to enable a key combination (no, I'm not going to give it here) that will *force* a memory dump and system halt. If you ever see a "blue screen of death" with the text "the end-user manually generated the crashdump," then you are under attack. In fact, it's best to make sure that "feature" is not enabled on any production server.
2. See http://www.tripwire.com/.
3. See http://www.sourceforge.net/projects/tripwire.

CHAPTER 13

Availability

Divorcing a "want" from its cost always leads to unrealistic desires. Ask a group of children how much ice cream they want, and the answer is usually, "All of it." The young ones have no concept of the various costs of eating a gallon of ice cream: there's the direct cost of paying for the ice cream and the indirect costs of damaged health, weight gain, and that queasy, flip-floppy feeling in your tummy.

This section discusses the difficult feat of balancing the tension between the dual forces of desire for greater availability and desire to minimize cost. These forces are in direct opposition; guaranteed availability necessarily increases costs.

13.1 Gathering Availability Requirements

Asking the sponsors of your system, "How highly available should this be?" probably results in one of two answers. The less experienced sponsors will simply reply, "100%." The more knowledgeable will say, "five nines" because it sounds cool and technical. But are five nines *really* required?

The proper way to frame the availability decision is in straightforward financial terms: actual cost vs. avoided losses. For example, "98% availability" translates to 864 minutes of downtime each month. That downtime has a direct cost because of lost revenue. Suppose the site brings in $1,500 per hour during the peak of the day—the worst possible time to be down. Then the worst-case loss with 98% availability is about $21,600. Now compare the minutes of downtime avoided by building a more reliable system. Improving the availability to 99.99% reduces the expected cost of downtime to just $108 per month —gaining $21,492 per month over the 98% availability case.

So, should the system be built to achieve 99.99% availability? It's like that ice cream question. Without considering the cost, of course the desire will be unlimited. Each "9" of availability increases the implementation cost by about a factor of ten and the operational cost per year by about a factor of two. In this example, the additional lifecycle cost—implementation cost plus operational cost for the five-year life span of the system—amounted to $98,700. Spending $98,700 to save $1,289,520 seems like a sound financial choice.

Availability	98%	99.99%
Downtime Min/Month	864	4
Downtime $/Month	$21,600	$108
Added Cost	$0	$98,700
Net Savings	$0	$1,289,520

13.2 Documenting Availability Requirements

Want to guarantee nasty conflicts? Take a word with multiple, fuzzy definitions, force people to strike an agreement about it, attach large amounts of money to it, and then watch them fight about it a year or two later.

I'm describing, of course, the inevitable effect of poorly defined service-level agreements about availability. SLA definitions are like the details in your medical insurance plan. Nobody reads them too closely until something awful happens. If you're having a conversation about SLA definitions a year after the system launched, odds are it's a heated discussion following an incident. Once you're in that situation, it's too late.

You can prevent (or at least diminish) the blamestorming by working out a precise service-level agreement with the system's sponsors in the beginning. It is not enough to write down, "The system shall be available 99.9% of the time" on a piece of paper. Vagueness lurks behind every word of that sentence.

What is "the system?" Unless it is trivial, "the system" probably includes calls to other systems inside and outside the enterprise. Are you really going to take accountability for all of those? I wouldn't! Also, if the system employs stability patterns like Circuit Breaker, then at any given time, the system as a whole might be up and running—responding to requests or generating web pages—but specific features might not be working. Rather than stating that "the system" will be available, it is better to define the SLAs in terms of specific features or functions of the system. A hotel chain, for example, might be interested in several key functions of its website: property locator, online reservations, subscription to the loyalty club, event bookings, and so on. Each of these features has different levels of importance to the business. Event bookings and online reservations both generate revenue, so they are likely to have the highest SLAs attached to them. Beware of the SLA Inversion antipattern (see *SLA Inversion*, on page 81); you cannot offer a better SLA than the *worst* of the external dependencies involved in a feature. For example, loyalty club programs are often handled by a third party, so this SLA can only be a pass-through, at best, of the vendor's own SLA.

Once you've isolated each feature or business process, you can define the required level of availability. Not to sound too much like a lawyer, but "availability" itself needs to be defined. How is the feature being checked? Is it a human clicking a mouse around? (I hope not.) Maybe it's the army of users, and problems are reported via a help desk. (I really hope not!) It's best to have some automated system checking the availability of a feature by executing synthetic transactions against it. The SLA should define what device or devices will be monitoring the availability of the feature. Furthermore, it should define how that monitoring device will report problems.

Synthetic transaction: work submitted to a system that emulates a real user. You must have some way to indicate this is for monitoring— such as a designated user ID —to avoid pol- luting the production data.

If a feature is functioning but takes twenty-seven-and-a-half minutes to respond, most users would not consider it to be "available." So, there's a time component involved. What if the transaction responds in fifty milliseconds but returns errors to everyone? That's also not really available, so there must be some definition about what a good response looks like. How about a feature that's wobbling up and down but acts like a car at the mechanic and seems OK whenever the monitoring device checks it? A good definition should nail down each of these variables:

- How often will the monitoring device execute its synthetic transaction?
- What is the maximum acceptable response time for each step of the transaction?
- What response codes or text patterns indicate success?
- What response codes or text patterns indicate failure?
- How frequently should the synthetic transaction be executed?
- From how many locations?
- Where will the data be recorded?
- What formula will be used to compute the percentage availability? Based on time or number of samples?

When the fur flies, paper makes a thin shield, but having this definition might help focus attention on the data rather than making it a personal issue.

13.3 Load Balancing

Horizontally scalable systems achieve both availability and scalability through multiplicity. Adding more machines to increase capacity simultaneous improves resiliency to impulses. The smaller servers used in horizontally scalable architectures also cost far less and allow you to add capacity in small increments. What's not to like?

Building systems for horizontal scaling automatically implies some form of load balancing. Load balancing is all about distributing requests across a pool or farm of servers to serve all requests correctly in the shortest feasible time. Throughout the remainder of this book, I will commonly refer to designs and situations involving one of these forms of load balancing.

DNS Round-Robin

DNS *round-robin* load balancing is the oldest of the techniques I'll discuss here—dating back to the early days of the web. It operates at the application layer (layer 7) of the OSI stack, but instead of operating during an actual request, it operates during address resolution.

This technique simply associates several IP addresses with the service name. This is most commonly used with small-to-medium business websites, so instead of finding a single IP address for "bobscleaners.example.com," a client would get one of several addresses. Each IP address points to a single server. The client therefore connects to one out of a pool of servers, as shown in Figure 29, *DNS Round-Robin Load Balancing*, on page 201.

Although this serves the basic purpose of distributing work across a group of machines, it does poorly on other essential criteria. For one thing, all the servers in the pool must be "routable." That is, though they can sit behind a firewall, their front-end IP addresses are visible and reachable from clients. These days, that just invites attacks.

In addition to the security concerns, the DNS round-robin approach suffers from putting too much control in the client's hands. Since the client connects directly to one of the servers, there is no opportunity to redirect that traffic if one particular server is down. The DNS server has no information about the health of the web servers, so it can keep vending out IP addresses for web servers that are toast. Furthermore, doling out IP addresses in round-robin style does not guarantee that the *load* is distributed evenly, just the initial connections. Some clients consume more resources than others, leading to unbalanced workloads. Again, when one of the servers gets busy, the DNS

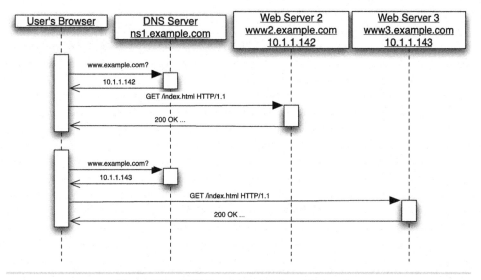

Figure 29—DNS Round-Robin Load Balancing

server has no way to know, so it just keeps sending every eleventh connection (or whatever) to the staggering server.

DNS round-robin load balancing is inappropriate whenever the calling system is another long-running enterprise system. Anything built on Java will cache the first IP address received from DNS, guaranteeing that every future connection targets the same host and completely defeating load balancing.

Some Apache configurations also perform round-robin style URL rewriting. This is visible to the user, when "www.example.com" suddenly becomes "www7.example.com." Unfortunately, this approach performs even worse than DNS round-robin, because of a user's tendency to bookmark individual servers instead of the "front door" address.

Reverse Proxy

A reverse proxy server addresses limitation in the DNS round-robin approach by acting as an interceptor for every request. In this case, DNS resolves the service name to exactly one IP address. The device listening to that IP address will be a typical host, running a proxy server configured in "reverse proxy server" mode, as shown in Figure 30, *Reverse Proxy Server*, on page 202.

A normal proxy multiplexes many outgoing calls into a single source IP address. A reverse proxy server does the opposite: it demultiplexes calls coming in to a single IP address and fans them out to multiple addresses. In

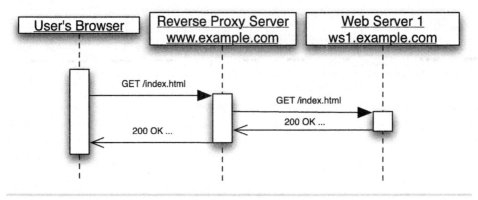

Figure 30—Reverse Proxy Server

the case of web servers, Squid, the popular open source proxy server, makes a great reverse proxy server.[1] Apache's mod_proxy also allows a special-purpose server to act as a reverse proxy for a farm or cluster of other Apache servers.

Like the DNS round-robin trick, reverse proxy servers do their magic at the application layer. As such, they are not transparent, but adapting to them is not onerous. Application servers and web servers must be configured to generate URLs for hostnames not their own. Logging the source address of the request (as is done by Apache's "Common" log format) is useless, because it will represent only the proxy server.[2]

In addition to load balancing, you can configure reverse proxy servers to reduce the load on the web servers by caching static content. This provides some benefits in reducing the traffic on the internal network. (By sending static content from the reverse proxy server, it traverses only one or two links on its way out of the network. Coming from the web server, it would probably cross two or three.) If the web servers are the capacity constraint in the system (see Section 8.2, *Constraints*, on page 136), then offloading this traffic will improve the system's overall capacity. Of course, if the proxy server itself is the constraint, then this will not help or hurt.

---

1.   See http://www.squid-cache.org/ for configuration instructions.
2.   It is possible, however, to use a custom log format to log the X-Forwarded-For header that Akamai and other well-behaved proxies add to the request. Note that ill-behaved or malicious proxies are unlikely to conform to that part of the standard. As a result, that header will be least reliable when you most need to trace the origin of some traffic, such as an attack. In such cases, you have to rely on correlating your log files with the proxy's log files.

The biggest reverse proxy server "cluster" in the world is Akamai. Akamai's basic service functions exactly like Squid, configured as a caching proxy. Akamai has certain advantages over Squid, including a large number of servers located near the end users, but is otherwise logically equivalent.[3]

Because the reverse proxy server is involved in every request, it can get burdened very quickly. Once you start having to add a layer of load balancing *in front of* your reverse proxy servers, it's time to look at other options. Also, because the proxy server is in the middle of every request, it should be able to keep track of which origin servers are healthy and responsive. Unfortunately, the most commonly used reverse proxy servers—Squid and Apache—do not. They will happily direct an incoming request to a dead server, wait for a timeout, and then return an error to the caller.

Hardware Load Balancer

Hardware load balancers are specialized network devices that serve a similar role to the reverse proxy server. These devices, such as Cisco's 11500 Series Content Services Switch or F5's BigIP products, provide the same kind of interception and redirection capabilities as the reverse proxy software. Because the operate closer to the network, hardware load balancers frequently provide better administration and redundancy features. For example, the CSS can periodically check on the health of the servers in its pool, as shown in Figure 31, *Hardware Load Balancer*, on page 204. The load balancer removes dead servers from its service pool, directing connections to the healthy ones.

Hardware load balancers are application-aware and can provide switching at layers 4 through 7 of the OSI stack. In practice, this means they can load balance any connection-oriented protocol, not just HTTP or FTP. I have seen these successfully employed to load balance a group of search servers that didn't have their own load managers. They can also hand off traffic from one entire site to another, which is particularly useful for diverting traffic to a failover site for disaster recovery.

SSL poses challenges for any of these solutions. Hardware load balancer are often used as SSL "accelerators." Frankly, in my opinion, that puts the load balancer on the wrong end of both Moore's law—that web servers can be replaced with faster machines every eighteen months—and scalability; after all, there are going to be more web servers than hardware load balancers. Furthermore, the web servers are probably not doing much, whereas the load

SSL: Secure Sockets Layer. Connections encrypted for confidentiality and integrity. Relatively CPU intensive.

---

3.   Please note, I'm talking only about Akamai's basic service, currently called Web Application Accelerator. Its *other* services go far beyond Squid!

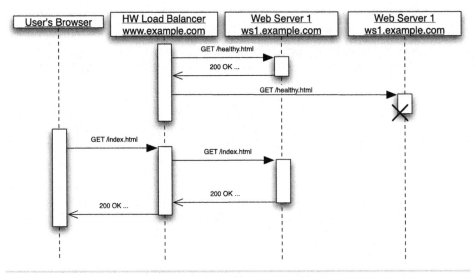

Figure 31—Hardware Load Balancer

balancer is involved in every single request. Using the load balancer to handle SSL decryption does make managing SSL certificates easier, since there is just a pair of devices to update, rather than a dozen or so web servers. In fact, if the load balancers handle multiple VIPs for different domains, then all of your SSL certificates could be on the same pair of machines (assuming they're big enough to handle the load!).

Hardware load balancers can provide a number of application-level services, including checking for HTTP error codes and redirecting to different error pages based on the web servers' reply. For HTTPS, you have two choices: you can use the load balancer for SSL and keep the application-level services, or you can terminate SSL connections at the web servers, essentially using the load balancer as a smart switch and giving up the application-level services. If it tried to pass SSL connections directly to web servers while also examining the content, then the load balancer would essentially be performing a man-in-the-middle attack against the encrypted channel between the browser and server.

The big drawback to these machines is—of course—their price. Expect to pay in the five digits for a low-end configuration. High-end configurations, such as those needed for a first-tier retailer, easily run into the six digits.

Load Balancing with Apache 2.2

As of version 2.2, Apache includes the new mod_proxy_balancer module. This is a very intelligent load-balancing module with more capability. It can "balance" a load proportionally to the capacity of the web servers behind it—although you have to configure the proportions yourself.

Apache operates at layer 7 of the venerable OSI model;[a] it's an application. Dedicated hardware will tend to be faster and reach higher volumes. For many sites, however, avoiding the $50,000 expense of a pair of dedicated hardware load balancers will matter more than the reduced ceiling. Besides, no design is static, so if the site starts to bump up against a constraint in the open source load balancers, they can always be replaced with the higher-capacity hardware solution.

---

a.   See http://en.wikipedia.org/wiki/OSI_model.

13.4 Clustering

Load balancing does not require collaboration between the separate servers. When the servers are aware of each other and actively participate in distributing load, then they form a cluster. Clusters can be used for load balancing, in the case of *active/active* clusters. They can also be used for redundancy in the case of failure. These are called *active/passive* clusters, meaning that one server handles all the load until it fails and then the passive one takes over and becomes active.

Fully load-balanced farms scale close to linearly. Load-balanced clusters do not. Clusters incur some communication overhead in heartbeats and state synchronization. As a result of this overhead, the capacity of a cluster scales less than linearly and might flatten out severely as the number of servers increases. This imposes a practical size limit on clusters, though the limit varies depending on the servers being clustered.

> Heartbeat: packets sent between clustered servers, usually on a separate network, indicating "I'm still alive."

Some applications build in their own clustering. WebSphere, WebLogic, Oracle, and Microsoft SQL Server all have their own clustering technology built in. With these, the application software coordinates its own availability and failover. Such applications inevitably have certain "master control" nodes responsible for directing work to different nodes in the cluster. These control nodes can be a weak point in the architecture—for example, if there is only one—and will usually be the first nodes to hit capacity limitations.

For applications that do not have their own native clustering, it is possible to run them under the control of a cluster server, such as Veritas Cluster Server or Microsoft Windows Server Clustering Services (whew). The cluster server acts like an exoskeleton, running the clustered application as a child process. The cluster servers pass heartbeats between themselves and often use a "quorum volume" on a network drive to synchronize their activities. If the cluster servers detect that a node has failed, they run a predetermined sequence of actions to bring the clusters applications back up on a surviving node. These actions include some variation of taking over one or more filesystems, starting an application from scratch or activating an application from memory image, and taking over a virtual IP address.

I am ambivalent about cluster servers. At the same time, they are marvelous and kludgy. They can add redundancy and failover to applications that weren't designed for it. Configuring the cluster server itself is finicky, though, and applications usually have a few small glitches when failing over. The biggest drawback is probably that these run in active/passive mode. So, redundancy is achieved, but scalability is not. I consider cluster servers a Band-Aid for applications that don't do it themselves.

CHAPTER 14

Administration

If your system is easy to administer, it will have good uptime. What's more, you'll find it easy to get help and resources from operations. On the other hand, if your system is difficult or annoying to administer, it will be neglected, deprecated, and probably implemented incorrectly. It might even get sabotaged.

Administrators have a difficult, thankless job. They're almost never consulted or involved during the design and architecture of a system. Instead, they get some partially baked software thrown over the wall at them, which they must then somehow fit into their routine of operations.

There's another, more fundamental conflict, too. Developers and users both view change as positive. Each new release means new features—with corresponding increases in revenue—bugs corrected and design improvements. Releases add value. For administrators, it's exactly the opposite. They have to do more work to deploy the new release. Furthermore, after each release, the system will behave differently than it did before. Old log messages or commands disappear, replaced by new ones. Old failure modes might be fixed, but there might be new ones, too, that nobody knows how to detect. When every lesson has to be learned the hard way, you become very conservative. Both views are simultaneously correct!

Administrators can be powerful allies or enemies. (After all, they probably talk to the IT managers much more often than you do.) The good news is that it doesn't require bribes or loyalty oaths to win their allegiance. Just understand their motivations, and commit to making their work easier. When their work is easier, they will do a better job—both because they can and because they will want to do so.

Here are some ways you can make your administrators happy by making your software easier to administer.

14.1 "Does QA Match Production?"

File this question under, "I wish I had a nickel." Anytime a deployment fails or some bug surfaces in production, people will naturally ask why the issue wasn't discovered during testing. It is an important question to ask and answer. Nine times out of ten, the immediate corollary question will be, "Are there any differences in configuration between QA and production?"

This question is what I call a "gimme." It is easy to ask, very expensive to answer, and guaranteed to find *something* different such as hostnames and IP addresses, if nothing else. You might be thinking, "Why should that be expensive to answer? Isn't that what configuration management systems are all about?" Yes and no. Configuration management systems can tell you exactly when a change was made, who made it, and sometimes why. Some of the good ones have operational modules that can interrogate systems and identify discrepancies. The expensive part is figuring out which discrepancies are known, expected, and harmless and which are unexpected and risky. For instance, it is common for QA to run on scaled-down hardware. Some vendors, typically integrated hardware/software vendors such as HP, deliver firmware patches, device driver patches, operating system functionality upgrades, and security patches through the same patch bundle mechanism. In these cases, different hardware models might require entirely different patch sets.

At another level, you can also say that QA *must* differ from production. After all, if it were identical down to the last hostname and port number, then it wouldn't be QA...it would be production!

In my experience, the most common causes of failure are not configurations anyway. I've spent at least of hours scrubbing configuration files, reconciling expected differences, and highlighting unexpected differences. Once in a while that will turn up something significant, but configuration discrepancies are usually not the culprit.

Most of the time, the real culprit is a mismatch in topology between QA and production. What do I mean by topology? *Topology* is the connectivity and number of the servers and applications. If you consider each server and application instance to be a node and each connection or dependency to be an arc, you can define a graph that represents the system topology. UML deployment diagrams are a useful, but underused, way to depict this.

Obviously, the main barrier to making QA's topology match production is cost. Here are some ways to make the production topology match QA without busting the budget.

Keep Them Separated

Keep them separated. Often, applications will share hosts in QA that run separately in production. This can lead to hidden dependencies: two applications might expect a directory to have synchronized content. They would just work in QA, since it's the same directory. In production, however, there would be no mechanism to keep them in sync. (Last-minute cron jobs running rsync don't count!) Assuming that you cannot simply buy the same number of servers for QA that you will have in production, what can you do to avoid this kind of hidden dependency?

In cases like this, I recommend VMware. VMware allows you to create multiple virtual hosts on a single physical machine. Each virtual machine looks and acts like its own independent server, complete with its own operating system installation, IP address, and hostname. If two applications will run on separate hosts in production but must share the same hardware in QA, you can run them in separate VMware instances on the shared machine. (This also has the nice benefit of allowing you to keep snapshots of particular versions of the applications, which can be a huge help when you are testing deployment processes!)

Zero, One, Many

There's an old saying that the only sensible numbers in computer science are 0, 1, and many. There is a fundamental difference between one-to-one and one-to-many. Sometimes, you will find a single instance in QA where production will run multiple instances in a cluster or farm. This can make the difference between a point-to-point cache invalidation strategy and a multicast or broadcast strategy, for example. This is another case where server virtualization such as VMware will allow you to match the production multiplicity in QA. If you are going to run a dozen instances in production, you probably don't need to run a full dozen in QA (though see my later remarks about proportionality). You should definitely run more than one, however.

Just Buy the Gear

I've seen hours of downtime result from the presence of firewalls or load balancers in production that did not exist in QA. The cost of this downtime exceeds the cost of the network gear. QA probably doesn't need the top-of-the-line model, but it should have a product from the same vendor and product line. After all, where are you testing your firewall configuration changes?

> ## You Play the Way You Practice
>
> In sports, a team will play the real game the same way it practices. Likewise, if the development team works with firewalls in the architecture from day one, the team will design accordingly. There's almost nothing as painful as sitting down with a system that's 95% complete and trying to identify all the firewall rules needed to let it function in production. If the development team has been working with the firewalls all along, however, they will already have the rules documented.
>
> Keeping track of the firewall rules goes right along with keeping track of integration points. (See *Integration Points*, on page 33.) Why would there be a hole in the firewall if not to call some other system? That's an integration point. An added benefit: these are also the configuration parameters most likely to need changes for production.

14.2 Configuration Files

Ruby on Rails might favor convention over configuration, but every piece of enterprise-class software I've seen has scads of configuration files containing hostnames, port numbers, filesystem locations, ID numbers, magic keys, usernames, passwords, and lottery numbers. (I made that last one up.) Get any of these properties wrong, and the system is broken. Even if the system seems to work, it could be broken without anyone knowing it!

Configuration files are often obscurely named, buried deep in the directory structure of the code base, or just plain inscrutable. When a property is named hostname, is that "my hostname," "the name of the authorized caller," or "the host I call during the autumnal solstice?" Property files suffer from hidden linkages and high complexity—two of the biggest factors leading to operator error. These files contain the most sensitive information in the entire enterprise, short of the CEO's actual compensation—production database passwords. Therefore, they are highly secret and accidental errors in other parts of the configuration aren't likely to be discovered by the developers who know and care about the difference between "wsdlServer" and "uddlServer."

One of the most common errors I see in designing a configuration scheme is mixing production configuration with basic plumbing. For instance, using the Spring framework to wire beans is wonderful, but Spring wants me to put *all* of my configuration in a single file.[1] That includes not only the properties that should change between development and production but also vital details such as object instantiation and relationship. As a result, administrators have to edit, by hand, 5,000-line XML files to update a single database

---

1. There are ways to modularize these files, but I think the cure is as bad as the disease.

password, and 4,999 of those lines are just land mines, waiting for an errant edit. All that painful-sounding "dependency injection" turns out to be pretty important for the application to work. Mess it up by accidentally editing something other than the password, and the application breaks in obtuse ways. The opportunities for collateral damage are endless.

It should never be possible for an administrator to break object associations inside the application. That's just wearing your guts on the outside. Whenever possible, keep production configuration properties separate from the basic wiring and plumbing of the application. They should be in separate files so the administrators do not accidentally edit internals.

Equally importantly, the production configuration files should not be anywhere underneath the installation directory of the software itself. The installation directory is likely to be overwritten on the next upgrade. Would you really want to count on the administrators remembering *every* change they made to configurations over the past six months and reapplying them manually after installing the update? Not to mention, admins commonly copy entire install trees from one server to another to skip the time-consuming installation process. (For example, the first step of installation BEA WebLogic 9 is uncompressing the entire 500MB file. This step alone takes ten minutes on a 2GHz x86 pizza box.) Backups and restores are issues, too. A restore from tape can easily overwrite the latest production configuration with something much older.

Because the same application probably runs on several machines, it is likely that some subset of the configuration properties should be the same on each machine and some subset should differ. Keep these properties in separate places so nobody ever has to ask, "Are those supposed to be different?" Also, I've found it helpful to have some periodic verification that the machines in a horizontally scaled layer—which should remain synchronized—actually are synchronized. Even with strong change management procedures, the rule should be, "Trust, but verify."

Finally, configuration properties are part of the system's user interface. They are the interface the system provides to one of its most overlooked constituency: the people who keep it running every day. As such, property names should be clear enough to help the user (the administrator) do her job without making "unforced errors."

One helpful convention is to name the properties according to their function, not their nature. Don't call it hostname just because it *is* a hostname. That's like naming a variable integer because it's an integer or string because it's a

> \|/   **Joe asks:**
> ~J   ## Why Don't They Keep Config Files in Version Control?
>
> Long ago, programmers coded themselves a solution to the problem of lost files and missing revisions: version control. If configuration files are such a big issue for administrators, why don't they just use version control to manage them?
>
> Some do. In some more advanced shops, administrators use tools such as Subversion[a] and cfengine[b] to manage and deploy configurations. An increasing number of IT shops use system management suites such as HP OpenView, BladeLogic, and Opsware to control configurations.
>
> In many cases, though, administrators in IT operations haven't had the time to implement and roll out version control, or they are not aware of the concept. Some are aware of version control but have never thought of applying it to system configuration files. (I didn't say it would be a good reason.)
>
> In any case, I definitely recommend using version control for configuration files, with a few constraints:
>
> - Use a secure repository. These files have database passwords in them!
>
> - Link version control with a larger change control process. You should be able to see *why* a configuration change was made, not just that one happened.
>
> - Automate the deployment of authorized changes, directly from the repository.
>
> - Make an automated audit process. Files sometimes get changed during incident management to restore service in a crisis. They sometimes don't get updated in version control afterward. You need to be able to find the deltas without automatically overwriting them.
>
> As an alternative, you could buy and deploy the twenty-seven products from BMC that do all of that for you.
>
> ---
> a.   See http://subversion.tigris.org.
> b.   See http://www.cfengine.org.

string. It might be true, but it isn't helpful. Instead, name the property authenticationServer. If an administrator sees that, she will go looking for an LDAP or Active Directory host.

The most popular Java application servers are a mixed bag when it comes to managing configuration. WebLogic, WebSphere, and JBoss each provide spiffy HTML GUIs for editing configurations.

WebSphere and WebLogic do a credible job of identifying the properties that belong to your application rather than to the system. JBoss encourages somewhat more mixing. All of these keep configurations thoroughly mixed within the application server installation directory. WebSphere at least has a notion of a "configuration repository," which can be used as a master copy of the properties and a source for deployment when promoting applications from one environment to the next. Still, none of them has separate locations for storing application-specific properties and system-level properties.

.NET developers have a better picture, but only when using the latest version of Visual Studio to manage configurations. Of course, only the bravest (and most foolhardy) developers would attempt .NET development without Visual Studio anyway.

14.3 Start-up and Shutdown

When a developer starts up an application and it bonks, the developer sees the error, kills the app, and fixes the error. When a host gets rebooted in the middle of the night and an application fails on start-up, nobody is going to know unless the application itself announces the problem. This can be as simple as an error in a log file, if a monitoring system (see Chapter 17, *Transparency*, on page 231) is already in place. Of course, for the application to announce that it failed to start up correctly, it first has to *know* that it failed to start up correctly.

Build a clean start-up sequence into applications to ensure that components are started in the right order and that the start-up sequence must complete successfully before the application starts accepting work. It can bind to sockets, for example, but should not accept any connections until the master switch is flipped. Think of it as like getting a store ready to open in the morning. You don't start letting people in through the doors just because one employee arrives. Instead, you wait until everyone is in place and ready to serve customers properly.

Don't accept connections until start-up is complete.

If the application requires a connection pool, at least some of the connections should be initialized when the application boots up. This is another form of Fail Fast (see *Fail Fast*, on page 105) and provides a useful self-test. The app certainly won't be able to process transactions very well without the database! Therefore, if the connection pool initialization fails because it cannot create any connections, the entire application should be in a failure state.

Note that this is *very* different from aborting and exiting if something fails during start-up. A running application can be interrogated for its internal state (see Chapter 17, *Transparency*, on page 231), but a halted one cannot.

Clean shutdown is equally important to production readiness. Just as that hypothetical retailer wouldn't lock the doors while customers were still inside, applications should not shut down by rudely aborting. Instead, each application needs a mode in which it will complete existing transactions but will not accept any new work. Once the in-flight transactions have all completed, then the application can exit. Be sure to moderate this rule with a timeout (see *Use Timeouts*, on page 89), however, or shutdown might never finish.

14.4 Administrative Interfaces

Spiffy Java GUIs demo very well. They make software look more "enterprisey." Unfortunately, they are a nightmare in production. The chief problem with a GUI is all the dang clicking. I can't script a bunch of clicking. Java GUIs will slow down operations by forcing administrators to do the same manual process on each server (there might be many!) every time the process is needed. For example, the clean shutdown sequence on a particular order management system I worked on required clicking—and waiting several minutes—on each of six different servers. Guess how often the clean shutdown sequence was observed? If the change window is only one hour long, I cannot afford to spend half of it waiting on a GUI.

Remote access to Java GUIs can be a challenge, too. Administrators often reach their boxes through a tortured route of SSH tunnels. Routing either X connections or HTTP connections through those tunnels is a big pain. There's no way that something so difficult will be used. So much for clean shutdown —I predict a lot of kill -9 commands.

The net result is that Java GUIs make terrible administrative interfaces for long-term production operation. The best interface for long-term operation is the command line. Given a command line, admins can easily build a scaffolding of scripts, logging, and automated actions to keep your software happy. A big step back, but still workable, is the pure HTML administrative GUI. Because Perl and Ruby have such great client libraries for HTTP, it is not too hard to script against an HTML administrative interface.

CHAPTER 15

Design Summary

It can be hard to draw attention to these topics during the hustle and rush of a development project, especially once crunch mode begins. There's good and bad news here; you can choose not to deal with these issues during development. If so, you will deal with them in production...time and time again. Dealing with these issues in development does not necessarily cost much, in time or effort, and what it does cost is far outweighed by the long-term cost of ignoring them.

Remember that your application will run on a server with multiple network interfaces. Be sure it binds to the correct address for any sockets it listens to, and be sure that any special routing requirements are set up and documented. Administrative functions should be exposed on the administration and monitoring network, not the production network.

Be sure to use virtual IP addresses to access clustered services, such as database servers or web services provided by other systems. Using the VIP allows the service provider to fail over—whether planned or unplanned—without necessitating the reconfiguration of your system.

Applications should be able to run as application users; they should not require root or Administrator permissions. Sensitive configuration parameters, such as database passwords or encryption keys, should be kept in their own configuration files.

Not all systems require five nines of availability. The cost of greater availability increases radically at each level. Considering the availability requirements as a cost/benefit trade-off (well, a cost/cost trade-off, really) with the sponsors helps move the discussion forward.

Rather than defining the availability of the entire system as a whole, I prefer to define the availability of specific features or functions performed by the system. Be sure to write exclusions for loss of availability caused by external systems.

Load balancing and clustering are two prerequisites for high availability. You can employ a variety of techniques, with a *wide* range of costs. Armed with your availability requirements, you can apply various load-balancing and clustering solutions as needed to meet the requirements at efficient cost. Each of these solutions has its own unique set of considerations, so defining the high-availability architecture early makes development and deployment much easier.

Your application's administrators will never know as much about its internals as you will. You can help reduce the likelihood of operator error by making your application obvious to configure. This means separating essential plumbing, such as Spring's beans.xml files, from environment-specific configuration. Mixing them is the equivalent of putting the ejection seat button next to the radio tuner. Sooner or later, something bad will happen.

Spend some time making your application simple to operate. Start-up and shutdown should be nondisruptive to users, and any administration duty *must* be scriptable. Pretty Java desktop administration GUIs help the novice learn his way around, but nobody wants to click through the pretty GUI for the thousandth time.

Part IV

Operations

CHAPTER 16

Case Study: Phenomenal Cosmic Powers, Itty-Bitty Living Space

16.1 Peak Season

In the middle 1500s, a Calabrian doctor named Aloysius Lilius invented a new calendar to fix a bug in the widely used Julian calendar. The Julian calendar had an accumulating drift. After a few hundred years, the official calendar date for the solstice would occur weeks before the actual event. Lilius's calendar used an elaborate system of corrections and countercorrections to keep the official calendar dates for the equinoxes and solstices close to the astronomical events. Over a 400-year cycle, the calendar dates vary by as much as 2.25 days, but they vary predictably and periodically; overall, the error is cyclic, not cumulative. This calendar, decreed by Pope Gregory XIII, was eventually adopted by all European nations, although not without struggles, and even by Egypt, China, Korea, and Japan (with modifications for the latter three). Some nations adopted the Gregorian calendar as early as 1582, while others adopted it in only the 1920s.

It's no wonder that the Catholic church created the calendar. The Gregorian calendar, like most calendars, was created to mark holy days (that is, holidays). It has since been used to mark useful recurring events in certain other domains that depend on the annual solar cycle, such as agriculture. No business in the world actually lives by the Gregorian calendar, though. The business community uses the dates as a convenient marker for its own internal business cycle.

Each industry has its own internal almanac. For an insurance company, the year is structured around "open enrollment." All plans take their bearings from the open enrollment period. Florists' thinking is dominated by Mother's Day and Valentine's Day. These landmarks happen to be marked with specific dates on the Gregorian calendar, but in the minds of florists, and their entire extended supply chain, those seasons have their own significance, with no bearing on the official calendar date.

For retailers, the year begins and ends with the euphemistically called "holiday season." Here we see a correspondence between various religious calendars and the retail calendar. Christmas, Hanukkah, and Kwanzaa all occur relatively close together. Since "Christmahannukwanzaakah" turns out to be difficult to say in meetings with a straight face, they call it "holiday season" instead. Don't be fooled, though. Retailers' interest in the holiday season is strictly ecumenical—some might even call it cynical. Up to 50% of a retailer's entire annual revenue occurs between November 1 and December 31.

In the United States, Thanksgiving—the fourth Thursday[1] in November—is the de facto start of the retail holiday season. By long tradition, this is when consumers start getting serious about gift shopping, because there are usually a little less than 30 days left at that point. Apparently, motivation by deadline crosses religious boundaries. Shopper panic sets in, resulting in a collective phenomenon known as Black Friday. Retailers encourage and reinforce this by changing their assortment, increasing stocks in stores, and advertising wondrous things. Traffic in physical stores can quadruple overnight. Traffic at online stores can increase by 1,000%. This is the real load test, the only one that matters.

16.2 Baby's First Christmas

My client had launched a new online store in the summer. The weeks and months following launch proved, time and time again, why launching a new site is like having a baby. You must expect certain things, such as being awakened in the middle of the night and routinely uncovering horrifying discoveries (as in, "Dear God! What have you been feeding this child? Orange Play-Doh?" or "What? Why would they parse content during page rendering?") Still, for all the problems we experienced following the launch, we approached the holiday season with cautious optimism.

---

1. Some retailers have lobbied Congress asking the government to move Thanksgiving two weeks earlier.

Our optimism was rooted in several factors. First, we had nearly doubled the number of servers in production. Second, we had hard data showing that the site was stable at current loads. A few burst events (mispriced items, mainly) had given us some traffic spikes to measure. The spikes were large enough to see where page latency started to climb, so we had a good feel for what level of load would cause the site to bog down. The third reason for our optimism sprang from the confidence that we could handle whatever the site decided to throw at us. Between the inherent capabilities of the application server and the tools we had built around the application server, we had more visibility and control over the online store internals than any other system on which I've worked. This would ultimately prove to be the difference between a difficult but successful Thanksgiving weekend and an unmitigated disaster.

A few of us who had pulled weekend duty through Labor Day had been granted weekend passes. I had a four-day furlough to take my family to my parents' house three states away for Thanksgiving dinner. We had also scheduled a twenty-four-hour onsite presence through the weekend. As I said, we were executing *cautious* optimism. Bear in mind, we were the local engineering team; the main Site Operations Center (SOC)—a facility staffed with highly skilled engineers twenty-four hours a day—was in another city. Ordinarily, they were the ones monitoring and managing sites during the nights and weekends. Local engineering was there to provide backup for the SOC, an escalation path when they encounter problems that have no known solution. Our local team was far too small to be on-site twenty-four hours a day all the time, but we worked out a way to do it for the limited span of the Thanksgiving weekend. Of course, as a former Boy Scout ("Be prepared"), I crammed my laptop into the packed family van, just in case.

16.3 Taking the Pulse

When we arrived on Wednesday night, I immediately set up my laptop in my parents' home office. I can work anywhere I have broadband and a cell phone. Using their 3Mb cable broadband, I used Putty—my favorite SSH client—to log into our jumphost and start up my sampling scripts.

Jumphost: a single machine, very tightly secured, that is allowed to connect via SSH to the production servers.

Back during the run-up to launch, I was part of load testing this new site. Most load tests deliver results after the test is done. Since the data come from the load generators rather than inside the systems under test, it is a "black-box" test. To get more information out of the load test, I had started off using the application server's HTML administration GUI to check vitals like latency, free heap memory, active request-handling threads, and active sessions.

If you don't know in advance what you are looking for, then a GUI is a great way to explore the system.[2] If you know exactly what you want, the GUI gets tedious. On the other hand, if you need to look at thirty or forty servers at a time, the GUI gets downright impractical.

To get more out of our load tests, I wrote a collection of Perl modules that would screen-scrape the admin GUI for me, parsing the HTML for values. These modules would let me get and set property values and invoke methods on the components of the application server—built-in as well as custom. Because the entire admin GUI was HTML based, the application server never knew the difference between a Perl module or a web browser. Armed with these Perl modules, I was able to create a set of scripts that would sample all the application servers for their vital stats, print out detail and summary results, sleep a while, and loop.

They were simple indicators, but in the time since site launch, all of us had learned the normal rhythm and pulse of the site by watching these stats. We knew, with a single glance, what was normal for noon on Tuesday in July. If session counts went up or down from the usual envelope, if the count of orders placed just looked wrong, we would know. It's really surprising how quickly you can learn to smell problems. Monitoring technology[3] provides a great safety net, pinpointing problems when they occur, but nothing beats the pattern-matching power of the human brain.

16.4 Thanksgiving Day

As soon as I woke up Thanksgiving morning, before I even had a cup of coffee, I hopped into my parents' office to check the stats windows that I left running all night. I had to look twice to be sure of what I saw. The session count in the early morning already rivaled peak time of the busiest day in a normal week. The order counts were so high that I called our DBA to verify orders were not being double-submitted. They weren't.

By noon, customers had placed as many orders as in a typical week. Page latency, our summary indicator of response time and overall site performance,

---

2. This particular application server, ATG Dynamo, still has the best admin GUI. It's not as pretty as WebLogic or WebSphere, but it exposes every single component of the application server. Like the original Volkswagen Beetle engine, you can see every part, how well it's working, and how it's wired to other components. ATG was doing dependency injection long before Martin Fowler coined the term and way, way before Spring had sprung.

3. See *Transparency* for a discussion of various monitoring technologies.

was clearly stressed but still nominal. Better still, it was holding steady over time, even as the number of sessions and orders mounted. I was one happy camper over turkey dinner. By evening, we had taken as many orders in one day as in the entire month to date. By midnight, we had taken as many orders as in the entire month of October—and the site held up. It passed the first killer load test.

16.5 Black Friday

The next morning, on Black Friday, I ambled into the office after breakfast to glance at the stats. Orders were trending even higher than the day before. Session counts were up, but page latency was still down around 250 milliseconds, right where we knew it should be. I decided to head out around town with my mom to pick up the ingredients for chicken curry. (It would be Thanksgiving leftovers for dinner on Friday, but I wanted to make the curry on Saturday, and our favorite Thai market was closed on Saturday.)

Of course, I wouldn't be telling this story if things didn't go horribly wrong. And, things wouldn't go horribly wrong until I was well away from my access point. Sure enough, I got the call when I was halfway across town.

"Good morning, Michael. This is Daniel from the Site Operations Center," said Daniel.

"I'm not going to like this, am I Daniel?" I asked.

"SiteScope is currently showing red on all DRPs. We've been doing rolling restarts of DRPs, but they are failing immediately. David has a conference call going and has asked for you to join the bridge."

In the terse code we've evolved in our hundreds of calls, Daniel was telling me that the site was down, and down hard. SiteScope—our external monitoring tool—shown in Figure 32, *SiteScope Hits Front-End Store, Simulates Users*, on page 225 access the site the same way that real customer's access it. When SiteScope goes red, we know that customers aren't able to shop and we're losing revenue. In an ATG site,[4] page requests are handled by instances that do nothing but serve pages. The web server calls the application server via the Dynamo Request Protocol, so it's common to refer to the request-handling instances as DRPs. A red DRP indicates that one of those request-handling instances stopped responding to page requests. "All DRPs red" meant the site

---

4. A J2EE application server that is well-suited to commerce applications. See the site at http://www.atg.com.

was down, losing orders at the rate of about a million dollars an hour. "Rolling restart" meant they were shutting down and restarting the application servers as fast as possible. It takes about ten minutes to bring up all the application servers on a single host. You can do up to four or five hosts at a time, but more than that and the database response time starts to suffer, which makes the start-up process take longer. All together, it meant they were trying to tread water but were still sinking.

"OK. I'll dial in now, but I'm thirty minutes from hands on keyboard," I told him.

Daniel said, "I have the conference bridge and passcode for you."

"Never mind. I've got it memorized," I said.

I dialed in and got a babel of voices. Clearly, a speakerphone in a conference room was dialed in to the bridge as well. There's nothing like trying to sort out fifteen different voices in an echoing conference room, especially when other people keep popping in and out of the call from their desks, announcing such helpful information as, "There's a problem with the site." Yes, we know. Thank you, and hang up, please.

16.6 Vital Signs

The incident had started about twenty minutes before Daniel called me. The operations center had escalated to the on-site team. David, the operations manager, had made the choice to bring me in as well.

Too much was on the line for our client to worry about interrupting a vacation day. Besides, I had told them not to hesitate to call me if I was needed.

We knew a few things at this point, twenty minutes into the incident:

- Session counts were very high, higher than the day before.
- Network bandwidth usage was high but not hitting a limit.
- Application server page latency (response time) was high.
- Web, application, and database CPU usage were low—really low.
- Search servers, our usual culprit, were responding well. System stats looked healthy.
- Request-handling threads were almost all busy. Many of them had been working on their requests for more than five seconds.

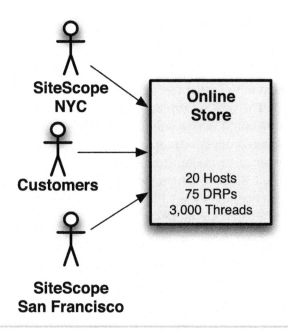

SiteScope
NYC

Customers

SiteScope
San Francisco

Online
Store

20 Hosts
75 DRPs
3,000 Threads

Figure 32—SiteScope Hits Front-End Store, Simulates Users

In fact, the page latency wasn't just high. Because requests were timing out, it was effectively infinite. The statistics showed us only the average of requests that completed.

Requests that didn't complete never got averaged in. Other than the long response time, which we already knew about since SiteScope was failing to complete its synthetic transactions, none of our usual suspects looked guilty.

To get more information, I started taking thread dumps of the application servers that were misbehaving. While I was doing that, I asked Ashok, one of our rock-star engineers who was on-site in the conference room, to check the back-end order management system. He saw similar patterns on the back end as on the front end: low CPU usage and most threads busy for a long time.

It was now almost an hour since I got the call, or ninety minutes since the site went down. This means not only lost orders for my client but also that we were coming close to missing our SLA for resolving a high severity incident. I hate missing an SLA. I take it personally, as do all of my colleagues.

16.7 Diagnostic Tests

The thread dumps on the front-end applications servers revealed a similar pattern across all the DRPs. A few threads were busy making a call to the back end, and most of the others were waiting for an available connection to call the back end. The waiting threads were all blocked on a resource pool, one that had no timeout. If the back end stopped responding, then the threads making the calls would never return, and the ones that were blocked would never get their chance to make their calls. In short, every single request-handling thread, all 3,000 of them, were tied up doing nothing, perfectly explaining our observation of low CPU usage: all 100 DRPs were idle, waiting forever for an answer that would never come.

Attention swung to the order management system. Thread dumps on that system revealed that some of its 450 threads were occupied making calls to an external integration point, as shown in Figure 33, *Front-End Store Hits Back-End Order Management*, on page 227. As you probably have guessed, all other threads were blocked waiting to make calls to that external integration point. That system handles scheduling for home delivery. We immediately paged the operations team for that system. (It's managed by a different group that does not have 24/7 support staff. They pass a pager around on rotation.)

I think it was about this time that my wife brought me a plate of leftover turkey and stuffing for dinner. Between status reports, I muted the phone to take quick bites. By that point, I had used up the battery on my cell phone and was close to draining the cordless phone. (I couldn't use a regular phone because none of them took my headset plug.) I crossed my fingers that my cell phone would get enough of a charge before the cordless phone ran out.

16.8 Call in a Specialist

It felt like half of forever (but was probably only half an hour) when the support engineer dialed in to the bridge. He explained that of the four servers that normally handle scheduling, two were down for maintenance over the holiday weekend, and one of the others was malfunctioning for reasons unknown. To this day, I have no idea why they would schedule maintenance for that weekend of all weekends! Figure 34, *Order Management Hits ``Enterprise" Scheduling System*, on page 228 shows the relative sizes of the three systems involved.

The sole remaining server could handle up to twenty-five concurrent requests before it started to slow down and hang. We estimated that right at that

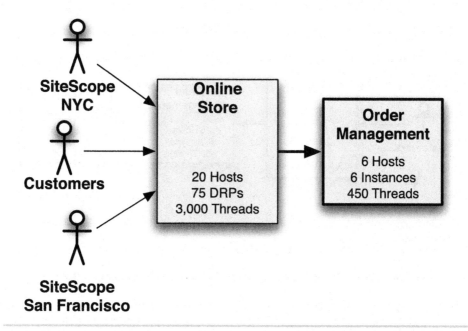

Figure 33—Front-End Store Hits Back-End Order Management

moment, the order management system was probably sending it ninety requests. Sure enough, when the on-call engineer checked the lone scheduling server, it was stuck at 100% CPU. He had gotten paged a few times about the high CPU condition but had not responded, since that group routinely gets paged for transient spikes in CPU usage that turn out to be false alarms. All the false positives had quite effectively trained them to ignore high CPU conditions.

Our business sponsor, on the conference call, gravely informed us that marketing had prepared a new insert that hit newspapers Friday morning. The ad offered free home delivery for all online orders placed before Monday. The entire line, with fifteen people in a conference room on speakerphone and a dozen more dialed in from their desks, went silent for the first time in four hours.

So, to recap, we have the front-end system, the online store, with 3,000 threads on 100 servers and a radically changed traffic pattern. It's swamping the order management system, which has 450 threads that are shared between handling requests from the front end and processing orders. The order management system is swamping the scheduling system, which can barely handle twenty-five requests at a time.

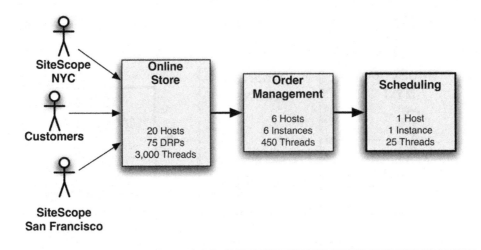

Figure 34—Order Management Hits "Enterprise" Scheduling System

And it's going to continue until Monday. It's the nightmare scenario. The site is down, and there's no playbook for this situation. We're in the middle of an incident, and we have to improvise a solution.

16.9 Compare Treatment Options

Brainstorming ensued. Numerous proposals were thrown up and shot down, generally because the application code's behavior under that circumstance is unknown. It quickly became clear that the only answer was to stop making so many requests to check schedule availability. With the weekend's marketing campaign centered around free home delivery, we knew requests from the users were not about to slow down. We had to find a way to throttle the calls. The order management system had no way to do that.

We saw a glimmer of hope when we looked at the code for the store. It used a subclass of the standard resource pool to manage connections to order management. In fact, it had a separate connection pool just for scheduling requests. I'm not sure why the code was designed with a separate connection pool for that, probably an example of Conway's law, but it saved the day— and the retail weekend. Because it had a component just for those connections, we could use that component as our throttle.

If the developers had added an enabled property, it would have been a simple thing to set that to false. Maybe we could do the next best thing, though. A resource pool with a zero maximum is effectively disabled anyway. I asked the developers what would happen if the pool started returning null instead of a connection. They replied that the code would handle that and present the user with a polite message stating that delivery scheduling was not available for the time being. Good enough.

16.10 Does the Condition Respond to Treatment?

One of my Perl scripts could set the value of any property on any component. As an experiment, I used the script to set max for that resource pool (on just one DRP) to zero, and I set checkoutBlockTime to zero. Nothing happened. No change in behavior at all. Then I remembered that max has an effect only when the pool is starting up.

I used another script, one that could invoke methods on the component, to call its stopService() and startService() methods. Voila! That DRP started handling requests again! There was much rejoicing.

Of course, because only one DRP was responding, the load manager started sending every single page request to that one DRP. It was crushed like the last open beer stand at a World Cup match. But at least we had a strategy.

I ran my scripts, this time with the flag that said "all DRPs." They set max and checkoutBlockTime to zero and then recycled the service.

The ability to restart components, instead of entire servers, is a key concept of *recovery-oriented computing*. (See the "Recovery-Oriented Computing" sidebar.) Although we did not have the level of automation that ROC proposes, we were able to recover service without rebooting the world. If we had needed to change the configuration files and restart all the servers, it would have taken more than six hours under that level of load. Dynamically reconfiguring and restarting just the connection pool took less than five minutes (once we knew what to do).

Almost immediately after my scripts finished, we saw user traffic getting through. Page latency started to drop. About ninety seconds later, the DRPs went green in SiteScope. The site was back up and running.

16.11 Winding Down

I wrote a new script that would do all the actions needed to reset that connection pool's maximum. It set the max property, stopped the service, and then restarted the service. With one command, an engineer in the operations center or in the "command post" (that is, the conference room) at the client's site

Recovery-Oriented Computing

The Recovery-Oriented Computing (ROC) project is a joint Berkley and Stanford research project.[a] The project's founding principles are as follows:

- Failures are inevitable, in both hardware and software.

- Modeling and analysis can never be sufficiently complete. *A priori* prediction of all failure modes is not possible.

- Human action is a major source of system failures.

Their research runs contrary to most work in system reliability. Whereas most work focuses on eliminating the sources of failure, ROC accepts that failures will inevitably happen—a major theme in this book! Their investigations aim to improve survivability in the face of failures.

Many of the concepts of ROC can be implemented in today's languages and platforms. Follow their focus on damage containment, automatic fault detection, and component-level restartability, and you'll derive great benefits.

_____

a.   See http://roc.cs.berkeley.edu/.

could reset the maximum connections to whatever it needed to be. I would later learn that script was used constantly through the weekend. Because setting the max to zero completely disabled home delivery, the business sponsor wanted it increased when load was light and decreased to one (not zero) when load got heavy.

We closed out the call. I hung up and went to tuck my kids into bed. It took a while. They were full of news about going to the park, playing in the sprinkler, and seeing baby rabbits in the backyard. I wanted to hear all about it.

CHAPTER 17

Transparency

Experienced engineers on ships can tell when something is about to go wrong by the sound of the giant diesel engines. They've learned, by living with their engines, to recognize normal, nominal, and abnormal. In their case, they cannot help being surrounded by the sounds and rhythms of their environment. When something is wrong, the engineers' knowledge of the linkages within the engines can lead them to the problem with a speed and accuracy —and with just one or two clues—in a way that can seem psychic.

Our systems are not so naturally exposed. They run in faceless boxes. There are no moving parts to watch, and the steady whir of the fans communicates little about what's happening. (Though, if the fans *stop*, we do know there's a problem!) We sit in different rooms from the hardware, often in different buildings, and sometimes even in different cities. If we are to get the kind of "environmental awareness" that the shipboard engineers naturally acquire, we must facilitate that awareness by building *transparency* into our systems.

Transparency refers to the qualities that allow operators, developers, and business sponsors to gain understanding of the system's historical trends, present conditions, instantaneous state, and future projections. Transparent systems communicate, and in communicating, they train their attendant humans. The giant diesel power plant in a cruise ship radiates information through ambient sounds and vibration, through gauges with quantitative information, and in extreme (usually bad) cases through smell.

In debugging the "Black Friday problem" (see Section 16.1, *Peak Season*, on page 219), we relied on component-level visibility into the system's current behavior. That visibility was no accident. It was the product of enabling technologies implemented with transparency and feedback in mind. Without that level of visibility, we probably could have told that the site was slow (if a disgruntled user called us or someone in the business happened to hit the site) but with no idea why. It would be like having a sick goldfish—nothing you do can help, so you just wait and see whether it lives or dies.

Transparency has practical and psychological benefits. On the practical side, debugging a transparent system is vastly easier, so transparent systems will mature faster than opaque ones. Psychologically speaking, imagine sitting down once a year to have your future determined by peeking at the top face of a die labeled "Bonus," "Promotion," "Layoff," "Massive Overtime," "Public Scorn," and "Peer Acclaim," but someone else has either rolled the die for you or placed it with one face up. You don't know and have no control. Anyone accountable for the success of the system—from application development to business analysts to the project sponsors—has a large part of their future predicated on the system's behavior but with no idea how it will turn out.

When you have to add capacity, you are totally dependent on data collected from the existing infrastructure. You will need a combination of technical data and business metrics to understand the past and present state of your system in order to predict the future. Good data enables good decision making. In the absence of trusted data, decisions will be made for you, based on somebody's political clout, prejudices, or hair styles.

Finally, a system without transparency cannot survive long in production. If administrators do not know what it is doing, it cannot be tuned and optimized. If developers do not know what works and does not work in production, they cannot increase its reliability or resilience over time. And, if the business sponsors do not know whether they are making money on it, they will not fund future work. Without transparency, the system will drift into decay, functioning a bit worse with each release. Systems can mature well if, and only if, they have some degree of transparency.

This chapter discusses the four perspectives of transparency: historical trending, predictive forecasting, present status, and instantaneous behavior. It also examines existing technology that enables transparency and gaps in the technology that have yet to be filled. For web systems, a number of vendors smelled opportunity around performance measurement and reporting. These are currently undergoing a wave of consolidation to create integrated "enterprise application management" suites. This is a rich space, so I will be talking about specific products more than usual. It is likely that, by the time you read this, many of these companies will have been acquired and integrated with some larger suite.

17.1 Perspectives

Different constituencies require different perspectives. These perspectives will not all be served by the same views into the systems. Just as the question, "How's the weather?" means very different things to a gardener, a pilot, and a meteorologist, the question, "How's it going?" means something decidedly distinct when coming from the CEO or the system administrator.

Historical Trending

History is a fairly plastic word. There aren't too many fields in which "last week" is a plausible definition of "history." That might be the only connection between the worlds of IT operations and high fashion.

Still, even if myopic, we have to be concerned about historical views. Despite the Wall Street–style disclaimers,[1] it is possible to predict tomorrow's system behavior by extrapolating yesterday's results. This applies to business metrics (customers, orders, conversion rate, revenue, cost of delivering service, and so on) as well as system metrics (free storage, average CPU utilization, network bandwidth, and number of errors logged).

Obviously, historical records have to be stored somewhere for a period of time. The historical perspective is best served by a database. Section 17.2, *Designing for Transparency*, on page 240 refers to this as the OpsDB. The OpsDB can be used to investigate anomalies or trends. Because it contains system- and business-level metrics, it can be used to identify correlations in time and across layers.

The historical perspective can be represented by spreadsheets, charts, Microsoft PowerPoint presentations, or analysis reports. It lacks the immediacy of the present and is usually not appropriate for a dashboard view.

Because it can be used to discover new and interesting relationships, the historical data should be broadly available through tools such as Microsoft Access and Microsoft Excel. If your company has purchased a business intelligence (BI) or reporting tool, it should clearly be using the historical data. Just beware the temptation to have these tools directly access the production transactional database. (See *Historical Data*, on page 167.)

Some common questions indicate the historical perspective:

---

1. You know, "Past performance is no guarantee of future results."

- How many orders did we take yesterday?

- How does that compare to this day last year?[2]

- How much disk space did we consume during the first quarter?

- The last time we had a spike in traffic, which system was the limiting factor?

- How does the growth in customer traffic compare to the growth in CPU usage over the past three years?

Predicting the Future

In *Planning Extreme Programming [BF01]*, Kent Beck and Martin Fowler popularized the expression "yesterday's weather." They relate an apocryphal story about a sophisticated weather prediction system beaten by a much simpler algorithm: a prediction that today's weather will be the same as yesterday's weather will be accurate about 70% of the time. However shaky the meteorological foundation might be, the concept nicely encapsulates the recognition that we *can* predict the future by extrapolating the past.

In the case of our systems, the backward-facing historical information is also our crystal ball. Future predictions are almost always about correlations and linkages, rather than direct measurements. By far, the most common question is, "What's our capacity?" (See Section 8.1, *Defining Capacity*, on page 135 and Section 8.3, *Interrelations*, on page 138.) Although this appears to be a question about a single metric, the implied qualifier is "if the next N users have a proportional impact to the previous N users."

Predictions are always built on a model of the system. Bad predictions result from bad models (for example, linear projections). Really excellent models are hard to develop. They require people with deep understanding of wicked topics such as queuing theory and stochastic modeling—operations research specialists. These folks can build a model to predict system performance to three decimal places—based on just the architecture diagrams. I'm not convinced that the level of effort (and cost) is worth it for well-trodden territory like web-based ebusiness systems. I would probably reserve this for jobs such as modeling global communication networks.

On the other hand, it's possible to develop "good enough" models by finding correlations in past data, which can then be used—within a certain domain

---

2. Note that "this day" doesn't always mean the same calendar date—the correspondence almost certainly is with the same day of the week rather than the day of the month.

of applicability[3]—to make predictions. These correlative models can be built into spreadsheets to allow less technical users to perform "what if" scenarios.

Projections into the future tend to be sensitive information. They also do not have the urgency of immediate data. Therefore, they should generally not be built into a dashboard.

An application release can alter or invalidate the correlations on which the projections are built. Since these projections act like derivatives of the system's behavior, they must be reexamined after each application release to see whether they still apply. (Of course, you must wait for an adequate body of new measurements to build up before you can tell.) This also implies that anything based on these projections should include a reference to indicate which set of projections were used.[4]

Here are some common questions that indicate the future perspective:

- How many customers per day can we handle?

- When do I have to buy more servers (or disk, bandwidth, or any other computing resource)?

- Can we make it through this holiday season? (Notice that this requires a projection about a projection, which doesn't just double the possibility for error but squares it.)

Present Status

The distinction between the present status and the behavior at this instant can be illustrated by imagining a fat man jogging. The instantaneous behavior is one associated with improving health, but his present status might be one "thump" away from a heart attack.

"Present status" describes the overall state of the system. This is not so much about what it is doing as what it *has* done. This should include the state of each piece of hardware and every application server, application, and batch job.

The status of each component is defined by a combination of events and parameters. Events are point-in-time occurrences. Some indicate normal, or

---

3. However, please note that Newton's Laws of Motion are applicable only within a certain domain...but that domain works well enough to get a spacecraft to Neptune after a twenty-year flight!

4. I know, spoken like an academic. I don't expect business sponsors to be rigorous about their methodology, but I do hope that the developers and system engineers will be!

even required, occurrences, while others indicate abnormalities of concern. A daily inventory feed is an example of a required event. The occurrence of that event is expected; its absence should be cause for alarm. Abnormal events are commonly categorized as "low-medium-high" or "warn-severe-critical."

Parameters are continuous metrics or discrete states that can be observed about the system. This is where transparency is most vital. Applications that reveal more of their internal state provide more accurate, actionable parameters. At the most basic level, we have the operating system metrics: CPU usage, memory free, memory swap rate, network bandwidth per interface, and disk space free. Within an application server, a large number of metrics and states are generally applicable.

Memory
   Minimum heap size, maximum heap size, generation sizes

Garbage collection
   Type, frequency, memory reclaimed, size of request

Worker threads, for each thread pool
   Number of threads, threads busy, threads busy more than five seconds, high-water mark (maximum concurrent threads in use), low-water mark, number of times a thread was not available, request backlog

Database connection pools, for each pool
   Number of connections, connections in use, high-water mark, low-water mark, number of times a connection was not available, request backlog

Traffic statistics, for each request channel
   Total requests processed, average response time, requests aborted, requests per second, time of last request, accepting traffic or not

The application itself should reveal plenty of information about its own metrics.

Business transaction, for each type
   Number processed, number aborted, dollar value, transaction aging, conversion rate, completion rate

Users
   Demographics or classification, technographics, percentage of users who are registered, number of users, usage patterns, errors encountered

Integration points
   Current state, manual override applied, number of times used, average response time from remote system, number of failures

Circuit breakers

Current state, manual override applied, number of failed calls, time of last successful call, number of state transitions

As you can see, for even a medium-sized application, there could be hundreds of parameters. For each one, there is some range normal and acceptable values. This might be a tolerance around a discrete value, or it might be a threshold that should not be exceeded. The parameter is nominal as long as its metric is within acceptable range. Often, a second, tighter range will indicate a "caution" signal, warning that the parameter is approaching its threshold.

For continuous metrics, a handy rule-of-thumb definition for nominal would be "the mean value for this time period plus or minus two standard deviations." The choice of time period is where it gets interesting. For most traffic-driven metrics, the time period that shows the most stable correlation will be the "hour of the week"—that is, 2 p.m. on Tuesday. The day of the month means little. In certain industries—such as travel, floral, and sports—the most relevant measurement is counting backward from a holiday or event.

For a retailer, the "day of week" pattern will be overlaid on a strong "week of year" cycle. There is no one right answer for all organizations.[5]

The Infamous Dashboard

Status is commonly represented on a dashboard in the familiar "red-yellow-green" schema. Categorizing the entire state of a complex, multilayered distributed system with a three-level color coding system might seem like oversimplification, but it certainly has the virtue of familiarity. It helps if everyone has a common agreement about what the colors *mean*. Table 1, *Color Coding for Accuracy*, on page 238 shows a definition that has worked for me in the past. In particular, this definition accommodates an often-overlooked trouble condition: too much of a good thing.

The present status of the system is obviously amenable to a dashboard presentation. (It practically *defines* a dashboard.) The dashboard should be broadly visible; projecting it on a wall in the lunchroom isn't out of the question. The more people who understand the normal daily behavior of the system, the better. For the most utility, the dashboard should be able to present different facets of the overall system to different users. An engineer in operations

---

5. For a vivid illustration, sample the literature on "automatic workload characterization." Though it might be couched in the dry language of academics, a heated battle has raged for years.

Green   All of the following must be true:

- All expected events have occurred.
- No abnormal events have occurred.
- All metrics are nominal.
- All states are fully operational.

Yellow   At least one of the following is true:

- An expected event has not occurred.
- At least one abnormal event, with a medium severity, has occurred.
- One or more parameters is above or below nominal.
- A noncritical state is not fully operational. (For example, a circuit breaker has cut off a noncritical feature.)

Red   At least one of the following is true:

- A required event has not occurred.
- At least one abnormal event, with high severity, has occurred.
- One or more parameters is far above or below nominal.
- A critical state is not at its expected value. (For example, "accepting requests" is false when it should be true.)

Table 1—Color Coding for Accuracy

probably cares first about the component-level view. A developer is more likely to want an application-centric view, whereas a business sponsor probably wants a view rolled up to the feature or business process level. Clearly, this implies that the dashboard should know the linkages between these different views. When observing a component-level outage—for example, a network failure—an administrator should be able to see which business processes are affected. This facilitates both communication with the sponsors and proper prioritization of the problem.

Most systems have a daily rhythm of expected events. Those might be feeds from other systems, extracts to ship out to other systems, or just batch jobs to integrate with legacy systems. Whatever the purpose, those jobs become just as much a part of the system as the web or database servers. Their execution falls in the category of "required expected events." The dashboard should be able to represent those expected events, whether or not they've occurred, and whether they succeeded or not. A startling number of business-level issues can be traced back to batch jobs failing invisibly for 33 days straight.

Present status will be important to anyone with a financial or career stake in the day-to-day function of the systems. IT obviously falls in this category. There are certainly sponsors outside of IT who have their careers tied to the systems. All of these people will develop their situational awareness by spending time observing the present status of the system at various times and under various conditions.

Instantaneous Behavior

Instantaneous behavior answers the question, "What the **** is going on?" People will be most interested in instantaneous behavior when an incident is already underway.

Obviously, instantaneous behavior relates to present status. Anomalies in instantaneous behavior often, but not always, result in incorrect status. Stack traces, thread dumps, errors thrown in log files, and bad responses to users are all examples of behavior problems that might or might not show up in the status perspective. For example, users don't like having errors thrown at them. They tend to leave when that happens. As a result, errors to users will eventually result in a "transactions per hour" metric dropping below its nominal range. It's better to catch the aberrant behavior before users start walking away.

Instantaneous behavior is the realm of monitoring systems. Ranging from homegrown log file scraping to multimillion-dollar HP OpenView installations, monitoring systems sit outside your system, watching like Big Brother for conformance to the plan.

This is also the realm of thread dumps (see *Getting Thread Dumps*, on page 17). Frameworks such as JMX also enable a view into instantaneous behavior, because they allow administrators to see the internals of running applications.

Who gets to see the instantaneous behavior? Some portions have to be restricted because of their potential for harm. Not everyone will get access to the JMX console, because they could do bad things like shut down servers or change vital parameters. Some methods of gathering status (thread dumps, for instance) require privileged access to servers. Outside of those clearly dangerous channels, however, be aware that the operations department often feels threatened when developers or business sponsors ask for a view into the system's immediate behavior, especially if there is already a lack of trust or even a hostile atmosphere. Operations worries that they will be deluged with inquiries about every blip and anomaly. Worse yet, they fear that their customers—the people who pay for the systems—will spot problems before they do. Nothing is more embarrassing than getting a call from some director of marketing asking, "Why is one server's CPU running higher than all the others?" and having to reply, "I don't know. I haven't looked at the chart all day."

One way to defuse that tension is to improve the transparency of the present status. When sponsors ask for more information, what they usually want is status, not instantaneous behavior. (This is one of the reasons I separate these two concerns in the first place.) Standing in their shoes, it's totally understandable. They are accountable for the financial success of this system, so they should have some idea of what's happening with it. But, they don't really need to know every time an application burps out a stack trace in a log file. What they need to know is, "Is our revenue tracking to plan?" or "Did our last campaign increase conversion rates?" or "Should we buy more kiosks or staff more agents?" These concerns are served with a status dashboard, historical trends, and future projections. They are not served by looking at SNMP traps and thread dumps.

17.2 Designing for Transparency

Transparency arises from deliberate design and architecture. "Adding transparency" late in development is about as effective as "adding quality." Maybe it can be done, but only with greater effort and cost than if it had been built in from the beginning.

Visibility inside one application or server is not enough. Strictly local visibility leads to strictly local optimization. For example, a retailer ran a major project to get items appearing on the site faster. The nightly update was running until 5 or 6 a.m., when it needed to complete closer to midnight. This project optimized the string of batch jobs that fed content to the site. The project met its goals, in that the batch jobs finished two hours earlier. Items still did not appear on the site, however, until a long-running parallel process finished, at 5 or 6 a.m. The local optimization on the batch jobs had no global effect.

Visibility into one application at a time can also mask problems with scaling effects. For instance, observing cache flushes on one application server would not reveal that each server was knocking items out of all the other servers' caches. Every time an item was displayed, it was accidentally being updated, therefore causing a cache invalidation notice to all other servers. As soon as all the caches' statistics appeared on one page, the problem was obvious. Without that visibility, we would have added many servers to reach the necessary capacity—and each server would have made the problem worse.

In designing for transparency, keep a close eye on coupling. It's relatively easy for the monitoring framework to intrude on the internals of the system. Use the standards discussed next to avoid this excessively tight coupling. The monitoring and reporting systems should be like an exoskeleton built around your system, not woven into it. In particular, decisions about what metrics should trigger alerts, where to set the thresholds, and how to "roll up" state variables into an overall system health status should all be left outside of the application itself. These are policy decisions that will change at a very different rate than the application code itself will.

17.3 Enabling Technologies

By nature, a process running on a server is totally opaque. Unless you're running a debugger on the process, it reveals practically nothing about itself. It might be working fine, it might be running on its very last thread, or it might be spinning in circles doing nothing. Like Schrodinger's cat, it is impossible to tell whether the process is alive or dead until you look at it.

The very first trick, then, is getting information out of the process. This section examines the most important enabling technologies that reduce the opacity of that process boundary. You can classify these as either "white-box" or "black-box" technologies.

A black-box technology sits outside the process, examining it through externally observable things. Black-box technologies can be implemented after the system is delivered, usually by operations. Even though black-box technologies are unknown to the system being observed, there are still helpful things you can do during development to facilitate the use of these tools.

By contrast, white-box technology runs inside the thing being observed—either a process or a whole system. The system deliberately exposes itself through these tools. These must be integrated during development. White-box technologies necessarily have tighter coupling to the system than black-box technologies.

17.4 Logging

Despite millions of R&D dollars on "enterprise application management" suites and spiffy operations centers with giant plasma monitors showing color-coded network maps, good old log files are still the most reliable, versatile information vehicle. It's worth a chuckle once in a while to realize that here we are, in the 21st century, and log files are still one of our most valuable tools.

Logging is certainly a white-box technology; it must be integrated pervasively into the source code. Nevertheless, logging is ubiquitous for a number of good reasons. Log files reflect activity within an application. Therefore, they reveal the instantaneous behavior of that application. They are also persistent, so they can be examined to understand the system's status—though that often requires some "digestion" to trace state transitions into current states.

If you want to avoid tight coupling to a particular monitoring tool or framework (see *Commercial Monitoring Systems*, on page 250), then log files are the way to go. Nothing is more loosely coupled than log files; every framework or tool that exists can scrape log files. This loose coupling means log files are also valuable in development, where you are unlikely to find OpenView or its kin.

Despite this value, log files are badly abused. Here are some keys to successful logging.

Configuration

Despite the developer's instinct to put a logs directory under the application's install directory, administrators often want to keep logs on a different "spindle" (hard drive or LUN) than the operating system or content. Log files can be large. They grow rapidly and consume lots of I/O. Keeping them on a separate drive uses more I/O bandwidth in parallel and reduces contention for the busy drives.

If you make the log file locations configurable, the administrator can just set the right property to locate the files. If you don't make the location configurable, then they'll probably relocate the files anyway, but you might not like how it gets done.

On UNIX systems, symlinks are the most common workaround. This involves creating a symbolic link from the logs directory to the actual location of the files. There's a small I/O penalty on each file open, but not much compared to the penalty of contention for a busy drive. I've also seen a separate filesystem dedicated to logs, mounted directly underneath the installation directory.

Fortunately, all the common logging frameworks support configurable paths (which is reason number 72 *not* to roll your own logging).

Logging Levels

As humans read (or even just scan) log files for a new system, they are learning what "normal" means for that system. Some applications, particularly young ecommerce applications, are very noisy; they generate a lot of errors in their logs. Some are quiet, reporting nothing during normal operation. In either case, the applications will train their humans on what's healthy or normal.

Most developers implement logging as though they are the primary consumer of the log files. In fact, administrators and engineers in operations will spend far more time with these log files than developers will. Logging should be aimed at production operations rather than development or testing. One consequence is that anything logged at level "ERROR" or "SEVERE" should be something that requires action on the part of operations. Not every exception needs to be logged as an error. Just because a user entered a bad credit card number and the validation component threw an exception doesn't mean anything has to be done about it. Log errors in business logic or user input as warnings (if at all). Reserve "ERROR" for a serious system problem. For example, a circuit breaker tripping to "open" is an error. It's something that should not happen under normal circumstances, and it probably means action is required on the other end of the connection. Failure to connect to a database is an error—there's a problem with either the network or the database server. A NullPointerException isn't automatically an error.

Catalog of Messages

One of the common requests from operations is a list of all the log messages the system can produce. This always used to make me groan. These days, though, a few hours with the internationalization tools in IDEs such as Eclipse, IDEA, and NetBeans are all it takes to externalize all the log messages. Once they've been collected into a single resource bundle, it's easy to send it to operations.

What's more, you can even add unambiguous codes to each message. There are two great things about message codes. First, they make for accurate communications between operations and development. If you've ever been told, "I'm not sure what the whole message was, but it said something about a fatal system error," you need message codes. Second, message codes are easy for operations to look up in a run book or knowledge base. Suppose your code has many occurrences of the following pattern:

```
try {
  ...
} catch (TimeoutException e) {
  LOGGER.log(Level.SEVERE, "Timeout failure connecting to fulfillment system.", e);
}
```

Debug Logs in Production

While I'm on the subject of logging levels, I'll address a pet peeve of mine: "debug" logs in production. This is rarely a good idea and can create so much noise that real issues get buried in tons of method traces or trivial checkpoints. It's easy to leave debug messages turned on in production. All it takes is one cvs or svn commit while the logging configuration has some debug levels enabled. I recommend adding a step to your build process that automatically removes any configs that enable debug or trace log levels.

Applying Eclipse's "Externalize Strings" command results in a new file, messages.properties, and a new class, Messages. Here is what Eclipse put into messages.properties:

transparency/messages.properties
```
FulfillmentClient.0=Connection refused.
FulfillmentClient.1=Authorization failed. Credentials refused.
FulfillmentClient.2=Timeout failure connecting to fulfillment system.
```

These messages are accessed via getString(String key) on the new utility class Messages, which Eclipse created in the same package as the original class:

transparency/Messages.java
```java
public static String getString(String key) {
    // TODO Auto-generated method stub
    try {
        return RESOURCE_BUNDLE.getString(key);
    } catch (MissingResourceException e) {
        return '!' + key + '!';
    }
}
```

Even though "Externalize Strings" was created to make internationalization easier, you can use it for a different type of interface. Once Eclipse collects all the strings together in a single file, with a utility method to return them, you have a great leverage point to make changes. For instance, the key parameter to getString(String key) makes a great message code, with just one small tweak to Messages:

transparency/Messages.java
```java
public static String getString(String key) {
    // TODO Auto-generated method stub
    try {
        return "(" + key + ") " + RESOURCE_BUNDLE.getString(key);
    } catch (MissingResourceException e) {
        return '!' + key + '!';
    }
}
```

Human Factors

Above all else, log files are human-readable. That means they constitute a human-computer interface and should be examined in terms of human factors. This might sound trivial—even laughable—but in a stressful situation, such as a Severity 1 incident, human misinterpretation of status information can prolong or aggravate the problem. Operators in the Three Mile Island reactor misinterpreted the meaning of coolant pressure and temperature values, leading them to take exactly the wrong action at every turn. (See *Inviting Disaster [Chi01]*, pages 49–63.) Although most of our systems will not vent radioactive steam when they break, they will take thousands of dollars with them. Therefore, it behooves us to ensure that log files convey clear, accurate, and actionable information to the humans who read them.

If log files are a human interface, then they should also be written such that humans can recognize and interpret them as rapidly as possible. The format should be as readable as possible. The human visual system is a pattern-matching machine of unparalleled speed and sophistication. Why do so many vendors work so hard to defeat that ability? Figure 36, *Impossible to Scan*, on page 246, shows an example of a log format that was made for computers or perhaps Martians to read—not humans. This is from the start-up log of WebLogic 9.2. How rapidly can you spot the warning message?

Figure 37, *A Format That Aids Scanning*, on page 246 comes from WebSphere 6.1. It uses the same java.util.logging API that the previous example used, but it replaces the awful default format with a much more helpful one. This is a format that the human eye can scan. Once you know that I, W, and A indicate different severity levels ("information," "warning," and "audit"), then scanning for warnings and errors becomes trivial. The space-padded, columnar format helps humans read the file. Note the message code field, which aids in auto-mated parsing of the file. This log format helps both humans and computers.

Figure 38, *java.util.logging Default Format*, on page 246, shows the same output as from WebSphere's start-up sequence but using the default format for JDK's java.util.logging package.

I don't know who thought up this two-line format, but it makes scanning through logs utterly impossible. For that matter, the two-line format makes parsing the logs with other programs difficult, too. grep has no idea how to deal with two-line formats. You'll have to dig up an old-school UNIX hacker to do some awk trickery. This format defeats man and machine.

```
<Aug 13, 2006 7:24:53 PM CDT> <Notice> <Log Management> <BEA-170027> <The server
<Aug 13, 2006 7:24:54 PM CDT> <Notice> <WebLogicServer> <BEA-000365> <Server stat
<Aug 13, 2006 7:24:54 PM CDT> <Notice> <WebLogicServer> <BEA-000365> <Server stat
<Aug 13, 2006 7:24:57 PM CDT> <Notice> <Security> <BEA-090171> <Loading the ident
A-000331> <Started WebLogic Admin Server "examplesServer" for domain "wl_server"
<Aug 13, 2006 7:25:00 PM CDT> <Warning> <WorkManager> <BEA-002919> <Unable to fin
map to the default WorkManager for the application bea_wls9_async_response>
<Aug 13, 2006 7:25:00 PM CDT> <Warning> <EJB> <BEA-014014> <The message driven be
chPolicy" that refers to an unknown work manager. The default work manager will b
Could not invoke browser, command=netscape -remote openURL(http://192.168.1.98:70
can open from the cmd-line.
java.io.IOException: java.io.IOException: netscape: not found
<Aug 13, 2006 7:25:00 PM CDT> <Notice> <WebLogicServer> <BEA-000365> <Server stat
<Aug 13, 2006 7:25:00 PM CDT> <Notice> <WebLogicServer> <BEA-000360> <Server star
```

Figure 36—Impossible to Scan

```
[8/14/06 8:22:14:653 CDT] 0000000a SSLComponentI I    CWPKI0001I: SSL service is
[8/14/06 8:22:14:813 CDT] 0000000a WSKeyStore      W    CWPKI0041W: One or more key
[8/14/06 8:22:14:848 CDT] 0000000a SSLConfigMana  I    CWPKI0027I: Disabling defau
[8/14/06 8:22:24:639 CDT] 0000000a WorkSpaceMana  A    WKSP0500I: Workspace config
[8/14/06 8:22:25:508 CDT] 0000000a FileRepositor  A    ADMR0010I: Document cells/t
[8/14/06 8:22:25:961 CDT] 0000000a SSLDiagnostic  I    CWPKI0014I: The SSL componer
[8/14/06 8:22:26:325 CDT] 0000000a FileRepositor  A    ADMR0010I: Document cells/t
[8/14/06 8:22:26:670 CDT] 0000000a SSLComponentI I    CWPKI0002I: SSL service init
```

Figure 37—A Format That Aids Scanning

```
Aug 19, 2006 7:13:25 PM com.example.server.SSLComponentIdentity emit
INFO: SSL service is initializing the configuration
Aug 19, 2006 7:13:25 PM com.example.server.WSKeyStore emit
WARNING: One or more key stores are using the default password.
Aug 19, 2006 7:13:25 PM com.example.server.SSLConfigManager emit
INFO: Disabling default hostname verification for HTTPS URL connections.
Aug 19, 2006 7:13:25 PM com.example.server.WorkSpaceManager emit
INFO: Workspace configuration consistency check is false.
Aug 19, 2006 7:13:25 PM com.example.server.FileRepository emit
INFO: Document cells/trozNode01Cell/security.xml is modified.
Aug 19, 2006 7:13:25 PM com.example.server.SSLDiagnostic emit
INFO: The SSL component's FFDC Diagnostic Module com.ibm.ws.ssl.core.SSLDiagnosti
Aug 19, 2006 7:13:25 PM com.example.server.FileRepository emit
INFO: Document cells/trozNode01Cell/security.xml is modified.
Aug 19, 2006 7:13:25 PM com.example.server.SSLComponentIdentity emit
INFO: SSL service initialization completed successfully
```

Figure 38—java.util.logging Default Format

Voodoo Operations

As I said before, humans are very good at detecting patterns. In fact, we appear to have a natural bias toward detecting patterns, even when they aren't there. In *Why People Believe Weird Things* *[She97]*, Michael Shermer discusses the evolutionary impact of pattern detection. Early humans who failed to detect a real pattern—such as a pattern of light and shadow that turned out to be a leopard—were less likely to pass on their genes than those who detected patterns that weren't there and ran away from a clump of bushes that happened to look like a leopard.

In other words, the cost of a false positive—"detecting" a pattern that wasn't—was minimal, whereas the cost of a false negative—failing to detect a pattern that was there—was high. Shermer claims that this evolutionary pressure creates a tendency toward superstitions. I've seen it in action.

Given a system on the verge of failure, administrators in operations have to proceed through observation, analysis, hypothesis, and action very quickly. If that action appears to resolve the issue, it becomes part of the lore, possibly even part of a documented knowledge base. Who says it was the right action, though? What if it's just a coincidence?

I once found a practice in the operations group for one of my early commerce applications that was no better than witchcraft. I happened to be in one of the administrator's cubicle when her pager went off. On seeing the message, she immediately logged into the production server and started a database failover. Curious, and more than a little alarmed, I asked what was going on. She told me that this one message showed that a database server was about to fail, so they had to fail over to the other node and restart the primary database. When I looked at the actual message, I got cold shivers. It said, "Data channel lifetime limit reached. Reset required."

Naturally, I recognized that message, having written it myself. The thing was, it had nothing at all to do with the database. It was a debug message (see *Debug Logs in Production*, on page 244!) informing me that an encrypted channel to an outside vendor had been up and running long enough that the encryption key would soon be vulnerable to discovery, just because of the amount of encrypted data that the channel had served. It happened about once a week.

Part of the problem was the wording of the message. "Reset required" doesn't say *who* has to do the reset. If you looked at the code, it was clear that the application itself reset the channel right after emitting that message—but the consumers of the message didn't have the code. Also, it was a debug message that I had left enabled so I could get an idea of how often it happened at normal volumes. I just forgot to ever turn it off.

I traced the origin of this myth back about six months to a system failure that had happened shortly after launch. That "Reset required" message was the last thing logged before the Sybase server went down. There was no causal connection, but there was a temporal connection. (There was no advance warning about the database crash—it required a patch from Sybase, which we had applied shortly after the outage.) That temporal connection, combined with an ambiguous, obscurely worded message, led the administrators to perform weekly database failovers during peak hours for six months.

Final Notes

Messages should include an identifier that can be used to trace the steps of a transaction. This might be a user's ID, a session ID, a transaction ID, or even an arbitrary number assigned when the request comes in. When it's time to read 10,000 lines of a log file (after an outage, for example), having a string to grep will save tons of time.

Interesting state transitions should be logged, even if you plan to use SNMP traps or JMX notifications to inform monitoring about them. Logging the state transitions takes a few seconds of additional coding, but it leaves options open downstream. Besides, the record of state transitions will be important during post-mortem investigations.

17.5 Monitoring Systems

Even the best use of logging can help only when the application is actually running. Dead processes log no tales. Neither do hung processes. For those, some entity outside the process itself must be watching—some black-box tool monitoring the health and well-being of the application and its host.

This is the domain of monitoring systems. Figure 39, *Conceptual View of a Monitoring System*, on page 249 depicts a vastly simplified view of a monitoring system. The essential components of this third-party inspector are agents that collect information, a reliable transport mechanism, and the display and processing of the information.

Most monitoring systems run agents on the hosts being observed. These agents perform periodic observations, including at least operating system performance statistics, process health, log file pattern matching, and port listeners. For UNIX hosts, they scan syslog and any other log files the administrator configures. On Windows hosts, the agents also scan the Windows event logs. In this example, an agent on the database server detects that the database is down. It fires an event to the message broker—an embedded component running as part of the monitoring system itself. The message broker notifies all active clients about the alert. In this case, an administrator's monitoring console—a client application that accesses the monitoring system —shows the alert as a textual message and a color change on the icon representing the database.

These agents are very good at detecting events they've been told to look for: patterns in log files, SNMP traps (covered in a moment), processes that are down or consuming more than their fair share of resources, filesystems that

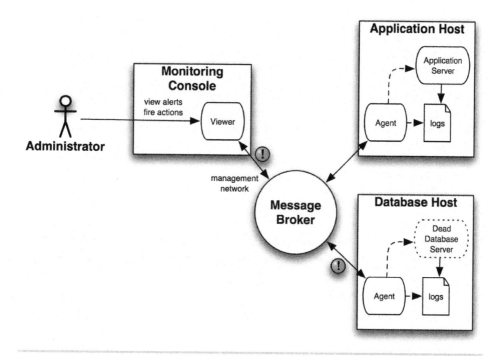

Figure 39—Conceptual View of a Monitoring System

are close to full, and so on. Unanticipated or novel behavior might not be detected, unless it triggers one of these events. For example, if all errors in a log file are reported with the same format, then unexpected errors can be caught. On the other hand, if one type of error isn't logged or is logged with a different format, then the monitoring system cannot catch it.

The agents are like reporters embedded with Army units. They are close to the action. One implication is that the agents themselves are at risk. Should the entire host go down, the agent surely goes with it. Therefore, monitoring systems always use some kind of heartbeat to detect a failed agent—or a network failure between the agent and the mothership.

Embedded reporters must have some way to submit their stories; the same is true for monitoring agents. Monitoring systems are critically dependent on their reliable message transport. In small-to-medium-sized corporate deployments, monitoring traffic sometimes crosses the same network segments as production traffic. This is a bad idea. For one thing, it means a problem with the production network—such as a network worm, DDoS attack, or plain old configuration error—automatically disables monitoring. Monitoring traffic often contains sensitive information. Even though it doesn't contain passwords,

Agentless Monitoring

Some monitoring systems advertise "agentless" installations, with the premise that obviating the need for agents on the hosts under observation reduces the CPU overhead of monitoring them. This is essentially a marketing ploy. Even if observations are collected from another host, they still require collaboration by the operating system on the observed host. For example, Microsoft's Operations Manager, MS MOM, can run in agentless mode. In this configuration, the management server uses the built-in event log and remote administration capabilities of the host under observation. So, the information gathering still happens, and it still consumes resources on the host under observation.

it often has hostnames, user names, internal IP addresses, snippets of log files, process names, and process IDs, among other things. None of these should be public, so they should not cross VLANs that carry public traffic.

Commercial Monitoring Systems

Previously, only massive enterprises were interested in the big commercial monitoring systems. Vendors such as IBM, Computer Associates, and Hewlett-Packard went after only multimillion-dollar deals in the Fortune 500. As the entire business world has shifted onto a 24-by-7 schedule, the systems have gotten bigger. At the same time, the vendors have discovered opportunities in new segments of the market. Hurricane Katrina in 2005 and the 9/11 attacks of 2001 raised awareness of the urgent need for business continuance plans and disaster recovery. (Many IT operations managers had been trying to raise this alarm well before Katrina, but disaster recovery planning never had "sex appeal" to CEOs and boards of directors until they saw companies going out of business for the lack of a plan.) The strict regulatory environment created by totalitarian implementations of Sarbanes-Oxley section 404[6] has also made security controls and monitoring more important than ever. This convergence of forces means that the commercial monitoring systems are now a standard part of doing business.

Gaps in Commercial Systems

The big vendors toolsets are stable, mature, and well supported. In the language of *Crossing the Chasm [Moo91]*, these systems have now penetrated

---

6. I find it endlessly entertaining that section 404 requires controls on sensitive information, and the ability to verify where every piece of financial information has come from, when a "404 error" means "not found" on the web. I'll warn you, though, that this joke seems to fall flat at most parties I've attended.

Enterprise Application Management

By and large, these systems focus on network and server management. A quick crop of smaller companies sprang up in the late 90s that focused on applications. Unlike their pre-Cambrian cousins, these considered application availability and performance primary determinants of the user's experience. Big fish ate small fish, and these small companies have disappeared from the market. The major vendors—HP, EMC, BMC, IBM, CA (you can't play in this space unless you're big enough to be known by just two or three letters)—are now integrating these application-aware products with their flagship suites to create the emerging enterprise application management (EAM) suites.

EAM suites combine network, server, and application awareness to (in theory) deliver complete visibility into your systems. They support the automatic discovery of dependencies by sniffing network packets and automatic performance baselining. EAM holds promise and might deliver great things, especially as they begin to further annex application lifecycle features such as configuration management, automated deployments, and load and stress testing. This segment of the market is evolving quickly.

even the "late mainstream"—absolutely the toughest market to sell technology to. If they have a flaw, it is in their orientation toward IT (but see *Enterprise Application Management*, on page 251). It is no longer acceptable—and, indeed, was never a good idea—to divorce the operation of production systems from business results.

Linking operations to business results requires the ability to correlate "systems" information with "business" information. For example, in a typical distributed system today, can you always identify which server provides a particular feature? Probably not. More likely, a single feature is served by groups of servers across multiple tiers. Therefore, the monitoring system should be aware not only of the systems but also of the business features those systems serve. In fact, it should be able to identify the impact to those features anytime there is a system event—whether that event is a problem or metric deviating from normal. So far, most of the commercial systems seem to assume that the application does not provide any visibility of its own. They are beginning to implement this type of awareness but have far to go.

If there's another major gap in these systems, it is that they can tell you only what the systems think is happening. It is totally possible for every component in the environment to be up and running by itself but still have bad results for the end user. This often happens in the event of blocked threads or cascading failures. Even if most users are served correctly, some users might have problems because of issues with their profiles, browsers, cookies, or other external factors. So far, the major systems do not represent an individual user's perspective on the system; they just represent the system's view of itself. There are some newer products (not yet swallowed by big fish) that put themselves in the users' perspective.[7]

Designing for Monitoring Systems

In almost every case, the selection of a monitoring system will be done for you. These are expensive systems that require pervasive implementation to deliver value. Once chosen and implemented, the system will be embedded deeply into IT operations for many years. That decision will outlast corporate commitments to operating systems, programming languages, hardware vendors, and org charts. In other words, the probability of the monitoring system being "in play" at the same time as you are designing a new system is vanishingly small. Therefore, the monitoring system becomes part of the environment for which you design.

In such an environment, it would be easy to build in support for that particular monitoring system, resulting in tight coupling and vendor lock-in. You can avoid those pitfalls by designing to a small set of applicable standards, both official and de facto.

17.6 Standards, De Jure and De Facto

The world of monitoring systems is dominated by standards. Oddly, these standards don't seem to provide as much interoperability as you might expect. Let's look at SNMP, the 800-pound gorilla of monitoring standards, as well as some up and coming contenders.

Simple Network Management Protocol

The granddaddy of standards around monitoring and system management is definitely the Simple Network Management Protocol (SNMP). SNMP dates back to 1988, with SNMP version 1. Although it was originally written specifically for management of network devices (which is why "Network" appears in the name), SNMP has expanded far beyond its original boundaries. It can now be used with everything from carrier-grade Cisco routers that handle half the traffic of the Internet down to USB peripherals.

Even in its first version, the "Simple" in SNMP really was a bit of spin. SNMP has a conceptual elegance that makes it simple in the same sense that LISP

---

7. Tealeaf, for example. See http://www.tealeaf.com/.

Ambient Awareness

In *Ambient Displays: Turning Architectural Space into an Interface between People and Digital Information [WIDG98]*, some researchers from MIT's Media Lab argue for ambient displays. These include subtle sounds, lighting, and patterns of movement such as ripples in water, each mapped to some piece of data. For example, a pinwheel might map to incoming traffic on a website. The soundscape could represent the internal health of the systems.

When everything is normal, the inhabitant's perception of the sounds fades into the background, just as the sound of crickets on a summer evening fades into the background. Part of the human brain's great pattern recognition system suppresses unchanging input, at least when it is nonthreatening. Even better, after a day or two in the environment, the inhabitant will automatically understand what "normal" sounds like, just like the shipboard engineer.

When the underlying data changes, the ambient display mapped to that data changes its sound or pattern. Imagine those crickets suddenly fell silent. The crickets chirping might fade into the background but would not disappear entirely. At some level, awareness remains, and the sudden silence would seem shockingly loud.

Not everyone can live in the MIT Media Lab, but there is an open source project to provide ambient awareness through soundscapes. Peep[a] can monitor states and events on a network and turn them into pleasant sounds of brooks and birds. That project hasn't seen a new release in more than four years. It seems to be languishing in neglect, just waiting for someone new to pick up the torch.

The *Pragmatic Project Automation [Cla04]* site has many posts about physical devices used to monitor the health of a system (typically a build server). See http://www.pragmaticautomation.com/cgi-bin/pragauto.cgi/Monitor/Devices for lots of ideas. On a previous project, my team was inspired by this site. We wired up a stoplight to monitor our build server. "When the light is green, the build is clean."

---

a.   See http://peep.sourceforge.net/.

is simple: it's one idea, distilled to its purest essence and then applied to every possible problem. Internalize that concept, *grok* it, and the rest becomes clear and simple. Before you grok it, it just seems kludgy. SNMP's essential concept is "Everything is a variable." Everything a node can report on or do is a variable. There are no commands, just variable assignments.

Instead of telling a device to do something, SNMP sends a "set request" asking the device to set the variable to a desired state. For example, using SNMP to tell a Packeteer traffic shaper about a new trap receiver looks like a write to a variable called 1.3.6.1.4.1.2334.2.1.6.2.0, also known as trapDestAdd. (You have to be part of a standards committee to come up with names like 1.3.6.1.4.1.2334.2.1.6.2.0.)

Although SNMP refers to itself as a protocol, the full standards define much more than just a network protocol. The RFCs that define SNMP also define an information model and a kind of metastandard about how new modular portions of the information model might be defined.

The information model is called the Structure of Management Information. It defines the Management Information Base (MIB). The Internet Assigned Numbers Authority[8] (IANA) maintains the master list of module owners at http://www.iana.org/assignments/smi-numbers. In another display of overloaded nomenclature, the modular definitions are usually also referred to as MIBs. Vendors provide MIBs to describe the management interface to their devices and software. Here is a portion of the MIB defined by Packeteer:[9]

transparency/packeteer.mib
```
trapDestAdd OBJECT-TYPE
    SYNTAX DisplayString
    ACCESS write-only
    STATUS mandatory
    DESCRIPTION
        "A shortcut for adding a host to trapDestTable.  If the name is not
        in n.n.n.n IP address form, then the agent attempts to look it up
        via DNS.  If the operation fails with BADVALUE, try again with
        an IP address.  The associated
        IP address is added to the trapDestTable if the operation succeeded.
        The table should be queried afterward to
        insure that the action took place.  "
    ::= { psAdmin 2}
```

As you can see, MIBs are defined by a portable language.[10] Given a MIB, the monitoring system knows how to talk with a device or application. (The MIB usually has to be compiled into a proprietary format first, as part of importing it into the monitoring system.) Armed with the MIB's definitions of tables, types, and variables, the monitoring system can define thresholds, triggers, and alerts based on the present status of the observed system. SNMP also allows the "agent"—the daemon or library on the server that handles SNMP itself—to notify the monitoring system asynchronously when interesting or alarming events occur. These alerts are referred to as *traps*. Traps are less versatile than variables; they mainly serve to get the monitoring system's attention.

---

8. See http://www.iana.org.

9. From http://www.packeteer.com/support/resources/utilities/mibs/8.0/packeteer.mib.

10. ASN.1, if you're interested. See http://www.asn1.org/.

Many software vendors have gotten on board with SNMP. Microsoft has an SNMP service available for Windows that allows any Windows 2000 (or later) computer to expose itself (as if they weren't exposed enough already). There's an SNMP module for Apache. It's built in to both WebSphere and WebLogic. Oracle supports several MIBs, both standard and private.

So, what does all this mean for your systems? Using any of these platforms automatically brings a high degree of SNMP support and, therefore, immediate transparency. Using an SNMP-based monitoring system together with SNMP-supporting platforms provides immediate exposure for thousands of variables. The monitoring system will also allow you to define the thresholds and policies about alerts that reveal both instantaneous behavior and abnormal status.

For your application code, however, the picture is far less rosy. The trouble is that creating a MIB for custom software is a huge undertaking of a very specialized nature. Even if you do write your own MIB, the administrators of the monitoring system are often reluctant to install MIBs from "untrusted" parties. (I don't know why it should be the case that a development group can be trusted to create applications responsible for millions of dollars in revenue but cannot be trusted to create a plug-in MIB for the monitoring system. Nevertheless, I've often seen strenuous resistance from these administrators.)

Beyond that, after you create the MIB, you must have an SNMP agent embedded in your application that can bridge between the SNMP variables and the objects in your application, as shown in Figure 40, *SNMP Communication Structure*, on page 256. (Even though the standards define port 161 as standard for an agent, it is possible to run multiple SNMP agents, each on their own port.) Even though SNMP refers to MIB variables as *objects*, they're really more like C structs. A MIB essentially defines a big pile of global variables —some are arrays, and some are structs—that don't necessarily map well into objects.

In the Java community, SNMP compatibility is best achieved by writing application code to support the Java Management Extensions (JMX) and by using a JMX-to-SNMP connector.

CIM

In 1996, the Distributed Management Task Force[11] (DMTF) introduced a successor and competitor to SNMP in 1996. Called the Common Information Model (CIM), this model replaces the awkward ASN.1 and MIB structure with

---

11. See http://www.dmtf.org.

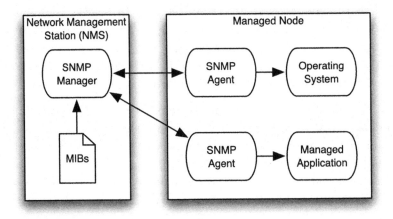

Figure 40—SNMP Communication Structure

a metaobject protocol and a brokered structure that allows for the dynamic registration and discovery of managed resources.

In many ways, CIM is technically superior to SNMP. CIM's object-oriented model is a more natural fit for today's programming styles, and its dynamic discovery of capabilities means that management platforms will no longer need to be "big-bang" purchases.

At this point, CIM is far less widely implemented than SNMP. So far, most operating system vendors are supporting CIM, including Microsoft, Sun, HP, and IBM. Linux support exists but is not generally integrated into distributions. Many hardware vendors are supporting CIM for their enterprise-class lines. Some application vendors support it, notably Oracle. Application-level support is far from widespread, however, which is the major reason that I still regard CIM as a future concern rather than something to address today.

JMX

Java Management Extensions (JMX) has historically been one of the most overlooked, underappreciated APIs in Java. Introduced in 1998 as JSR 3, it was initially expected to be part of the Java Enterprise Edition only. As time has passed, JMX has proven its value to such a degree that it became part of the Standard Edition as of JDK 1.5. Every JVM running Java 5 or later will automatically be JMX-enabled.

Where SNMP resembles procedural languages, with its global variables, structs, and tables, JMX presents an object-oriented view of managing applications. The fundamental unit of management is an MBean, a kind of "management

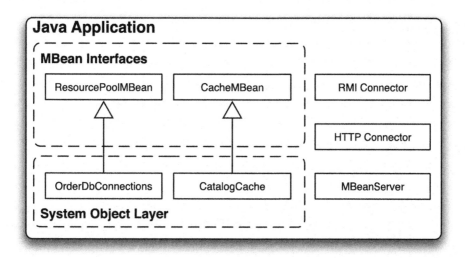

Figure 41—MBeans as Proxies

proxy" for some underlying system object, as shown in Figure 41, *MBeans as Proxies*, on page 257. Public properties—in the JavaBean sense of the word—and methods of the MBeans can be invoked remotely.

MBeans have names, registered with an MBeanServer. It sits between the external connectors that allow remote access and the internal MBeans. External connectors adapt protocols such as HTTP and RMI to calls on the MBeanServer itself. (It is also possible to call the MBeanServer from within the same JVM as the managed resources. Application code should not be doing this. It is an utterly circuitous way of talking to yourself.) Using the RMI connector, it is possible to retrieve a remote proxy representing the managed bean. Methods invoked on the remote proxy get invoked on the managed bean itself. These can be simple property accessors or control methods.

Figure 42, *Sample MBean Interface*, on page 258, shows a simple management interface for a circuit breaker component. The setResetTime(long timestamp) and getResetTime() methods define a property, JavaBeans style. The reset() method forces a state transition in the managed object. This is just an interface, so there must be some class implementing it. Indeed, the object being managed typically implements this interface. Figure 43, *MBean Interface Implemented*, on page 259, shows an example of a managed resource. This means that a direct use of JMX leaves the code "aware" of its future as a closely watched application under management.

transparency/CircuitBreakerMBean.java

```
package com.example.util;

import java.io.IOException;

public interface CircuitBreakerMBean {
        public void setResetTime(long timestamp) throws IOException;
        public long getResetTime() throws IOException;

        public CircuitBreakerState getState() throws IOException;

        public void reset() throws IOException;
}
```

Figure 42—Sample MBean Interface

Another type of MBean—the "dynamic MBean"—does not require compile-time information. Similar to CORBA's Dynamic Invocation Interface or Java's own reflection API, dynamic MBeans get to describe their own methods, rather than being stuck with a static, compile-time definition. This means that a sufficiently generic dynamic MBean should be able to act as a management proxy for any old Java object. Sure enough, the StandardMBean does exactly that. Given an object and an interface class, it becomes an MBean, exposing that interface on that object. This is absolutely the fastest way to add JMX support to your application, with the added benefit of removing the JMX pollution from the system objects themselves.

Prior to Java 5 (JDK 1.5), JMX was an extension. To use it, applications had to include some implementation of the JMX specification. The most common were the JMX Reference Implementation from Sun and the open source MX4J project. Since Java 5, JMX has been integrated into the JVM itself, so any application can now draw on the MBeanServer.

Although still little used by application developers, JMX has gained broad support among platform developers. JBoss's kernel has shrunk to nothing more than a JMX-based registry and module loader. IBM WebSphere uses JMX to expose itself. BEA WebLogic sits somewhere in the middle; significant parts of WebLogic are activated and managed by JMX, but not to the radical extreme of JBoss. Since version 1.2, the Spring framework has provided an automatic dynamic MBean generator. In typical Spring fashion, it requires a bunch of squirrely XML and no code. (OK, the XML eventually makes sense, but like an Oracular prophecy, it makes sense only in retrospect.)

```
transparency/CircuitBreaker.java
package com.example.util;

public class CircuitBreaker implements CircuitBreakerMBean {
        private CircuitBreakerState state = CircuitBreakerState.CLOSED;
        private long resetTime = -1;

        public void setResetTime(long timestamp) {
                this.resetTime = timestamp;
                checkForReset();
        }

        public long getResetTime() {
                return resetTime;
        }

        public CircuitBreakerState getState() {
                return state;
        }

        public void reset() {
                setState(CircuitBreakerState.CLOSED);
        }

        ...
}
```

Figure 43—MBean Interface Implemented

JMX support in these platforms brings one of the best benefits: scriptability. Oracle and IBM have both created command-line shells that access MBeans through the remote connectors. Oracles's WSLT and IBM's wsadmin both provide scriptable shell interfaces to MBean-enabled application servers. (See Section 14.4, *Administrative Interfaces*, on page 214 for my rant about graphical administration interfaces.) JBoss has "twiddle," which is not a complete shell but does allow invocation of commands on arbitrary beans.

Make administration interfaces scriptable.

It's remarkably tough to get praise from people in operations. They're a hard-bitten lot. Nevertheless, make your application's administrative functions scriptable, and they will bless your name. I cannot overstate the value of a scriptable administration interface. Providing a useful set of MBeans through JMX is the easiest way you can offer scriptable administration for Java applications.

JMX Gone Berserk

The full JMX specification permits much more sophisticated behavior than most application developers will ever need. MBeans can be instantiated dynamically, which might cause entire subsystems to be activated. Domain objects can have their own MBeans, which pop up and disappear dynamically. Model MBeans are so dynamic that they don't even exist at compile time—they are assembled by defining the interface programmatically and attaching any object whatsoever.

In terms of creating a transparent application, MBeans serve well when attached to long-lived components of the application's architecture: resource pools, caches, repositories, interfaces to external systems, and so on.

These dynamic, whizzy features really pay off for platform developers—the open source crew working on JBoss, the hordes of true-blue WebSphere developers in IBM—but they have little value for application developers. Odds are, if you're *that* far into JMX, you've gotten lost in the weeds. Back up, take a cleansing breath, and start working on a story card instead of polishing JMX's tail fins.

What to Expose

If you could predict which metrics would limit capacity, reveal stability problems, or expose other cracks in the system, then you could monitor only those. There are two problems with that prediction. First, you're likely to guess wrong. Second, even if you guess right, the key metrics change over time. Code changes and demand patterns change. The linchpin a year from now might not even exist now.

Within the application, the ideal is to expose every state variable, counter, and metric. Since you don't know what you'll need down the road, expose everything. Since you can't predict what the thresholds should be or how to react when they're breached, you should stick to providing visibility. Leave the policy for later. Provide universal visibility now, but externalize the policy so you can defer those decisions.

Of course, you could spend an unlimited amount of effort creating MBeans or SNMP variables for absolutely everything. Since your system still has to *do* something other than just collecting data, I've found a few heuristics to help decide which variables or metrics to expose. Some of these will be available right away. For others, you might need to add code to collect the data in the first place. Here are some things I've consistently found useful.

Traffic indicators

Page requests total, page requests, transaction counts, concurrent sessions

Resource pool health

Enabled state, total resources,[12] resources checked out, high-water mark, number of resources created, number of resources destroyed, number of times checked out, number of threads blocked waiting for a resource, number of times a thread has blocked waiting

Database connection health

Number of SQLExceptions thrown, number of queries, average response time to queries

Integration point health

State of circuit breaker, number of timeouts, number of requests, average response time, number of good responses, number of network errors, number of protocol errors, number of application errors, actual IP address of the remote endpoint, current number of concurrent requests, concurrent request high-water mark

Cache health

Items in cache, memory used by cache, cache hit rate, items flushed by garbage collector, configured upper limit, time spent creating items

All of the counters have an implied time component. You should read them as if they all end with "in the last n minutes" or "since the last reset."

JMX and SNMP Together

JMX was built to support different connectors and protocol adapters. It seems only natural to open Java applications up to SNMP through JMX itself. Indeed, several JMX-to-SNMP connectors are available, of varying quality. AdventNet (http://www.adventnet.com) appears to be the market leader in this (admittedly small) space.

The largest challenge such a connector must overcome is not bridging the protocols. Mapping the protocol operations between SNMP and JMX is trivial. After all, SNMP really has only three types of operation: get variable, set variable, and enumerate variables. Recall that SNMP's information model is based on a schema of variables, tables, and structures. JMX is object-oriented. The JMX-to-SNMP connector bridges this impedance mismatch. It must determine which variables map to properties on MBeans, which variables will trigger method calls, and how to turn collections of objects into entries in a table. Finally, the JMX-to-SNMP connector must also map JMX's notifications (asynchronous events) to SNMP traps.

---

12. This applies to connection pools, worker thread pools, and any other resource pools.

The result is a fully configured SNMP agent that uses the MBeanServer inside the JVM, and a MIB for import into the monitoring system. Once that hurdle is cleared, integrating a JMX-enabled Java application into an SNMP-based monitoring system is trivial.

17.7 Operations Database

Logging and monitoring are both good for exposing and understanding the immediate behavior of an application or system. Neither is particularly good at serving the historical or future perspective. Figure 44, *Suitability for Purpose of Transparency Technologies*, on page 263, judges each of these approaches against the four perspectives. It is possible to derive a system's current status from log files alone, but it's very difficult, since it requires tracing backward for the last state transition for each relevant status variable. (Of course, spitting out the status variables on a recurring timer would aid this analysis.)

Monitoring systems are great at representing instantaneous behavior. They do a good job of representing present status, but, as I discussed in *Gaps in Commercial Systems*, on page 250, they serve only one constituency. When it comes to historical and future trends, they have a way to go. Until the enterprise application management suites mature, I have to consider this a gap.

Figure 45, *Role of the Operations Database*, on page 263, introduces a complementary technology that serves the time-oriented views of the system. This "operations database"[13] (OpsDB) accumulates status and metrics from all the servers, applications, batch jobs, and feeds that make up the extended system. It provides the "single pane of glass" that can present business-oriented metrics in the dashboard, system statistics, and, best of all, the correlations between them. Whereas logging provides visibility into a single application, the broader view of the OpsDb unifies status and metrics reporting across the entire system.

The OpsDB serves as a source for the ever-popular dashboard, for the present status crowd. Because it contains demand metrics as well as system metrics, a few exercises in data mining will reveal the correlation factors needed for capacity planning. The historical record contained in the OpsDB also allows automatic baselining to determine what "normal" looks like for the metrics across the site.

---

13. I'd love to call it an "operational data store," but that name is already taken for something else.

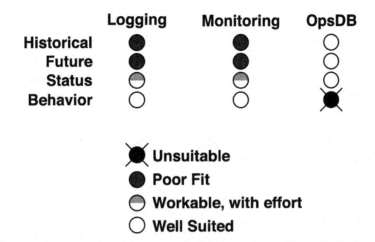

	Logging	Monitoring	OpsDB
Historical	●	●	○
Future	●	●	○
Status	◒	◒	○
Behavior	○	○	✖

✖ **Unsuitable**

● **Poor Fit**

◒ **Workable, with effort**

○ **Well Suited**

Figure 44—Suitability for Purpose of Transparency Technologies

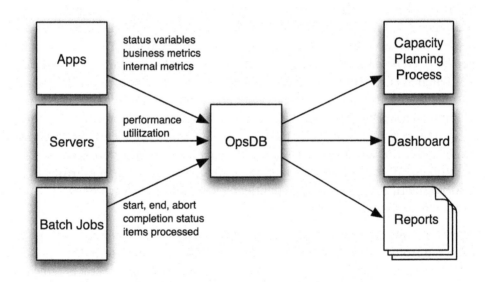

Figure 45—Role of the Operations Database

The records of job execution make troubleshooting faster when application-level problems arise, such as stale data from a channel partner. Examining the normal start and end times, and correlating them with the number of items processed, also illustrates when we should expect jobs to complete and if any of them are in danger of breaking their windows.

OpsDb High-Level Structure

Figure 46, *OpsDb Object Model: Observations*, on page 265 shows the UML class diagram representing the information in the OpsDb.[14] Mapping this object model to a SQL schema is left as an exercise for the reader (in part, because the form of that mapping should be driven by your particular ORM tool and database server).

A Feature represents a unit of business-significant functionality. These should be the same features the system's availability SLAs are written about and the same ones that capacity planning will be measuring.

A Feature does not come from a server. A single Feature is probably implemented across at least three hosts (web, application, and database), applications on each tier, a pair of firewalls, a network switch, and a storage array or SAN. The Node class represents any of these active nodes. In practice, it is usually sufficient to represent the hosts and applications. If the system includes hardware firewalls, SSL accelerators, content caching servers, or other network equipment that plays an active role in delivering the application (mainly with respect to layer 7 interactions), then it probably pays to include them as nodes. Each Node has its own unique ID. The individual servers, applications, and batch jobs use this ID when reporting their observations, so it is important to track them carefully. (I find that assigning blocks of IDs to particular teams or subteams works well. That keeps their node IDs contiguous and lets them use up their node IDs without having to wait for a new allocation.) Nodes use other Nodes, but capturing these dependencies can be burdensome, so this is optional. If you use them, Node dependencies can be a powerful aid to troubleshooting. Those same dependencies are the pathways by which cascading failures will propagate.

Observations are the heart of the OpsDb. Each Observation is a single data point collected from a Node. For server nodes, the observations are mainly performance statistics, which are recorded as Measurements. A Measurement is typically periodic, and all records are kept. For an application, these will include performance statistics as well as the status of important system objects. For example, an application server should record its database connection pool high-water mark and resources checked out (among other things), but it

---

14. Readers of Martin Fowler's *Analysis Patterns [Fow96]* will recognize this as similar to the Observation pattern. That pattern described a medical diagnosis system for assessing the health or diseases of a patient. The concepts transfer directly. Here, instead of a human patient, you are dealing with networked computer systems—a far less complex animal.

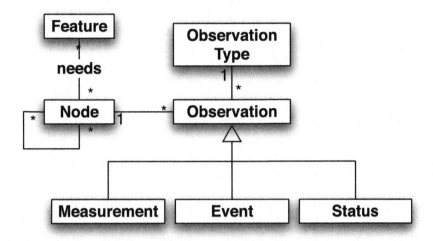

Figure 46—OpsDb Object Model: Observations

should also record the state change from "enabled" to "disabled." Likewise, a circuit breaker should record each of its state transitions. State transitions are recorded as Status objects. For a dashboard (present status), only the last Status entry is of interest. For troubleshooting or historical trending, the frequency and type of state changes is often significant.

Every Observation requires an ObservationType to make sense. The set of all ObservationTypes defines the universe of information in the OpsDb. ObservationType defines the name and concrete subtype of the Observation.

Feeding the Database

I recommend creating a client-side API to feed observations to the OpsDb. This should be in whatever language most of the system will be in. Above all, keep it simple. Everything can fail, including this new database. It is not critical to the financial success of the system, so there is absolutely no reason that a failure in the OpsDb should have a noticeable effect on the system's primary function.

If the system includes shell scripts or batch files, they will need to invoke some command-line utility for writing to the OpsDb.

The script should call the command-line at start-up time, with a record of how many items need work. When finished, it should record how many items were actually processed (as opposed to the number that had issues). If the job fails completely, it should record an abnormal termination.

If this is a Java system and you are feeling ambitious, you could write a generic MBean to record periodic samples. It could even receive notifications about state changes and record them, too. Then, instrumenting any application would just be a matter of instantiating and configuring that MBean.

Using the Operations Database

Once a body of data has built up in the OpsDb, it becomes even more useful. Figure 47, *OpsDb Expectations*, on page 267, adds new classes to the model from Figure 46, *OpsDb Object Model: Observations*, on page 265. (Feature and Node are omitted from this diagram, but they still exist.)

An ExpectationType corresponds to an ObservationType. It defines the name and characteristics of its Expectation. An Expectation represents an allowed range for a metric, a time frame in which an event must (or must not) occur, or an allowed status. Violating any of these expectations should trigger alerts in the monitoring system.

The best source for the expectations is the same historical data already contained in the database. Expectations should be set to match reality so you can avoid the negative effects of false positives.

In the beginning, expectations can be somewhat loose. Over time, as processes come under better control, those expectations can be tightened and made more sophisticated. For example, an early expectation for "web server CPU utilization" could state that ">0% and <80%" is acceptable. As you learn more about the system linkages, that expectation can be tightened to ">5% and <50%." At the next level of maturity, the business rhythm can come into it, either as a continuous envelope or as a step function. For example, as a step function, that expectation can require low CPU utilization during the night, moderate in the morning, and high in the mid-afternoon. Deviation greater than *or less than* that expectation would trigger alerts.

Over time, the OpsDb allows the system to grow more mature and introspective. It will know itself better and know how it should react to external stimuli.

For large systems, the OpsDb can accumulate a lot of data over time. Don't forget about the Steady State stability pattern. (See *Steady State*, on page 99.) If you don't condense the data, your system will eventually bog down in data collection. Obviously, it's not good to jeopardize capacity because you're keeping too much ancient performance data. (What's ancient? That depends on your system, but I'd say that minute-by-minute samples older than a week are not helpful.)

The Danger of False Positives

In *Inviting Disaster [Chi01]*, James Chiles relates the story of a plant supervisor who saw an operator reflexively override a warning chime in a control room. When confronted, the operator vehemently denied that he had done so, not because he feared consequences but because he had no conscious recollection of shutting off the warning. The system had trained him to so completely disregard the chime that he could shut it off without being aware of doing so.

I commonly hear from developers or managers who wear pagers. One woman told me that her pager went off three times every night. She knew that indicated normalcy. If the third page did not come in by a certain time of night, she knew there was a problem. If a fourth page arrived, she knew there was a problem. That's a form of situational awareness that might be better than nothing, but I can't endorse it as a way of life.

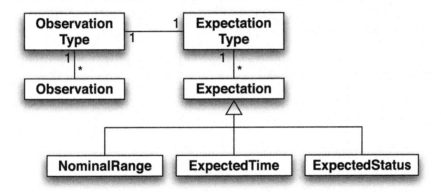

Figure 47—OpsDb Expectations

17.8 Supporting Processes

How many times have you seen this one: some reporting system generates a report and sends it to a distribution list, and half the people on the list have a rule in Microsoft Outlook that automatically deletes the report? It's classic. Of course, anytime I see that, I immediately know that the report is useless. In fact, it's probably worse than useless. Not only does it take time and effort to generate the report, but somebody has to maintain that report through changes in the underlying system. Worse still, once in a blue moon, the report might actually show something serious, but all of the supposed consumers of the report stopped reading it long ago.

That report is an example of transparency without a closed-loop feedback process. It costs money to implement and operate but provides no value. It creates a false sense of security. The best data in the world can't help if nobody is looking. In this section, I will take a step back from the systems themselves to discuss the larger dynamic system: the organization that is creating and operating these computer systems.

An effective feedback process can be described as "acting responsively to meaningful data." Transparency in the systems only provides access to the data. Humans in the loop still need to view and interpret the information.

Various forms of feedback loops exist in different schools of process, such as the Deming Cycle's[15] spiral through "Plan-Do-Check-Act" or John Boyd's nonlinear "O-O-D-A."[16] Ultimately, they all boil down to some execution of each of the following:

- Examine the system: current state, historical patterns, and future projections.

- Interpret the data. This always occurs within the context of some person's mental model of the system.

- Evaluate potential actions, including the costs of each and, perhaps, taking no action at all.

- Decide on a course of action.

- Implement the chosen course of action.

- Observe the new state of the system.

Keys to Observation

First and foremost, observers should watch for both trends and outliers. Both provide insight. It helps to build an operational rhythm that makes improvement a routine occurrence rather than a spasmic effort. Here are a few helpful routines to aid observations:

- Every week, review the past week's problem tickets. Look for recurring problems and those that consume the most time. Look for particular subsystems that cause a lot of problems or a development team (if there is more than one). Look for problems related to a particular third party or integration point.

---

15. See *Deming and Goldratt [LC99]*.
16. See *Certain to Win [Ric04]*.

Colonel John Boyd and O-O-D-A

This style of feedback process draws directly from the work of Colonel John Boyd, an Air Force pilot and strategist. Col. Boyd's key concept was the "O-O-D-A Loop," an acronym for Observe-Orient-Decide-Act. Boyd argued that complete knowledge of a situation is impossible and, even if it were attainable, quickly irrelevant. He viewed the battlefield situation as fluidly, even chaotically, changing. In that realm, victory would go to the force best able to react and control the changing tactical and strategic dynamics.

The O-O-D-A Loop requires correct observations, unclouded by wishful thinking or confirmation bias—definitely a tall order. Orientation is the process of updating a mental map of possibilities and options according to the previous map and the new observations.

Good orientation acknowledges what is possible and impossible. In the military and the corporation, political filtering of observations and orientation is fatal. "Spin" is antithetical to O-O-D-A, which requires engagement with the real environment, not a fanciful or idealized picture of the environment.

O-O-D-A contains many feedback steps. Observe, Decide, and Act all affect the actor's orientation. As you act, you change the external environment as well as your own understanding of the evolving conditions. In this way, the result of an iteration of O-O-D-A affects the next iteration in two ways: once through the environment itself and once through your own perception of the environment.

Each time through the loop, you know more than before, creating reinforcing feedback. Anytime you see reinforcing feedback loops, you should suspect that the system can go nonlinear and chaotic, in the modern sense of those words.

This capacity for chaos separates O-O-D-A from a mere stimulus/response reaction, where an increase in stimulus creates a proportional increase in response. Think trench warfare in World War I or trying to get faster software by "doing more process." You can gain tremendous creative power to disrupt your opponents by going through O-O-D-A faster than they can.

Boyd called this getting "inside" the enemy's decision cycle: both anticipating and constraining his actions.[a]

---

a.   I also view O-O-D-A as a powerful argument for agile development methods. Each development iteration should map to an iteration of O-O-D-A. The resulting control of the environment allows a company to take over the initiative and unravel the competition. See http://www.steveadolph.com/articles%20and%20papers/Adolph%202006%20agile%20lessons_final.pdf for a paper from Steve Adolph that further examines the connection between O-O-D-A and agile.

- Every month, look at the total volume of problems. Consider the distribution of problem types. The overall trend should be a decrease in severity as serious problems are corrected. There should also be an overall decrease in volume. (There will be a sawtooth pattern as new code releases introduce new problems.)

- Either daily or weekly, look for exceptions and stack traces in log files. Correlate these to find the most common sources of exceptions. Consider whether these indicate serious problems or just gaps in the code's error handling.

- Review help desk calls for common issues. These can point toward user interface improvements as well as places the system needs to be more robust.

- If there are too many tickets and help desk calls to review thoroughly, look for the top categories. Also sample tickets randomly to find the things that make you go "hmmm."

- Every four to six months, recheck that old correlations still hold true.

- At least monthly, look at data volumes and query statistics.

- Check the database server for the most expensive queries. Have the query plans changed for any of these? Has a new query hit the most expensive list? Either of these changes could indicate an accumulation of data somewhere. Do any of the most common queries cause a table scan? That probably indicates a missing index.

- Look at the daily and weekly envelope of demand (driving variables) and system metrics. Are traffic patterns changing? If you suddenly see that a popular time is dropping in popularity, it probably indicates that the system is too slow at those times. Is there a plateau in the driving variables? That indicates some limiting factor, probably responsiveness of the system.

Remember that the focus of interest will shift over time. In the early days, the issues will mainly be reactive. Ticket reviews, post-mortem reports from incidents, and recent trends will be of most interest. As root causes get corrected, as new code releases come out, and as traffic patterns change, the emphasis will shift from reactive to predictive analysis. What will happen next quarter? Where do you need to be this time next year? As this emphasis shifts, stop reviewing some old things, and start reviewing new trends. Once a metric stops producing useful information, stop reviewing it. Reports you live by one month after launch will be worthless—or even misleading—two years later.

For each metric being reviewed, consider each of the following. How does it compare to the historical norms? (This is easy if the OpsDb has enough data to start forming expectations.) If the metrics continues its recent trend, what happens to other correlated metrics? How long could the trend continue— what limiting factor will kick in? What will result from that limiting factor?

For example, consider the relationship between "orders received" and "application server CPU utilization." On any kind of retail site, these metrics will be correlated to some degree. ("Orders received" is a derivative of "unique visits." The beta of "orders received" to "unique visits" is just what the marketers call *conversion rate*.) Therefore, if you see "orders received" increasing, you can ask, "How long can that continue to increase?" The answer to this question should motivate interpretation and decision. The decision might be to do nothing, to add resources, to drive away customers, or to optimize the application code. Any of those decisions represent a successful conclusion of the feedback loop.

17.9 Summary

Strange things happen to systems when they encounter the real world. Anomalies and events can remain forever mysterious, or they can be valuable lessons learned. Transparency makes the difference between a system that improves over time in production and one that stagnates or decays.

Management systems are prevalent. SNMP version 3 currently dominates the landscape. CIM/WBEM overcomes many of SNMP's disadvantages and will be a major force in the near future. For Java developers, JMX offers a path into either the SNMP or CIM/WBEM world.

Transparency requires access to the internals of the computers and software. Exposing those internals is the first prerequisite. Next, some means for collecting and understanding the data points is required. This can be facilitated with the commercial monitoring systems and the OpsDb. Finally, some feedback process is needed to act on the acquired knowledge.

The next chapter examines what to do when transparency reveals a need for change. *Adaptation* takes the long view, examining how to build systems that can change gracefully over time.

... pity us all,
Who vainly the dreams of youth recall.
For of all sad words of tongue or pen,
The saddest are these: "It might have been!"

> *John Whittier*

CHAPTER **18**

Adaptation

No matter how bold the vision or how severe the crunch mode, the system that launches will always be less than it might have been. The new system is a flawed and diminished thing, barely suited to its purpose in life. Will it remain so, or will it grow into its creators' vision?

The true birth of a system comes not on the day that design and development begins, or even when the project is conceived, but on the day it launches into production. This is a beginning, not an end. Over time, the system will grow and mature. It will gain new features. It will lose defects and perhaps gain some, too. It will become what it was meant to be, or, even better, it will become what it needs to be. Most of all, it must change. A system that cannot adapt to its environment is stillborn.

18.1 Adaptation Over Time

The fledgling system must do some things right, or it would not have been launched, and it might do other things as well as the designers could conceive. Still other features might work as built but not as intended, or they might be more difficult than they should be. In essence, there are gaps and protrusions between the shape of the system and the solution space it is meant to occupy.

A new system does not automatically become better fitting through use. Most of the time, the system trains its users—painfully. The system can be changed to fit its solution space better—even as the solution space continues to change over time—thereby filling the gaps and filing the bumps, but only by deliberate action.

In *The Evolution of Useful Things [Pet92]*, Henry Petroski[1] argues that the old dictum "form follows function" is false. In its place, he offers the rule of design evolution, "form follows failure." That is, changes in the design of such commonplace things as forks and paper clips are motivated more by the things early designs do poorly than those things they do well. Not even the humble paper clip sprang into existence in its present form. Each new attempt differs from its predecessor mainly in its attempts to correct flaws.

In the world of software development, each new release is motivated by either new features (filling in gaps) or defects (filing down bumps). Just as the shape of the paper clip evolved over time, the architecture and design of software systems adapt over time in response to real and perceived failures in each iteration.

But, adaptation has a price. Any action to change the system has a cost: design, development, and testing effort, plus the cost of release. Physicists and chemists recognize this as "activation energy." If the cost of making these changes exceeds the value returned by filling a gap or removing a bump, then the rational choice is to *not* make the change. The value returned might be strictly in terms of cash flows. On the other hand, the value might lie in protecting the large investment already made in the system itself.

Cash flow: the lifeblood of every business. Money in, money out. Thanks to the time value of money, cash flows now are more valuable than cash flows in the future.

Finally, as a matter of simple economics, somewhere between 40% and 90% of a system's cost of development will be incurred after the first release. This might be labeled "maintenance," or it might be considered new development. Either way, development costs continue to appear long after release 1.0. This is an old, thoroughly recognized problem for design and architecture. The difficulty and cost incurred in releasing changes into the wild is less well understood.

The remainder of this chapter examines how small- and large-scale architecture choices affect a system's ability to adapt. These are the "implementation cost" portions of the activation energy. The balance of the activation energy requirement is the cost of releasing changes—a hidden cost that can mount to surprising levels. Our ultimate goal is to ensure that changes to our systems —filling the gaps and filing the bumps—release more cash than they consume.

Chemical reactions that produce more energy than is required to initiate them are called *exothermic*. We want changes to our systems to be exoeconomic, producing more money than is required to create them.

---

1. I have to admire any author who can enthrall me with eighteen pages on the emergence of the fork.

18.2 Adaptable Software Design

Thousands of pages have been written on the subject of adaptable software design. Dozens of named methodologies aim to produce software perfectly fitted to its functional space. Many of the newer of these even incorporate the principles of change over time under the rubric of "agile methods." It would be impossible to recapitulate them here.

The overwhelming majority of these methodologies focus on creating the correct functionality or allowing functionality to change over time. However, there are some other aspects of software design, related to a system's ability to adapt without disrupting production operations. We'll look at those aspects here. Think of these issues as an "overlay" that you should consider on top of whatever design methods you choose to employ.

Dependency Injection

There is power in names. When Martin Fowler gave a name to a relatively commonplace technique, the programming world suddenly blazed with "dependency injection" frameworks.[2] (See also AJAX.) The principle of dependency injection is simply that components should interact through interfaces and shouldn't directly instantiate each other. Instead, some other agency should "wire up" the application out of loosely coupled components.

Done well, dependency injection encourages loose coupling. To that extent, it has real power. It also facilitates unit testing, which is even better. Defining and using interfaces is the main key to successfully achieving flexibility with dependency injection. Objects collaborating through interfaces can have either endpoint swapped out without noticing. That swap can replace the existing endpoint with new functionality, or the substitute can be a mock object used for unit testing. Dependency injection using interfaces preserves your ability to make localized changes.

Object Design

It's amazing how much energy and emotion the phrase "good object-oriented design" can generate, even now, twenty years after the "object revolution" began. I will assert, without further proof, that there exists such a thing as good object-oriented design. Those who already believe in it will agree with me without evidence, and those who refute its existence would not be swayed by any argument I could offer.

---

2.   See http://www.martinfowler.com/articles/injection.html.

Dependency Injection

Back when J2EE started lumbering around the landscape, a number of framework developers started creating things such as Pico, Spring, and Apache Avalon. They had a markedly different quality to them than typical J2EE applications did. In particular, applications written with these "lightweight" frameworks tended to focus on small, stand-alone components that implemented interfaces. These components did not instantiate other components directly. Instead, they called other services through interfaces and just "assumed" that an implementation of that interface would be provided by the container.

At first, this was described as Inversion of Control, a commonly identified characteristic of application frameworks. Inversion of Control as commonly practiced in framework design, however, applies to the more general practice of extending a framework by plugging application code in as subclasses or callbacks, thereby placing the framework in control rather than the application code. (The framework calls into the application, which is the characteristic inversion that distinguishes a "framework" from a "class library.")

Martin Fowler popularized the term *dependency injection* to describe the case of, well, injecting references into components. The container wires components together at runtime based on a configuration file or application definition. The components themselves do not need to know exactly to whom they're talking. Dependency injection leads to highly adaptable code that can be easy to unit test and easy to "rewire" as requirements change over time.

In the context of adaptation, the best rules to follow are those crusty old proscriptions: loose coupling and tight cohesion. When originally written, those rules applied to source modules. Loose coupling meant "Don't touch another file's global variables." Tight cohesion meant "Most or all of the subroutines in this file should use most or all of the file's global variables." It seems that the rules could use a bit of updating.

The modern object-oriented definition of coupling has more to do with behavior than variables. Whenever a class uses behavior from another class, it is coupled by that behavior. The number of behaviors that one class requires from another class defines the "width" of the interface between those classes.

Obviously, some degree of coupling is required. Objects that don't call each other can't do very much. So, what does "loose coupling" mean in this context? Consider all the public methods exposed by a class. Now look at the subsets of those methods that are called by other classes. A perfectly cohesive class will have just one set, containing all the methods, that are called by all users of the class. This is highly unlikely. More likely, there are a small number of sets of methods. Different users of the class use different subsets of its methods. The more distinct these subsets are—that is, the fewer methods that are found across multiple subsets—the easier it will be to change the class's behavior later. It will be more adaptable. Not coincidentally, it will also be easier to create classless interfaces to group, name, and abstract out those subsets of methods.

With the methods grouped into subsets, cohesiveness describes how much of the object's internal state affects and is affected by the sets of methods. In other words, if a set of methods touches only a subset of the object's state but is unaffected by other aspects of the object's state, then the object is not cohesive. This might indicate there is another object hiding inside, waiting to be refactored into its own class.

Coupling affects adaptation more than cohesion. Highly coupled classes require more *external context* to be useful. For example, consider a simple geometry class representing a point in two dimensions. It is unlikely that the point requires any external context at all to function. It works fine by itself without the application setting up any other relationships or global state (such as singletons or object registries). In a sense, it is a brick; it can be used in the same way wherever you need something blocky to stack together.

Also, consider an overly smart domain object, such as a typical Customer object. It probably collaborates with three or four other classes, such as Account, Address, CreditCard, and perhaps others. If Customer also knows anything about its own persistence, it might collaborate with PersistenceManager, TableDataGateway, or others of that sort. Each of these collaborations is both necessary and problematic. Without them, the object is useless; with them, it depends on larger and larger substructures to be present and to be behaving in an expected manner. Rather than a brick, this is more like a jigsaw puzzle piece in many dimensions. It has knobs, sockets, and joints that must match up exactly with some other pieces to work.

A cluster of objects that can exist together only in a tight collaboration resembles a crystal in a metal. The objects stay together in a tightly bound relationship, just as the atoms in a crystal are tightly bound. In metal, small crystals mean greater malleability. More malleable metals recover from stress better. Large crystals encourage crack formation. In software, large "crystals" make it harder to change the software. When objects in one grain participate in multiple collaboration patterns, they bridge two crystals, forming a larger grained crystal—further reducing the malleability of the software.

There is no limit to how far this region of tightly bound crystals can spread. In the most extreme case, the crystal grows until it is the boundary of the

Collaborations and Design Patterns

It might sound as though I have a dim view of collaborations. Not at all. In fact, when it comes to object design, I am an avowed behaviorist. Collaborations are central. I do insist, however, that collaborations should be designed with an eye toward cohesiveness and reducing the crystal grain of the software. When I see an object that participates in multiple design patterns, each collaborating with a different group of objects, I see a Gordian knot that will be difficult or impossible to change.

Where different crystals need to be linked, those links should be minimized with as few ties across the boundary as possible.

This, by the way, is where many novices go wrong when applying newfound knowledge from the great book *Design Patterns [GHJV95]*. This book encourages a more collaborative, behavioral view of object interactions. The newly awakened object designer will be tempted to measure the quality of a design by how many patterns it employs, even though Gamma, et al, directly caution against this. Overloading pattern roles on a single object cause larger and larger crystal growth until the code base becomes one giant, rigid, rock.

application. When that happens, every object suits exactly one purpose to which it is supremely adapted. It fits perfectly into place and ultimately relates to every other object. These crystal palaces might even be beautiful in a baroque sort of way. They admit no improvement, in part, because no incremental change is possible and, in part, because nothing can be moved without moving every other object. These tend to be dead structures. Developers tiptoe through crystal palaces, speaking in hushed tones and trying not to touch anything.

XP Coding Practices

Programmers' religious wars are legendary: emacs vs. vi, tabs vs. spaces, VMS vs. UNIX, Java .vs .NET. To that list, we should now add agile methods vs. traditional methods.

Unfortunately, any religious war polarizes the passionate minority, leading the opposition—and the ambivalent majority that reacts with distaste—to reject an approach in its entirety. This clearly happens in the case of Extreme Programming (XP). Many developers and development managers have rejected XP as undisciplined or unrealistic. (They happen to be wrong, but that's a different book.) That's a shame, because they're cutting themselves off from two of the most valuable coding practices to be developed since object orientation was invented: refactoring and unit testing.

In *Refactoring [FBBO99]*, Martin Fowler collected and documented the growing practice. He called it "improving the design of existing code without changing its functionality." Far from an exercise in futility, refactoring is key to adaptability. Refactoring acts as a constant pressure to keep the design complexity at the minimum necessary to support the features of the software. It combats the spread of crystalization and promotes increasing levels of generalization in the core classes of the software.

Unit testing is the twin to refactoring. Indeed, many people argue that without unit tests, there is no such thing as refactoring. Changing designs without the safety net of the unit tests amounts to just random mucking around in the code base and is more likely to produce new bugs rather than design improvements.

The extreme form of unit testing is test-driven design (TDD). In TDD, you write the unit test first. It then serves as a functional specification. You write just enough code to make the test pass and not one line more. (See also YAGNI—"You Ain't Gonna Need It!") Once the test passes, you are allowed to refactor the code to improve the design, making sure that the unit tests always pass. The combination of TDD, refactoring, and YAGNI very naturally lead to a highly adaptable code base.

A second, more subtle effect is produced through consistent unit testing. You should never call an object "reusable" until it has been reused. When an object is subjected to unit testing, it is immediately used in two contexts: the production code and the unit test itself. This forces the object under test to be more reusable. Testing the object means you will need to supply stubs or mocks in place of real objects. That means the object must expose its dependencies as properties, thereby making them available for dependency injection in the production code. When an object requires extensive configuration in its external context (like the previously mentioned Customer object), it becomes difficult to unit test. One common—and unfortunate—response is to stop unit testing such objects. A better response is to reduce the amount of external context required. In the example of the Customer domain object, extracting its persistence responsibilities reduces the amount of external context you have to supply. This makes it easier to unit test and also reduces the size of Customer's crystal—thereby making Customer itself more malleable. The cumulative effect of many such small changes is profound.

Agile Databases

The term *agile databases* is not an oxymoron, but an agile database never happens accidentally. If there's an area of IT that resists change more than database schema definitions, it could only be CICS transactions on mainframes —you know, like the kind that can't be changed because the original programmer died in the late 70s.

If behavior is primary, then it is obvious that changing functionality in the application code requires corresponding changes to the database schema. Why then are databases so often resistant to change? First of all, beware that not everyone agrees that behavior is primary! Many organizations explicitly or tacitly argue that data is more important than application functionality.[3] Other organizations wall the database architects away from application developers. Each group thinks its needs trump the other's. Application developers want schema changes to adapt to the application's needs. Database architects view themselves as keepers of the data—not only its representation but also its essential meaning. What's more, the database itself often has multiple consumers, each with an embedded knowledge of the schema and its interpretation.

This is a false dichotomy. Neither behavior nor data can take absolute precedence. Programmers can and will invent their way around any obstructions, including a rigid schema. They will overload column definitions, add type indicators, or pack data into XML strings in CLOBs. They will implement relationships in code that have no referential integrity checking in the schema or invent coding schemes based on reference tables that exist only as "enum" types in the code. Changing behavior with an unchanging schema will result in ever more convoluted abuses of the schema, eventually resulting in uses that would make the data architect recoil in horror. This semantic pollution spreads to other consumers of the data, too, making their use of the data more complex and error-prone.

So, I have established that database schemas must change. Now, you need to consider how to make those changes as painless as possible. The first concern is the application code's own dependencies on the schema. Object/relational mapping makes it easy to update the application. There are, however, some limitations, particularly regarding versioning and version control. Starting an application against a database schema that doesn't match the ORM metadata produces unpredictable results. For example, Hibernate can be configured to verify that it's mapping files against the database's metadata at start-up, but this is time-consuming and depends on your database vendor's level of metadata support. If not verified at start-up, a

---

3. An early warning sign of these organizations will be data-flow diagrams or giant
    Zachman Framework charts.

schema-metadata mismatch will cause strange runtime errors that will either cause transaction rollbacks (with error reports to the users) or, worse, cause corrupted data.

Every schema should include a table that indicates the current structure revision. This table can be as simple as a single row with one column—the version number. At a minimum, applications should check for a compatible version number during start-up. Following the Fail Fast principle, the application should refuse to start if it can't use the database schema. The version number can also be used to trigger automated schema updates, such as Migrations in Ruby on Rails.[4] The version number will also be significant later in the zero-downtime deployment. Because the semantics of the data can change even without a direct change to the schema itself, be sure to bump the version number for changes in interpretation, too.

18.3 Adaptable Enterprise Architecture

Some architects aspire to create a modern day *Colossus: The Forbin Project* (or *Tron* if you're of my generation).[5] They labor under a vision of the seamless enterprise, working as a united machine. Every part is a necessary piece of the whole, perfectly suited to its role. Programs and programmers dwell inside the machine, serving its needs. I regard such utopians with deep suspicion.

Such an architecture proceeds from the top down, usually beginning with a giant framework like Zachman or TOGAF. They regard the architecture as an entity of its own, with mere systems filling in the cells of the enterprise architecture matrix. If this group has power, they will put projects on hold until the enterprise architecture is defined. If they do not have power, they will gnaw on their own livers as project after nonconforming project rolls into production without the benefit of their architecture.

This view rests atop two flawed assumptions. First, this assumes that the architecture can ever be finished. To state that the enterprise architecture is "in place" means an end to change. If the enterprise architecture stops changing, the organization will be frozen in time.

The only stasis is in death. Second, the top-down approach assumes that the organization can hold back time, denying change while the enterprise architecture is defined. This is costly in real terms and in opportunity cost.

---

4. See ActiveRecord::Migration in RDoc.
5. If *neither* of these rings a bell, then check out http://www.imdb.com.

To some extent, I'm exaggerating to make a point. My intention is not to create a straw man but to highlight the totalitarian tendency of the top-down architect. The notion of an enterprise as a cleanly integrated, well-defined whole implies a mechanistic view of systems. Large complex machines, however, exhibit many undesirable failure modes. They break often. They might be crippled when one part breaks. Designing and building such architectures *requires* the kind of command and control hierarchy that has failed time and time again.

Most damning, these require that changes occur simultaneously across widely separated groups—another application of Conway's law. As the number of these version-locked systems proliferates, the enterprise suffers from an exponential problem: each system is required to change when any of its counterparts changes (because that is the nature of tight coupling). In an extreme case, such as an enterprise service bus (ESB) protocol change, *every* participating system must upgrade simultaneously. Imagine the risks inherent in deploying a new release of every mission-critical enterprise system at the same time! In fact, the costs and risks associated with these changes are such that large-scale protocol changes will never happen. The ESB will either ossify or be subverted in the same way as the static database schema was at a smaller scale. Once it becomes sufficiently outdated, the ESB will be supplanted with some newer technology that claims to tame the cost of complexity.

Mechanistic metaphors for the enterprise trouble me. Mechanical systems exhibit exactly those attributes we don't want our organizations to share; they are both rigid and fragile. To avoid these attributes, we can draw inspiration from biological and ecological metaphors instead. I view an organization as an ecosystem. People and systems occupy niches in this ecosystem. They exchange resources with the environment, mainly in terms of information flows. Individual niches in the ecosystem might have more than one inhabitant. For instance, I've seen companies with no less than seven independent, partially interoperable implementations of SAP's ERP systems. Each one had its own geneaology, depending on which of the corporate acquisitions it came with. Each had its own constituents, food sources (systems that fed it data), and symbionts (systems that used its output). As is often the case, it was terribly inefficient but very robust. Each implementation could change independently of the others, allowing the individuals to adapt much more quickly than if they were developed under the "one and only one" view of the enterprise architects.

Real enterprises are always messier than the enterprise architecture would ever admit. New technologies never quite fully supplant old ones. A mishmash of integration technologies will be found, from flat-file transfer with batch processing to publish/subscribe messaging. Any strategy formulated predicated on creating a monoculture—whether it is a single integration technology or a single programming language—is doomed to be a costly failure. Imagine a company that *was* successful in imposing a single-language dictum. The entire company would be built on Ada, Smalltalk, Pascal, C, or some other old language. (The time needed for a language to gain enough currency to be selected ensures that it will be at least ten years old before it is a candidate for consideration. As an example of this pattern, I submit Java, which is now considered the "corporate-standard" language in a number of large IT shops.) Again, this artificial rigidity ensures that IT will not be serving its organization's needs.

> Ask, "Does this architecture make IT respond better to users' needs?"

In fact, the most useful criterion for evaluating architectures is this: "Does it make IT better at responding to its users' needs?" Most enterprise architectures are not constructed with this goal in mind. Rather, they are constructed with the needs of the IT group in mind. ("What's good for IT is good for the company.") With that end in mind, it's possible to let the enterprise architecture emerge from the patterns of interactions among the individual systems. I'm not suggesting total anarchy; that would not make IT better at responding to its users' needs either. Rather, there is a mix of forces in tension: budget pressure, schedule pressure, desire for features, direct and indirect costs of those features, technological mastery, and losses due to friction. Successful enterprise architecture requires a dynamic resolution of these forces—patterns of interactions that promote healthy organizations.

Dependencies Within a System

Systems should exhibit loose clustering. In a loose cluster, the loss of an individual is no more significant to the larger entity than the loss of a single tree in a forest. For example, losing one Apache instance out of a dozen has little impact on the overall service.[6] Likewise, losing a single application server instance should not matter to the health of the application or service being delivered.

---

6. Assuming adequate capacity exists (see Chapter 8, *Introducing Capacity*, on page 135).

This implies that individual servers do not have differentiated roles or at least that any differentiated roles are present in more than one service. WebLogic and WebSphere both violate this principle. They require the existence of unique nodes that manage clusters. Loss of these nodes is damaging to the overall service.

The members of a loose cluster can be brought up or down independently of each other. There should be no time-ordering requirements for the activation of the members of the cluster.

The members of one cluster or tier should have no specific dependencies—or knowledge of—the individual members of another tier. The dependencies should be on a virtual IP address or service name that represents the cluster as a whole. Direct member-to-member dependencies create hard linkages that prevent the endpoints from changing independently. Figure 48, *Dependencies on Services, Not Individual Instances*, on page 285, illustrates this notion. The calling application instances refer only to the service name provided by Cluster 2. The exact hosts and applications that supply this service should be unknown to the members of Cluster 1.

The members of a cluster should never need to know the identities of every other member in the cluster. This sets up an O(N^2) change requirement that makes it harder to add or remove members of the cluster. It also encourages one-to-many communication patterns, which are capacity killers. Broadcast notifications, such as cache invalidation messages, should go through a publish/subscribe topic or command queue.

Dependencies Between Systems: Protocols

Just as you saw with coupling between clusters of objects, coupling between systems in the enterprise can cause the same kind of calcification. Tight coupling among systems increases the barrier to change on each side of the interface. Once again, good architecture embraces the need for change as fundamental—an engine to drive improvement, rather than a beast to be controlled.

Any interface is defined by a protocol. It might be low-level, tossing packets at sockets; high-level, such as CORBA, DCOM, or RMI; or in between, such as XML over HTTPS. No matter the protocol, both ends of the interface must both speak and understand the same language. Sooner or later, the language will inevitably need to change. When that happens, one of two situations will result. In Figure 49, *Simultaneous Change at Both Endpoints*, on page 286, both systems change at the same time. This requires downtime for both

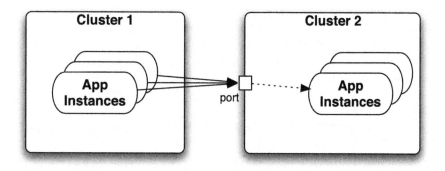

Figure 48—Dependencies on Services, Not Individual Instances

systems, since deployments are not instantaneous. If each system integrates with only the other, this might be acceptable (although it will make the zero-downtime deployment impossible). Once these systems develop the usual spiderweb of integrations with other systems, the change calendar starts to become untenable. Just the downtime required to support all the deployments becomes untenable.

Worse yet, each protocol revision requires enough lead time to get through a development cycle and a test cycle. Suppose that system Alpha from Figure 49, *Simultaneous Change at Both Endpoints*, on page 286, has a fast development team, using agile methods, on a two-week iteration. They will be able to adapt to the new protocol in about two weeks. But, if the development team behind Gamma takes anything more than two weeks, either because they have a longer iteration or because the current iteration is full, then Alpha must slow down to match Gamma's pace, and Gamma could be on a quarterly release cycle! Again, extrapolating to the other systems that Alpha integrates with shows that the fast, two-week development cycle will get throttled back to match the slowest development cycle in the enterprise.[7]

Clearly, there is value in avoiding this coupling. It has undesirable effects on the time to market, deployment cost, and system availability. We must design protocols so that either endpoint can change independently of the other. The solution lies in protocol versioning. Figure 50, *Independent Change at Each Endpoint*, on page 286, shows how Alpha and Gamma can change at different times. Clearly, there is a time during which Alpha is willing to speak and

---

7. In *The Goal [Gol04]*, Eli Goldratt describes this phenomenon when his character Alex watches a Boy Scout troop on a hike. No matter how the scouts are ordered, the fastest hiker ultimately gets throttled back to the speed of the slowest.

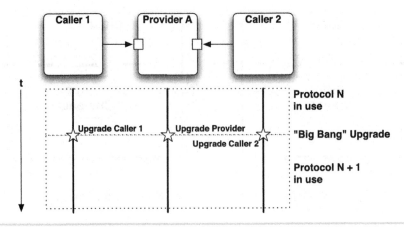

Figure 49—Simultaneous Change at Both Endpoints

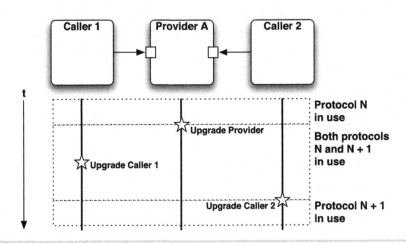

Figure 50—Independent Change at Each Endpoint

understand either version 1 or 2, but Gamma can speak and understand only version 1. Both systems have to agree on a compatible protocol version in order to work together. Good use of test harnesses (see *Test Harness*, on page 110) is helpful when ensuring that a system can handle all combinations of protocol versions it supports. The definition of a protocol version varies depending on the implementation technology. For low-level socket protocols —the kind that send a bag of bytes—the version should be part of early handshaking. Note that changes to the way the protocol version is sent will be next to impossible, so keep this part simple enough that it will not need to change. For remote object protocols, a system might expose multiple interface definitions simultaneously, bound to different names. XML-based protocols have an easy way to send and receive the protocol version and can be more challenging to implement internally, especially if using XML-to-object mapping tools.[8]

The same problem also holds for file format versions, though handshaking is not an option in that case. A system should be prepared to accept and generate old formats as needed. It should automatically detect the appropriate format on input. When the newer formats embody different semantics, there can be more than just a mapping problem here; defining format changes requires defining how to interpret older versions.

The duration of the overlap in Figure 50, *Independent Change at Each Endpoint*, on page 286 can be on the order of minutes or hours if it occurs only during the deployment of one of the systems. On the other hand, if Gamma's developers are on a quarterly (or worse) release cycle, it could be a long time.

Dependencies Between Systems: Databases

Integration databases—don't do it! Seriously! Not even with views. Not even with stored procedures. Take it up a level, and wrap a web service around the database. Then make the web service redundant and accessed through a virtual IP. Build a test harness to verify what happens when the web service is down. *That's* an enterprise integration technology. Reaching into another system's database is just...icky.

Nothing hobbles a system's ability to adapt quite like having other systems poking into its guts. Database "integrations" are pure evil. They violate encapsulation and information hiding by exposing the most intimate details about a system's inner workings. They encourage inappropriate coupling at both the structural and semantic levels.

Even worse, the system that hangs its database out for the world cannot trust the data in the database at all. Rows can be added or modified by other entities even while the owner has objects in memory mapped from those rows. Vital application logic can be bypassed, resulting in illegal or unreachable states.[9]

---

8. For example, JAXB generates XML schemas from objects, or vice versa. Keeping two sets of classes with the same names and different binding structures is really difficult. This is one reason I do not favor these tools.

9. The true database bigot will now pipe up that the database itself should be the repository of all business logic. I've heard that before. In principle, it seems plausible. Databases have Turing-complete languages available. In practice, it's the wrong logic in the wrong place with the wrong tools and processes for change.

A database with multiple systems accessing it becomes a nexus of rigidity. Every one of those systems must be upgraded simultaneously whenever the underlying schema changes. (Once again, the most likely outcome is that the schema just never changes.)

Still, sometimes other systems really do need access to large volumes of data from others. Maybe it's for reporting or business intelligence tools, or maybe it's for distribution to channel partners or financial analysis. In these cases, we can find a number of alternatives that do not incur the evil of reaching into the guts of another system.

Outside the trading floor, most purposes don't require immediate, up-to-the-second access to production data. If a need is expressed or perceived for that kind of immediacy, examine the latency inherent in the analysis and decision-making process. (See Section 17.8, *Supporting Processes*, on page 267.)

Odds are, the data will be hours stale (at least) by the time any action can be taken on it anyway. In that case, how important is it to get the production data? A snapshot from the previous hour would be just as timely. (If that feedback process takes only a few seconds to go around the loop, then you have a different story.)

Transporting large volumes of data out of production is sometimes necessary. In these cases, look toward extract-transform-load (ETL) tools to handle the physical and semantic mapping. Once the transforms are defined, they can be tuned and put under a quota to avoid risking production capacity. The ID that runs the extracts can be set to allow "select" but not "insert," "delete," or "update." Oracle's "materialized views" also serve well when transporting large volumes. Depending on your storage architecture, you might also be able to play games with so-called business continuance volumes (BCVs) to move data from one SAN to another.

18.4 Releases Shouldn't Hurt

One of my favorite retailers has a release process that rivals a NASA launch sequence. It starts in the afternoon and runs until the wee hours of the morning. In the early days, more than twenty people had active roles to play during the release. These days, that is down to less than a dozen. As you might imagine, any process involving that many people requires detailed planning and coordination. Because each release is arduous, they don't do many a year. Because there are so few releases, each one tends to be unique. That uniqueness requires additional planning with each release, making the release a bit more painful—further discouraging more frequent releases.

Releases should about as big an event as getting a haircut (or compiling a new kernel, for you gray-ponytailed UNIX hackers). The literature on agile methods, lean development, and incremental funding all make a powerful case for frequent releases in terms of user delight and business value.[10] With respect to production operations, however, there's an added benefit of frequent releases. It forces you to get really *good* at doing releases and deployments.

As discussed in Chapter 17, *Transparency*, on page 231, a closed feedback loop is essential to improvement. The faster that feedback loop operates, the more accurate those improvements will be. This demands frequent releases. Frequent releases with incremental functionality also allows your company to outpace its competitors and set the agenda in the marketplace.

As commonly practiced, releases cost too much and introduce too much risk. The kind of manual effort and coordination I described previously is barely sustainable for three or four releases a year. It could never work for twenty a year. One solution—the easy but harmful one—is to slow down the release calendar. Like going to the dentist less frequently because it hurts, this response to the problem can only exacerbate the issue. The right response is to reduce the effort needed, remove people from the process, and make the whole thing more automated and standardized.

Deployments Cost Too Much

Except for product companies, the cost of releasing software is almost never accounted for in budgeting. Planning, analysis, development, and testing all get recognized, but the release often has substantial direct and indirect costs.

The direct costs come primarily from the labor used during the run-up to the release. Aside from testing, there are tasks in four areas.

Configuration management
　Creating the release branch, labeling the code base, creating the release build

Documentation
　Release notes and new or updated training materials

Marketing communications
　Updated marketing materials and announcements inside and outside the company

---

10.　If *Agile Software Development* [Coc01], *Lean Software Development* [PP03], *Software by Numbers* [DC03], and *Extreme Programming Explained* [Bec00] don't convince you, nothing will.

The View from Operations

One of my favorite operations managers often reminds people to "assume positive intent"—that is, when conflict arises between people or groups, assume that all parties are motivated by the same desire to do good by the company. During the worst "us" vs. "them" conflicts, it can seem that so-and-so is "just out to screw us," but that's seldom the case. Conflict usually arises from different imperatives operating on the different groups.

Assuming positive intent is essential when discussing the frequency of releases. Business sponsors and development groups view new releases as the generator of positive change. When development looks at a release, they see requirements fulfilled, bugs fixed, and architecture improved. When the sponsors look at a new release, they see features to generate revenue, retain customers, and match or exceed their competitors. For them, change brings improvement.

When the operations department looks at a new release, they see the potential for new failure modes, the need for new procedures, and new monitoring. They see that old monitoring might not apply anymore. They see that the new release probably needs more of the "core four" resources: CPU, memory, storage, and bandwidth. Above all, they see *risk*. There's risk in the deployment itself, risk in the new release, and risk just because the release is an unknown quantity compared to the existing code base.

Business sponsors, development teams, and operations managers: they are all correct. A new release is all of these things to each of these people.

Deployment

Planning, executing, and verifying the deployment

Support

Emergency bug fixes, updates to monitoring, updates to the run book

The largest indirect cost of releases comes from downtime during the release. It is a rare system that operates only during "business hours." Or, looking at it from a different perspective, "business hours" have expanded to cover the entire clock. The days of nightly "system maintenance time" are long gone.

Operations probably computes availability based on unplanned downtime, so 99.5% availability means only that the system had less than 216 minutes of surprises that month. This is a dodge. The system might have been down for five hours during change windows. Do the users of the system care whether downtime is planned or unplanned? No! To a user, down is down. If I can't get my work done, the system is down! Always keep in mind that the users generally don't know the development or operations calendars. Users care only about their own calendars.

Timing Releases

Why do we place so much emphasis on release dates? For shrink-wrap product vendors such as Microsoft or Adobe, release dates matter. They are announced a year in advance, with giant product launch events, media attention, and massive planning and preparation from customers and the sales channel. Nobody is lining up at midnight to get their hands on the latest version of software from the other 99.9% of us.

Don't risk customers for an arbitrary release date.

For the most part, our customers don't even *know* the scheduled release dates. For web-based software, it just changes one day, without much ado on the customer's part. If the release is a day or a week late, the customer never knows or cares. The customer cares that the system is available and that it works without too many bugs.

Yet, I've seen organizations try to rush releases into production before they're ready. In one case, I was in a "go/no-go" meeting at 4 p.m. on the day of release. QA told us the release hadn't passed testing yet, but they would know more in an hour. Despite that, the table gave the release a thumbs-up! I objected, pointing out that the release couldn't be ready if it hadn't passed QA. Why jeopardize customers just to hit a release date that was chosen arbitrarily from a distance of several months? The answer is obvious, and it has nothing to do with what's best for the customer!

Zero Downtime Deployments

With high-availability servers and high-availability architectures, we no longer accept downtime for hardware maintenance, so why do we tolerate it for software changes?

Somehow, though, almost every code release requires downtime during the release. Whether that's an hour or a day, calling it "planned downtime" doesn't remove the cost. If the cost of downtime is $10,000 an hour, then a four-hour deployment costs $40,000 whether it's on the operations calendar or not.

Why do application releases seem to require downtime? Ironically, it's exactly because of the same architecture feature that is supposed to increase uptime: redundancy. The fact that multiple servers handle incoming requests means that during the deployment itself there will always be some servers on the new version of the code and some on the old version. During that period of overlap, version N and $N+1$ are both present. If the software is totally self-contained, then the presence of two versions doesn't pose a problem. Of course, enterprise applications are rarely self-contained. They use databases, web services, and search engines. For websites, they generate URLs that refer to style sheets, JavaScript files, and media files. All these external references leave plenty of opportunities for version conflict. The easiest approach is to just take downtime for the deployment.

It's possible, however, to execute a deployment over an extended period of time—days or even weeks—that avoids these version conflicts and allows two versions of the software to coexist (see Figure 51, *Zero-Downtime Deployment: Detailed Timeline*, on page 293). Structuring a zero-downtime deployment requires collaboration between development and operations, which is why it so seldom happens. Nevertheless, with a small bit of up-front architecture, you can eliminate deployment downtime.

The key is to break up the deployment into phases. Instead of adding, changing, and removing stuff—such as database columns and tables, constraints, services—all at once, add the new items early, with ways to ensure forward compatibility for the old version of the code. Later, after the release is rolled out, remove stuff that is no longer referenced, and add any new constraints that would have broken the old version. The next sections describe these phases in detail.

Expansion

The first step is to add new "stuff." The stuff consists of URL-based assets, web service endpoints, database tables and columns, and so on. All the stuff can be added without breaking the old version of the software, under certain conditions.

URL-based resources, such as style sheets, images, animations, or JavaScript files, should be given a new URL for each new revision. If the application generates web pages that refer to /static/styles.css, then any changes to styles.css is likely to cause a version conflict. On the other hand, if the application refers to /static/1.1/styles.css instead, then it's trivial to deploy /static/1.2/styles.css without conflicts.

For web services, each revision of the interface should be given a new endpoint name. Similarly, for remote object interfaces, defining a new interface name (for example, with a numeral after the interface name) for each version ensures that the old version of the software gets the interface it wants while the new version gets the interface it wants. A single implementation class can accommodate multiple interface definitions, as long as the changes are just adding or removing exposed methods. Changing the semantics of existing methods requires a different class definition, usually via an adapter or an extracted superclass.

Zero-Downtime Deployment Timeline

- Expansion
  - Deploy new static files (images, Javascript, stylesheets)
  - Create new service pools, if needed
  - Add new tables
  - Add new columns
  - Run data migration scripts
  - Add bridging triggers
  - Apply "recursive ZDD" to prepare secondary clusters
- Rollout
  - For each server
    - Unpack code on the server
    - Stop accepting new requests
    - Shutdown the server
    - Point to the new code
    - Start up the server
    - Verify clean startup
- Cleanup
  - Remove bridging triggers
  - Remove obsolete referential integrity relations
  - Remove obsolete columns
  - Remove obsolete tables
  - Add new referential integrity relations
  - Add NOT NULL constraints
  - Remove obsolete static files
  - Remove the old code
  - Remove old service pools

Figure 51—Zero-Downtime Deployment: Detailed Timeline

For socket-based protocols, the protocol itself should contain a version identifier. This definitely requires that the receiving applications must be updated before the senders. It also implies that the receiving application must support multiple versions of the protocol. If there are other callers of the receiving application, then this helps loosen the coupling with those systems, too. Deploying a new version of code to the servers that receive these calls can be done as its own "recursive zero-downtime deployment."

If it's simply impractical to support multiple protocol revisions, another option is to define multiple service pools in the load balancer on different ports. Then the old version of the calling application will hit the port number that maps to the original version of the receiving application, while the new version of the calling application will hit the new port number that maps to the new version of the receiving application.

By far, the most conflicts—and the most troublesome conflicts—will arise in the database. Schema changes are rarely forward compatible, and they're never by accident. Still, it is possible to break schema changes into phases. In the "expansion" phase, tables and columns get added. Any columns that will eventually be NOT NULL are added as nullable, because the old version doesn't know how to fill these in. Later, in the cleanup phase, constraints will be added. This goes for referential integrity rules, too. They cannot be added during expansion because the old version would immediately violate the relationships.

So, even if the old version of the application doesn't break because of the new tables and columns, it doesn't do anything useful with them either. The new version probably expects some meaningful data in these. It might even include a migration script to populate the new tables and columns with data from the old ones. The application probably just uses INSERT to create rows in the database.[11] You can use a trick to pass this data through to the new tables and columns: triggers. Assuming that the new structure can be filled in from the existing data—and there's an example of how to do that in the forward migration script—then a trigger can do the same thing, one row at a time. Thus, the old version of the application will create data that the new application can also use. After all, the new version will be creating data, too. It will use the new structure; so, if nothing is done, the old version would view data from the new version as corrupt or incomplete. Triggers can bridge this direction, too, by filling in the old structure based on the new data.

Of course, in order to prepare for this, any SQL INSERT or UPDATE statements must be explicit about columns and values. SELECT * is also unlikely to be helpful. Once again, ORM tools come to the rescue. They mechanically generate SQL statements that include the specific columns to select, insert, or update. Any ancillary queries—such as business intelligence or reporting—should also be specific about the columns of interest. This is not difficult to do if you do it consistently from the beginning. Trying to replace every SELECT * to get a release out the door will not be met well.

---

11. If the application uses stored procedures to add entries to the database, then the stored procedures should be updated at this point to fill in data when invoked by the old version of the application.

Rollout

With the preparations from the "expansion" phase in place, the actual rollout of the new software on the application servers should be trivial. This could take a few hours to a few days, depending on how cautiously you want to approach it. For example, this might include letting a couple of servers "bake" on the new code base for a day or more. (While both versions are in use, it might be helpful to create two service pools in the load balancers in order to keep request or session failover confined to the group of servers on the same version as the original session.)

If downtime were required for the deployment, then there would be a great deal of pressure to get this phase done in the minimum time possible. With that pressure removed, there is enough time for an orderly shutdown. This should follow good practices for clean shutdown and start-up, thereby avoiding the user frustration that accompanies abrupt shutdown.[12] (See Section 14.3, *Start-up and Shutdown*, on page 213.)

Cleanup

After the new release has baked long enough to be accepted, it is time to clean up. This includes removing the bridging triggers and extra service pools. Any columns or tables that are no longer being used can be removed. Old versions of static files can be removed, too.

At this point, all the application servers are running on the new version of the code. This is the time to convert columns to NOT NULL that need it, as well as to add referential integrity relations (though constraints enforced in the database can cause large problems for the ORM layer). This is also the time to drop any columns and tables that are no longer needed.

18.5 Summary

Change is the defining characteristic of software. That change—that adaptation—begins with release. Release is the beginning of the software's true life; everything before that release is gestation. Either systems grow over time, adapting to their changing environment, or they decay until their costs outweigh their benefits and then die.

---

12. Lost session state, mainly. I've never seen session failover work perfectly.

Bibliography

[BF01]   Kent Beck and Martin Fowler. *Planning Extreme Programming*. Addison-Wesley, Reading, MA, 2001.

[Bec00]   Kent Beck. *Extreme Programming Explained: Embrace Change*. Addison-Wesley Longman, Reading, MA, 2000.

[Chi01]   James R. Chiles. *Inviting Disaster: Lessons From the Edge of Technology*. Harper Business, New York, NY, USA, 2001.

[Cla04]   Mike Clark. *Pragmatic Project Automation. How to Build, Deploy, and Monitor Java Applications*. The Pragmatic Bookshelf, Raleigh, NC and Dallas, TX, 2004.

[Coc01]   Alistair Cockburn. *Agile Software Development*. Addison-Wesley Longman, Reading, MA, 2001.

[DC03]   Mark Denne and Jane Cleland-Huang. *Software by Numbers: Low-Risk, High-Return Development*. Prentice Hall, Englewood Cliffs, NJ, 2003.

[DeM95]   Tom DeMarco. *Why Does Software Cost So Much?*. Dorset House, New York, NY, USA, 1995.

[FBBO99]   Martin Fowler, Kent Beck, John Brant, William Opdyke, and Don Roberts. *Refactoring: Improving the Design of Existing Code*. Addison-Wesley, Reading, MA, 1999.

[Fow03]   Martin Fowler. *Patterns of Enterprise Application Architecture*. Addison-Wesley Longman, Reading, MA, 2003.

[Fow96]   Martin Fowler. *Analysis Patterns: Reusable Object Models*. Addison-Wesley Longman, Reading, MA, 1996.

[GGA06]   Justin Gehtland, Ben Galbraith, and Dion Almaer. *Pragmatic Ajax: A Web 2.0 Primer*. The Pragmatic Bookshelf, Raleigh, NC and Dallas, TX, 2006.

[GHJV95] Erich Gamma, Richard Helm, Ralph Johnson, and John Vlissides. *Design Patterns: Elements of Reusable Object-Oriented Software*. Addison-Wesley, Reading, MA, 1995.

[Gol04] Eliyahu Goldratt. *The Goal*. North River Press, Great Barrington, MA, Third, 2004.

[Koz05] Charles Kozierok. *The TCP/IP Guide: A Comprehensive, Illustrated Internet Protocols Reference*. No Starch Press, San Francisco, CA, 2005.

[LC99] Domenico Lepore and Oded Cohen. *Deming and Goldratt: The Theory of Constraints and the System of Profound Knowledge*. North River Press, Great Barrington, MA, 1999.

[LW93] Barbara Liskov and J. Wing. Family Values: A Behavioral Notion Of Subtyping. *citeseer.ist.psu.edu/liskov94family.html*. [MIT/LCS/TR-562b]:47, 1993.

[Lea00] Doug Lea. *Concurrent Programming in Java: Design Principles and Patterns*. Addison-Wesley, Reading, MA, Second, 2000.

[Moo91] Geoffrey A. Moore. *Crossing the Chasm*. Harper Business, New York, NY, USA, 1991.

[Nor88] Donald A. Norman. *The Design of Everyday Things*. Doubleday, New York, NY, USA, 1988.

[PP03] Mary Poppendieck and Tom Poppendieck. *Lean Software Development: An Agile Toolkit for Software Development Managers*. Addison-Wesley, Reading, MA, 2003.

[PP06] Mary Poppendieck and Tom Poppendieck. *Implementing Lean Software Development: From Concept to Cash*. Addison-Wesley, Reading, MA, 2006.

[Pet92] Henry Petroski. *The Evolution of Useful Things*. Alfred A. Knopf, Inc, New York, NY, 1992.

[Ric04] Chet Richards. *Certain To Win}*. Xlibris Corporation, Philadelphia, PA, 2004.

[Sen94] Peter M. Senge. *The Fifth Discipline: The Art & Practice of the Learning Organization* . Doubleday, New York, NY, USA, 1994.

[She97] Michael Shermer. *Why People Believe Weird Things*. W.H.Freeman and Company, New York, NY, 1997.

[Ste93] W. Richard Stevens. *TCP/IP Illustrated, Volume 1: The Protocols*. Addison-Wesley, Reading, MA, 1993.

[VCK96]   John Vlissides, James O. Coplien, and Norman L. Kerth. *Pattern Languages of Program Design 2*. Addison-Wesley, Reading, MA, 1996.

[WIDG98]   Craig Wisneski, Hiroshi Ishii, Andrew Dahley, Matt Gorbet, Scott Brave, Brygg Ullmer, and Paul Yarin. Ambient Displays: Turning Architectural Space into an Interface between People and Digital Information. *Lecture Notes in Computer Science*. 1370:22, 1998.

Index

The Pragmatic Bookshelf

The Pragmatic Bookshelf features books written by developers for developers. The titles continue the well-known Pragmatic Programmer style and continue to garner awards and rave reviews. As development gets more and more difficult, the Pragmatic Programmers will be there with more titles and products to help you stay on top of your game.

Visit Us Online

This Book's Home Page
http://pragprog.com/titles/mnee
Source code from this book, errata, and other resources. Come give us feedback, too!

Register for Updates
http://pragprog.com/updates
Be notified when updates and new books become available.

Join the Community
http://pragprog.com/community
Read our weblogs, join our online discussions, participate in our mailing list, interact with our wiki, and benefit from the experience of other Pragmatic Programmers.

New and Noteworthy
http://pragprog.com/news
Check out the latest pragmatic developments, new titles and other offerings.

Save on the eBook

Save on the eBook versions of this title. Owning the paper version of this book entitles you to purchase the electronic versions at a terrific discount.

PDFs are great for carrying around on your laptop—they are hyperlinked, have color, and are fully searchable. Most titles are also available for the iPhone and iPod touch, Amazon Kindle, and other popular e-book readers.

Buy now at *http://pragprog.com/coupon*

Contact Us

Online Orders:	*http://pragprog.com/catalog*
Customer Service:	*support@pragprog.com*
International Rights:	*translations@pragprog.com*
Academic Use:	*academic@pragprog.com*
Write for Us:	*http://pragprog.com/write-for-us*
Or Call:	+1 800-699-7764

CPSIA information can be obtained at www.ICGtesting.com
Printed in the USA
BVOW09s1705080316

439496BV00013B/61/P

Multilingual Multimedia

Bridging the Language Barrier with Intelligent Systems